SAGE

SAGE

A Journey to the Final Station—
My Years Working in
Assisted Living

By Liz Renshaw-Breen

Copyright © 2025 by Liz Renshaw-Breen.

All rights reserved.

ISBN 979-8-9898775-0-8 (paperback)

ISBN 979-8-9898775-3-9 (hardcover)

ISBN 979-8-9898775-1-5 (eBook)

ISBN 979-8-9898775-2-2 (audiobook)

Library of Congress Control Number: 2024901532

No portion of this book may be reproduced in any form without written permission from the publisher or author, except as permitted by U.S. copyright law.

This memoir is a truthful recollection of actual events in the author's life. Some conversations have been recreated and/or supplemented.

This publication is meant to provide valuable, accurate, and authoritative information. However, the content of this book is for informational purposes only and is not intended to diagnose, treat, cure, or prevent any condition or disease. Neither the author nor the publisher is engaged in rendering medical, legal, investment, accounting, or other professional services.

While the publisher and author have used their best efforts in preparing this book, they make no representations or warranties with respect to the accuracy or completeness of the contents of this book.

Neither the publisher nor the author shall be liable for any loss of profit or any other commercial damages, including but not limited to special, incidental, consequential, personal, or other damages.

First edition 2025.

Published by TiaMia Press.

Dedicated to:

Jordan Johnson
1988 – 2021

My heart

And

George Birimisa
1924 – 2012

One of the great loves of my life

Sage \saj\, *adj: wise through reflection and experience*

It takes a long time to become young.

— Pablo Picasso

Contents

Introduction 1

Chapter One: Old People 3

Chapter Two: Welcome to Assisted Living 15

Chapter Three: Falling Apart 49

Chapter Four: Dazed And Confused 59

Chapter Five: Caregivers: Angels on Earth 105

Chapter Six: Show Me the Money 127

Chapter Seven: We Are Family 203

Chapter Eight: Happily Ever After? 225

Chapter Nine: Last Man Standing 255

Chapter Ten: Life 285

Appendix: Research on Dementia and Brain Fitness 309

Bibliography 313

SAGE

Introduction

I began writing this book while lying on the beach in Mexico. I had spent years working with elders, and the experience changed me and afforded me insights on life and aging not common to a person in their 30s. I was staring at the waves, listening to classical music in my headphones, and the thought to write this book hit me like a lightning bolt. I went upstairs and began writing down my experiences.

I have changed the names and most of the identifying characteristics of all of the people in the book, with the exception of my nephew, Jordan, who was a son to me, my stepfather, Bob, my grandmother, Ruth, her sister, Ruby, my friend, George Birimisa, and historical figures such as Dr. Ethel Percy Andrus. I have changed the names of all of the assisted living communities with the exception of The Gables due to its historical significance as one of the first retirement homes in the United States and the birthplace of the American Association of Retired Persons.

Regarding dialogue, events, and conversations referenced in this memoir, I have a memory like an elephant, which people close to me will confirm. I remember conversations, events, and names in great detail. I have also kept a journal for the majority of my life. So these recollections are an accurate representation of what happened, from my point of view. The book is thematic. Because of that, I move around between venues and time in each section to illustrate experiences I had related to the themes of that particular chapter.

They say the journey of a thousand miles begins with one step. I had no idea that day on the beach that this writing journey would span many years and include additional experiences from subsequent positions in elder care. To that end, some information and research on dementia and brain fitness are dated, and therefore I have provided updated research in an appendix at the end of the book.

I am grateful to the many people who helped me along the way with writing guidance and emotional support in navigating life and completing this book. I would not have finished it without you. Thank you to my friends, family, and support network. To my mom, you always encouraged me to write. A special thank you to my two editors, Tom Bentley and Molly Silvestrini. Your input made this book so much better. I would also like to express my sincere gratitude to the many older adults who were my inspiration for this book. Throughout my journey, I met many people who were wise through reflection and experience. I met many sages.

Chapter One

Old People

> *Every man desires to live long,
> but no one would be old.*
>
> — Jonathan Swift

It was winter in San Francisco at eight o'clock on a Tuesday morning. I was 32 years old, sitting on the L-train headed downtown to my job at an advertising agency. I looked to my left and noticed an old woman standing in the aisle. She wore a baby-blue sweater with tan polyester pants and her hair was blown from the wind. Foundation and powder were caked into her wrinkles. Her jewelry, a ceramic gold necklace with bright pink stones, reminded me of thrift stores.

Holding a cane in one hand and two plastic grocery bags draped over the wrist of the other, she slumped over the metal bar she was holding onto for support as the train bumbled along. Glancing towards the front of the railcar, I saw that all of the seats reserved for seniors and disabled persons were occupied. I got up, offered my seat to the lady, and found another spot further back. As we got closer to downtown, several more seniors boarded the train and I ended up relinquishing my seat three more times, ultimately resolving to stand. This was my typical commute day.

I now stood wedged between an unkempt man who smelled like beer and garbage and a fit guy in a muscle t-shirt who was drenched in sweat. His perspiration was dripping on my designer suit. I looked around at all those comfortably seated seniors and thought, *Doesn't anyone die anymore? What happened to the days when the average life expectancy was 60? Who are all these old people and why are they taking this train? Is it like this on all trains, in all cities, or is this just a San Francisco phenomenon?*

I had flashbacks of a geography class from college that taught that the United States population growth was being affected less by birth rate and more by the fact that people just don't die anymore. *What is up with that?* I wondered.

My ride home that evening was similar. I got on at the front of the line and took a seat which I eventually gave up. Arriving home, I vented my frustration over cocktails with our neighbors, Alex and Sophie. It was not that I didn't *like* old people; it was just that I thought they had lived far too long and were a burden on society. "I'm not kidding," I complained to my neighbors. "There were NO seats available for anyone under 75." The neighbors, also in their 30s, laughed and got me another drink.

My grandparents had all died by the time I was 10. I was raised in the United States, a land obsessed with youth, a land where being old was just about the worst thing a person could be. Consequently, if I found myself behind an elderly person at the grocery store, my first thought was usually, *Come on lady, could you move a little faster, please?*

I had no inkling on the train that day that my life was about to change. I was about to head down a track which would lead me to spend the next several years *immersed* in a sea of old people.

A few weeks after that Tuesday morning train ride, I was sitting in my cubicle at 9:00 a.m., staring at story boards for a Teen Pregnancy Prevention television campaign. The drawings, which depicted two kids dancing and flirting, were leaning against file cabinets in a circle around me. I was not thinking of my client, nor the issue of teen pregnancy. I was obsessing about the bomb my husband, Dave, had dropped the night before. He announced that he wanted to move to Ojai, California, a small town six hours south of us. We had been to Ojai several times to visit his brother, Steve and sister-in-law, Trudy.

There was a house for sale there, a 1920s Craftsman-style fixer-upper, and Dave wanted to remodel it. The house had awakened his artistic passion. His career up until this point had been spent restoring Victorian homes in San Francisco. He loved building, loved antiques and all homes old. He also saw a great financial opportunity with the Ojai property. He explained that we would be buying the house with Steve and Trudy.

My thoughts went like this: *I love my husband. I love my job. I love our home and life in San Francisco. Why, why, why does he have to screw everything up like this?* Sitting in my cubicle, I flashed back to Dave's words over dinner the previous night. "It's an Arts and Crafts home, a total teardown on an acre of land right next door to Steve and Trudy's. The oak trees are beautiful. Wait until you see them. They're huge."

"Oak trees," I said. "Huh."

"Now, the house is unlivable and we'll need to live on-site," Dave continued, "so I can be close to the project. So, we'll get a trailer...." He kept talking, but I didn't hear anything after the word "trailer." *Did he just say he wants me to live in a* trailer?

I attempted to bring my focus back to the television campaign that would hopefully prevent teenage girls from getting knocked up. Instead, my thoughts ruminated:

> *I do not want to leave my friends of many years, the parties, my book club, my hairdresser, my dentist, my bikini waxer, my mechanic, my butcher, my therapist. I do not want to leave my job. I do not want to leave San Francisco, the only place that has ever felt like home. I like Steve and Trudy, but will I still like them if I live next door to them and buy a house with them? I do not want to leave my beautiful, Mediterranean, oceanfront home to live in a TRAILER.*

My jaw hurt from clenching it in my sleep the previous night. I often grind my teeth when I am trying to fix something in my life, trying to figure it out. But I couldn't figure this one out. I did not know what to do.

The ringing phone startled me. It was Dave.

"Hey," I said.

"So, are you moving to Ojai with me?"

"Do I have to decide now?" I asked, my voice raising an octave.

"Well, I need to let Steve know this week. The house won't be for sale forever. I need to send him $25,000 if we're going to do this ... Liz ... are you still there?"

"Yeah."

"Liz. Come on. You know our financial situation. We have to do something to get ahead. This is a great opportunity. That year in South America really set us back. Have you seen our credit card bills lately?"

"I know," I said, clutching the phone receiver tightly. He was right. I did not pull my weight with that trip. Part of the deal included me getting a job in South America, which never happened. Dave had also paid off my debts when we got married, to the tune of $14,000.

"*Do* you? Do you *really* know?"

"I can't think about this right now. I need to get back to work." I was raising my voice now, loud enough so that everyone around could hear. I didn't care.

Dave continued painting the bleak picture of our bank account. He reminded me again that we were in debt up to our ears due to the pursuit of my dream. Since getting my degree in Latin American Studies, I had always wanted to spend a year in Latin America. Three weeks after our wedding, that is what we did. We had been back in San Francisco for two years and were still trying to recover financially. Dave was convinced that flipping this house would turn things around for us.

"So, it sounds like you're going with or without me?"

"This is a great opportunity," he responded as I kicked one of the story boards near my feet.

"You love Ojai," he continued.

"Yeah, I love *visiting* Ojai." Ojai is a town of 8,000 people, a bucolic resort destination with spas, golf courses, and shops. "But do you seriously want to *live* there? What the hell am I going to do for a job? Work at Ojai Burger?"

"How do you know you won't find a job?"

"For fuckssake, Dave, I just got a promotion."

"You're being selfish," Dave said.

"I'M being selfish! You want to uproot me from my life, my friends, my career and *I'm* being selfish?"

"Yes, you are. You are a self-centered person."

"I have to go."

I stared at the wall and imagined another scenario. *It would be a different thing if I didn't have to work. If I could take a couple of years off and be a kept woman, greeting my husband at the door wearing lingerie. This, after a relaxing day of shopping, massages and lunch with the girls.* But that was not the case. Unemployment was not an option. I was appointed to be our steady paycheck while Dave worked full-time on our Ojai house. It was part of the master plan. The one that involved living in Ojai, in a trailer.

The week after our blow-up, Dave sent the money to his brother and let me know that he would be moving. He said we didn't have to split up, that we could have a long-distance marriage while he worked on this project. I felt certain, though, that our relationship would not survive that kind of separation.

I could not make up my mind and therefore I did what any sensible woman would do: I went to a psychic. Dakota May was her name and I was told she was quite gifted, a self-proclaimed channel for Native American spirits. She came highly recommended by my dear friend, Gabrielle. We made a phone date because Dakota lived 250 miles from San Francisco in a small town near Mount Shasta. One would think I could have found a decent psychic in San Francisco, but, no, I had already been to several and some had given me information which turned out to be *not true!* Charlatans. Gabrielle assured me Dakota was different. My phone date with Dakota went like this:

Me: Hi Dakota, it's Liz Breen, Gabrielle's friend.

Dakota: Nice to meet you. So, you're thinking of doing something drastic, making a huge decision.

Me: Did Gabrielle tell you that?

Dakota: No. I can see it. Don't do it. Whatever you're thinking of doing, don't do it.

Me: Well, I'm thinking of divorcing my husband. But, honestly Dakota, it isn't the first time I've considered this. We've been married three years and we have a lot of issues. *Here I go giving the psychic too much information instead of just letting her do her job. All right, I'm going to stop now. I'm going to let her figure it out.*

Dakota: I see your husband throwing tantrums. It's sort of like he's banging a trash can lid, figuratively speaking.

I told Dakota she was right, we did have a volatile relationship, but that we loved each other. She told me to work out this karma now or I would just end up marrying Dave again in the next lifetime and repeating the drama. She saw that he built things and was very good at it. She told me it was his third lifetime being a carpenter and our third lifetime being married.

Dakota: You need to stop engaging and reacting when he gets upset. Only you can break the cycle. He can't. He doesn't know how.

Me: How do I do that? Please tell me, Dakota.

Dakota: Move to Ojai with him.

She assured me I would find a job. She told me she saw me driving to Santa Barbara for work and she saw a swimming pool at my job. I waited two more weeks, then made my decision. I chose love over my career. I said to the universe, "Okay, fine, I don't want to leave this man. I will move to the damn trailer and get a damn job at the local diner if I have to." Even if I did find a job in my field, there was no way it would be on par with the level of positions available in San Francisco. I accepted that my career, for all intents and purposes, was over.

I began a thorough job search in Ojai and the surrounding areas: Ventura, Oxnard, Camarillo, Thousand Oaks, and Santa Barbara. Over the next few months, I applied for 30 jobs and landed 3 interviews. None of the jobs appealed to me and no offers came.

Another month went by and Dave and I took our annual vacation to Mazatlán, Mexico. On the third day of our trip, feeling at an all-time low about my job search, I strolled into Cyber Café and decided to check out the *Ventura County Star* newspaper's online edition. There it was, a two-line ad that jumped out at me: Marketing Director for The Gables of Ojai Retirement Community.

I walked into our hotel room, kissed Dave, sat down and said, "So, there's a marketing job at the old folks' home in Ojai."

"Cool."

"Yeah, it's cool that there's a sales job right in town, but not so cool that it's at a nursing home. I think the only time I've ever stepped foot in one of those places was in high school when I called Bingo on Thursdays for this place called Angelica Manor. It was creepy. Everyone was so pale, like their faces were covered in talcum powder."

"Well, you should at least check it out," Dave said.

After our vacation, we stopped in Ojai for a couple days to visit Steve and Trudy before heading back home to San Francisco. I went to The Gables and dropped off my resume. A week later the executive director, Sharon, called me. "I received your resume," she said. "I actually know your sister-in-law, Trudy, from Rotary Club. She put in a good word for you."

"So," Sharon continued. "Why are you moving to *Ojai?*" I explained the real estate project, my husband's dream to renovate a Craftsman-style home. "Well," she said "I'm very impressed with your background and interested in meeting you. The only bugaboo I can see is salary. I don't want to waste your time or mine if this isn't a fit."

"Look," I said, "I realize there is no way I'm going to make the same kind of money I make in San Francisco. I think we should at least meet and talk about it." Sharon told me the salary range and it was actually pretty good for Ojai. Two weeks later, I drove six hours south and met her in her office at The Gables.

Sharon sat behind her cedar desk and I sat in an antique chair across from her. Two sides of the office were made up of windows looking out on the front of the property. There was an expansive fresh-cut lawn with white and pink rose bushes framing it. I saw two large oak trees.

The buildings were all pink and on the front porch outside Sharon's window I saw a lady who looked to be in her 80s sitting with a younger woman. They were chatting and drinking lemonade. They looked happy. The Gables smelled clean. So far, it did not feel anything like Angelica Manor where I had volunteered in high school.

Sharon and I talked easily. Our conversation covered the basics of my experience and the responsibilities of the marketing director's job. We laughed and looked each other in the eye throughout the interview. Sharon was warm, articulate, and to the point. I could tell she loved her work.

Sharon reminded me of my mom. She was in her early 60s with strawberry blonde hair, fair skin, and laugh lines around her eyes. She was plump, with just enough cushion on her to give a good hug. I relaxed, unclasped my hands and sat back in my chair. From the kitchen down the hall, I could smell chocolate chip cookies baking.

Sharon told me how The Gables was the birthplace of the American Association of Retired Persons. The Gables had been in Ojai almost 50 years and was started by a woman named Dr. Ethel Percy Andrus. After retiring at age 62 from her job as a high-school principal, Dr. Andrus became an active lobbyist in Washington. She founded the National Retired Teachers Association (NRTA) in 1947 and AARP in 1954. I found this history intriguing.

"The most important quality I look for in a marketing person," Sharon explained, "is a sense of urgency. Can you tell me how you would go about tackling this position?"

I spoke about my approach to sales and marketing, including ideas for special events, public relations, and building relationships in the community. Sharon nodded her approval. I spoke of Dave's remodel project, my life in San Francisco, my nephew, Jordan, in San Diego who was a son to me, and my book club and friends. I, of course, did not tell Sharon of my slight *issues* with old people.

Then she asked if I had ever been around seniors. I told her my grandparents had all passed away by the time I was 10. I had a 78-year-old great uncle who was sweet, but I rarely saw him. I told her about Dave's 89-year-old grandma whom I had known for a few years and was growing fond of. Then she asked, "So, do you have any *discomfort* with the elderly?" *That* was a tricky question. I try hard not to lie, especially when posed a direct query. "Discomfort" wasn't the right word. Apathy, annoyance, and impatience, perhaps, but not discomfort. "No," I answered, shifting in my chair, "no discomfort."

We talked in Sharon's cozy office for more than an hour then took a tour of the property. It comprised eight beautifully landscaped acres with verdant lawns, pine, redwood, magnolia, and ginkgo trees. There were also roses, peonies, hibiscus, and crepe myrtle trees in full bloom with pink and purple flowers. We walked by a vegetable garden, fruit orchard, putting green, and pink bungalows with nicely painted white trim.

I felt the welcome heat of the sun wrapping around me. It was nice to be away from San Francisco's damp cold. The only sounds I heard were the songs and chirps of several birds. This was *not* what I had expected. The Gables felt more like a Hawaiian resort than a retirement home.

We walked into an apartment, "This is an example of what we call a Parlor," Sharon said. It had large windows, a kitchenette, and a half-wall divider between the living room and bedroom. I could see trees, flowers, and lawns from every direction. It felt peaceful. "It is less expensive than the one-bedroom because it doesn't have the full wall separating the living room and sleeping area." The walls were painted a pale green.

"It feels spacious," I said, stepping into the white tiled bathroom and peeking into the shower.

"We also have studios, which are just one room, one-bedrooms and two-bedrooms. So, there are lots of choices depending on how much people want to spend."

Leaving the apartment, we ran into a gentleman with a cane and Sharon introduced me. He was articulate and stood upright. We had a brief conversation and when he was out of earshot, Sharon said, "He's 89."

"Wow," I marveled. He didn't fit my image of an 89-year-old.

She explained that he lived in independent living because he didn't need help with much. "He's a widower and doesn't want to cook or clean. And he doesn't drive anymore."

The Gables had a total of 99 beds, some in independent living, some in assisted living, and some in the Alzheimer's care, which Sharon did not show me. She explained the dining room procedures, activity schedule, and transportation policy. "Local transportation is included," she said, "but if someone wants to go to LAX to catch a flight, they are on their own."

"They can *leave*?" I asked, incredulous. Never before having heard of assisted living, I had imagined a nursing home with restrictions, a prison for old people.

"Of *course* they can leave." Sharon responded. "They live their lives, do whatever they like. We're just here to offer whatever support they want." I wanted to know more, but didn't ask, concerned that Sharon would see just how unknowledgeable I was of this industry.

As we walked, Sharon told me, "Now, part of the job is two days a week of outside marketing. Networking with doctors and senior centers, things like that. You would have to drive to places like Santa Barbara and Camarillo, but the drive would be built into your workday." We walked by a swimming pool and Sharon paused to tell me about the water aerobics classes on Wednesdays and Saturdays. The pool was clean and bright blue, surrounded by comfortable looking chairs and potted plants. There were wooden tables with umbrellas. Looking at the pool and considering what she had just said about driving to Santa Barbara, I recalled Dakota May's words: *I see you driving to Santa Barbara for work. I see a swimming pool.* I caught my breath at the connection. *Hmm.*

Next, we walked through the lounge, where Sharon explained they held chair exercises in the morning and cocktail parties in the evening. The room was large with antique couches and cozy chairs. In one corner a group of four ladies were playing Bridge.

I noticed pictures of Dr. Andrus on the walls above the fireplace and next to the activity calendar. Not only did I see pictures of Dr. Andrus, I absolutely sensed her presence and thought about her the rest of the day. I was fascinated and inspired by this woman whose best life's work, her legacy, was accomplished *after* she retired. This struck me even more than the fact that she was a feminist long before the 1970's Women's Movement. I had always believed that meaningful life ended around age 50. It never occurred to me that people could continue to have goals, take risks and actually grow in their later years of life. I figured that I, like the rest of the world, would in my mid-50s begin a downward slope of *existing* rather than living.

Next, we visited the clubhouse, a modern-looking room with plush carpet, a large wooden fireplace, leather couches and a library. Sharon spotted a lady sitting near the books and whispered to me, "That's Gertrude Wilson, our librarian. She's 99 years old and has lived here since she was 80. She lives on the second floor of a building with no elevator and goes up and down the stairs every day. Come on, I'll introduce you." Gertrude had a very wrinkled face, as I would expect for a woman of her age. She was slender and decked out in purple from head to toe. Her movements were all very concentrated on the task of organizing books.

"Gertrude," Sharon said, "I'd like to introduce you to Liz. She's visiting today."

"Hello, it's nice to meet you," Gertrude said in a gorgeous Welsh accent, extending her hand. Where are you visiting from?" she asked.

"San Francisco."

"Oh, that's a lovely town. Great shopping."

"Sharon," Gertrude said, her tone slightly more edgy, "people are not signing the books out the way they're supposed to. And they're not returning them. It's very frustrating. I'm not sure I want to continue doing this job."

"Oh, Gertrude. I'm sorry. I'll bring it up at the Resident Council meeting. Please don't quit. You do a better job at this than anyone."

"Yes, well I've been at it five years and frankly, I'm not sure I want to continue if people aren't going to cooperate."

"All right, I'll see what I can do."

"She seems feisty for a 99-year-old," I said to Sharon as we walked away.

"Yes, she is, and incredibly astute," Sharon replied. "She has a glass of sherry every night, participates in most of the activities here, and thrives on a good political debate." I was amazed by Gertrude. I saw something in her face that I had not expected to see in the eyes of a woman who was almost a hundred. I saw life.

When the tour and interview ended, I looked at my watch and saw I had been there for over two hours. I drove back to San Francisco feeling exhilarated. I liked Sharon, The Gables, and the job description. Much to my own surprise, I realized that I *wanted* this job. I also felt something from the interview with Sharon, the tour of the property, hearing about Dr. Andrus, meeting Gertrude in her purple garb. There was something about that place that felt *special* and I wanted to be part of it.

Two weeks later, I interviewed with Rick Flores, one of the owners of The Gables, at his office in Santa Barbara. Rick was an affable guy, younger than I expected, a laid-back surfer who enjoyed caring for seniors. Driving home afterwards, I felt good about my second interview and hopeful about the prospect of this job. Halfway to the city, my cell phone rang. "Hi, Liz, it's Sharon from The Gables."

"Hi," I replied. "It's so nice to hear from you. I had a great meeting with Rick Flores this morning."

"Well, he enjoyed meeting you, too, and I'm calling to offer you the marketing director position." At that moment, I did something every professional should do when they *really* want to show how savvy they are: I screamed. I screamed loudly, right into Sharon's ear, because I was so elated and surprised that she had called less than two hours after my interview with Rick. I felt like I had won the lottery. I was on the 101 freeway and I looked for a place to pull over.

Once parked, I regained my composure and wrote down the specifics of the offer: salary, commission, vacation time, health insurance, start date. I thanked her profusely and then headed to the nearest shopping mall, where I spent a chunk of money on a celebration wardrobe.

I gave my notice at the advertising agency, found renters for our house in San Francisco, and packed my belongings. Dave planned to finish things up with his current remodel project and meet me a few weeks later. The night before my departure, the neighbors came over to say goodbye.

"It's so surprising that you're going to work at a retirement home," Alex said.

"I know," I replied.

"You don't even like old people," Alex said.

"I know."

Chapter Two

Welcome to Assisted Living

*Never lose sight of the fact that old age
needs so little,
but needs that little so much.*

— Margaret Willour

On my first day of work, I felt like an eager six-year-old, ready for first grade. While choosing my outfit the night before, I could hardly contain my enthusiasm. I slept very little, yet felt wide awake, pumped full of adrenaline. My coffee tasted especially good that morning and the air smelled sweet from the jasmine bush right outside the trailer window. Dixie Chicks songs were playing on the stereo and Dave called from San Francisco, to wish me luck.

I danced around the trailer, listening to the Chicks belt out "Wide Open Spaces," singing along with them. *She needed, Wiiide Ooopen Spaces . . . room to make her big miiistakes . . . she needed . . . neeew faces. . . ."*

At 10 minutes after 8, I put a final spritz of hairspray on, locked the trailer door, and headed to my car. My commute was three minutes. The weather was warm and I was wearing a short-sleeved shirt at 8:15 in the morning. "Thank you, God, thank you," I said out loud in my car. This was a welcome change from the cold weather and long commute in San Francisco.

I walked into The Gables and Mary Williams, the office manager, greeted me. She was at the front desk, answering the phone, writing a message, and watering a plant at the same time. I walked around the corner to my office. It was not the type of office one would expect for a marketing director. In fact, it wasn't really *my* office at all. It was the maintenance director's office and I had a desk in it.

The maintenance director, whom I had not yet met, was named John and his desk was kitty-corner to mine on the right. Directly behind my desk was a Xerox machine. I sat in my chair and Joan, the nurse, came in to make a copy. I was so close to the machine that I had to move my chair so she could use it. Joan greeted me, got her copy, and hurried out. There were no windows in the office and the walls looked as though they had not been painted since the 1950s when Dr. Andrus was here. I was staring at the ugly corn-colored walls when John walked in. He looked to be in his early 30s, fair skinned, medium height and build, an average-looking guy.

"Good morning," he grunted.

"Good morning," I said, standing up and extending my hand with a smile. "I'm Liz, the new marketing director."

"I kind of figured that, since you're sitting in that chair. Welcome to The Gables."

"Thanks. So, how long have you worked here?" I asked.

"Fifteen years. I started in the kitchen when I was 16 and worked my way up to maintenance director," he said, a tinge of pride in his voice.

"Wow. How long have you lived in Ojai?"

"My whole life. How long did you live in San Francisco?" he asks.

"Nine years."

"So, how do you like the job?"

"Well, I've only worked here about 20 minutes, but it's been great so far!"

"I swear, it seems like some of your predecessors barely lasted an hour." A twang of unease arose in me.

"Yeah, Sharon told me a bit about that. What happened to all of them?"

My first thought with every job I've had has always, been 'will I be able to keep this job and succeed here?' I have never been fired. Worrying is just part of who I am, part of my work ethic. With this job, I was especially concerned since I was our only paycheck and we were in debt. Also, Sharon sounded like she had very high standards. I was new to the industry. I had a lot to learn and it didn't sound like she was willing to cut any slack.

"Well, some quit and some got fired," he said. "Bill was a pretty good marketing director, but he was always shopping for stuff on the internet. He had all these college degrees, but he was actually kinda lazy."

"Oh," I said.

"Then there was Melissa. She was sweet. But she was off getting her nails done or going to the movies when she was supposed to be doing the outside sales. No wonder we weren't getting move-ins. Sharon found out about her escapades and that was the end of Melissa."

"Interesting," I said.

"Briana was trying to run her own massage business on the side instead of focusing on the marketing job. Also, every time they were in a marketing meeting, she would be looking out the window to see if her boyfriend drove by. So, Sharon fired her, too."

I could feel my breath getting shorter as John spoke. *I can't lose this job. I have to make this work.*

"Therese was too highfalutin for us," he continued. "She wanted all this money for advertising and doctor gifts. Then, one day, Sofia Flores, the co-owner of the property, saw her at Costco wearing shorts when she was supposed to be out marketing. The next day Sharon cut Therese's hours to part-time, you know, to kind of force her to quit, so they wouldn't have to pay unemployment."

"Hmm," I said.

"Julie was actually the best marketing director we had. She practically filled the place up. She had a lot of energy and enthusiasm. But then her parents offered to buy a house for her and her husband in Idaho, so she moved away. Sharon was really bummed when she left."

"Wow, thanks for the insights," I said as I nervously moved papers around on my desk. "I hope I last."

"Yeah, you'll do fine," he said.

How do you know? I wanted to ask him. *Maybe I won't do fine. Maybe I'll fail miserably at this job and get fired and Dave and I will lose everything because we are already hanging on by a thread.*

I looked around the office and asked, "So, what's that computer for?" pointing at a monitor which sat on a table about four feet from my desk.

"That's our internet server," he said. "It's also got all the phone logs, so Mary comes in here a lot to check it." John went on to give me a "tour" of our little office. There were numerous file cabinets which were used by many different people. The Xerox machine behind me was the only one on the property, so lots of people came in throughout the day to use it. Basically, our office was Grand Central Station. Due to my inexperience, it didn't even occur to me that this arrangement was odd. I just assumed that all marketing directors at all assisted living communities shared an office with the maintenance director, copy machine, internet server, and file storage.

"I gotta go now and check on my wife," John said. "She's due to have our third baby any day now." It turned out John lived right across the street with his wife and two small children. He walked to work, an even shorter commute than mine.

Sharon arrived soon after and found me sitting at my desk, looking bewildered. I wasn't sure what she wanted me to do for my first work tasks. I smiled and said, "Good morning," wondering to myself, *Does she think I'm a total freak because I screamed on the phone that day when she called to offer me the job? That was the last conversation we had until now. Does she regret hiring me? I have to redeem myself and show her I am actually a very professional person.*

"Let's get a cup of coffee and take a walk around," Sharon said. On our way to the kitchen, we ran into Olivia, who had worked at the Gables for 30 years. She began working there at age 16 and this was the only job Olivia had ever had. *Has everyone lived in Ojai and worked here their entire life?* She was beautiful and tan, with long thick hair and blue eyes.

Sharon and I continued her morning rounds, stopping to talk with residents and staff along the way. As we walked, I took a sip of my coffee and then a deep breath. *There is that smell of magnolias and roses again.*

Sharon joked with a resident about his wife bossing him around, ending with, "It's better if you just let her run the show, you know. Happy wife, happy life." She introduced me to the gentleman then reminded him of the next day's field trip to the county fair. *She's really got her finger on the pulse of this place.* Her energy felt a bit like the ocean, calm and yet powerful. It was odd: I felt relaxed with her and at the same time nervous about what she thought of me, afraid she would fire me if I missed a beat.

We went back to my office and Sharon handed me a five-by-seven index card with a woman's name and phone number on it. "This is an inquiry card," she said. "This lady called yesterday asking for information. Could you please send her a brochure and letter?"

"Sure," I said.

"Great. Well, I have a ton of paperwork and phone calls to take care of, so I'll leave you to it. Let me know if you need anything or have questions."

"Do you want to see the letter before I send it?" I asked.

"No. I wouldn't have hired you if I didn't think you could write a letter," she said with a smile and left. I sat there, looking at the card and realized I had no idea what assisted living was. I was supposed to sell this lady on it, but I didn't even know what I was selling. I had no idea where the brochures were or the letterhead. I was excited to do my first actual "work task," but I didn't want to look like an idiot. I didn't want to bug everyone who seemed quite busy, so I tried to find the brochures on my own and Mary saw me looking lost in the supply closet and asked, "What do you need?"

She helped me find the letterhead and then I wrote the best letter I could, which basically said, "Thanks for your interest. Here's the brochure. Come see the place sometime."

On my second day of work, I settled into my chair, picked up the phone, and started making calls to people who had toured during the previous months. Sharon had given me a box with index cards. Each card included the prospect's name, address, phone number, a brief synopsis of their background, and why they were looking into assisted living. Having almost no knowledge of elder care, I wasn't sure what to say on these calls, but somehow, I found a way to make conversation. "You've got the gift of gab, honey!" my stepmother, Anne, always said to me.

I convinced one lady to come back for a second tour and was quite proud of myself for *that* accomplishment. Sharon checked on me a few times throughout the morning and at 11:30, she popped her head in and said, "Why don't you have lunch in the dining room today so you can try the food and get to know some of the residents?" The blood drained from my face. I was not prepared for this suggestion, but tried not to show it. "Sure," I said with a big smile, then immediately called Dave.

"Oh my God," I whispered. "She wants me to eat lunch in the dining room. I didn't realize I was going to have to *eat* here—with the old people."

"Liz, you work in an old folks' home now. Did you think you could work there and not interact with seniors?"

"Well, I mean, I didn't think I would have to *eat* with them. And the food is probably like hospital food."

I took a deep breath and stepped into the dining room as though I were stepping into a cold pond. Entering that room was really the first moment for me, of walking *into their world*. It felt like another universe. I stood at the dining room entrance while everyone silently stared back at me: The New Girl.

The room was large and had about 50 elderly people sitting at tables of various sizes. The carpet was grey, the walls cream-colored. The tables had white linen. The décor reminded me a bit of a hotel restaurant, with its soft lighting and vinyl-covered chairs. Standing there, I felt more shell-shocked than nervous. They all looked different than me and the same as each other: a sea of old people.

I thought of my world: the staff I had met, my office with the maintenance director, my friends in San Francisco, my home, Jordan, Dave, my family, restaurants, airports, shops, movie theaters, coffee houses, bowling alleys, and parties.

And this was their world: an old folks' home.

Sharon stood next to me and said, "Why don't you sit with Clara Astor?"

"Which one is she?" I asked.

"The little lady over there with the grey hair and glasses." She had just described about 80 percent of the people in the room. Sharon pointed and I timidly approached Clara's table and sat down. There was one man at the table and two women, including Clara. I smelled a mixture of fresh bread, chicken soup, and bodies that were musty, old and shutting down. I recalled that distinct smell of bodies in their final years from my brief stint in high school volunteering at Angelica Manor. The scent overwhelmed me every time I entered the lobby. It smelled like something not quite dead but rapidly approaching the end.

Our main course, beef stroganoff, was served by Magdala, an elegant Egyptian woman in her 50s with a broad smile and very white teeth. As my table mates and I ate, food began flying from their mouths. Some seemed to have dentures which made chewing difficult. For others it seemed to be a challenge to breathe through their nose, which led to chewing with their mouth open. One woman seemed to have lost control over her lips, tongue, and the saliva escaping from her mouth.

It was gross, yet somehow, I still managed to enjoy the food, which was delicious. I had expected it to taste awful, but it was surprisingly on par with quality restaurants where I had eaten in San Francisco.

I tried to listen to the conversation, but all I could think was, *What is that strange growth on that guy's chin? Is it a mole?* I looked to my right and saw a man slumped in a wheelchair, trying futilely to feed himself soup. *This is depressing.* The walkers, hearing aids, odd skin growths, and airborne food left me in a state beyond discomfort.

"So, how's your new job going?" Clara asked, her voice quiet and crackly.

"Pretty good," I said. "I like it so far. Everyone has been really nice."

"You're the fifth marketing director we've been through in the past year and a half," she continued.

"So I've heard."

"Sharon is a tough boss," Joe Fontes, the guy with the mole, piped in.

"I guess so," I replied and then asked, "So how long have you lived here, Joe?"

"Two years."

"Do you like it?"

"Sure. The people are nice. The place is beautiful. Food's pretty good, too."

We sat in silence for the rest of the meal. They seemed comfortable to sit quietly and eat. I felt an urge to fill the silence, but did not know what to say.

The residents I ate lunch with that day lived in independent living, which provided the basics: meals, housekeeping, activities, transportation, and the comfort of knowing there was staff available 24 hours a day in the event of an emergency. Assisted Living offered this as well as personal care: help with bathing, dressing, medications, and going to the bathroom. Dementia Care was the highest and most expensive level of care, offering everything the first two gave plus 24-hour supervision and incontinence care when needed.

It was nice that my days were filled with work, learning my new job and getting to know all the players involved. I missed Dave and being busy with work helped. At night I talked on the phone with him and my friends in San Francisco and often wrote in my journal.

June 10th

I gave my first tour by myself today. Sharon or Olivia have done tours with me up until now. I got lost on the tour. The place is huge and all those pink and white bungalows look exactly the same. It was embarrassing. I stood there looking at this old lady and her daughter and had to tell them I had no idea how to get back to the main building or my office. Thank God we ran into the gardener, and he pointed the way back to Home Base.

The tour was cool. I showed them a few apartments and the clubhouse and pool. The daughter and I talked about what was going on with her mother. She had a stroke and, God, she walked so <u>slowly</u>. All I could think of was the pile of papers waiting for me on my desk. I've been at this job a week and already I'm behind. "Pick up the pace," I wanted to say to her, "This place is eight friggin' acres!"

I noticed when I toured with Sharon that she walked with the prospective resident, at <u>their</u> pace, even if their kids were young and agile and could walk faster. So, I did that, too. The tour took an hour and a half! I felt bad for the lady but I was also annoyed. She may be retired, but I'm not!

I'm going to Camarillo tomorrow to do my first day of outside sales. I guess I'm just supposed to schmooze with doctors and try to get them to send us people. I don't really even know where I'm going. I've only been to Camarillo once.

June 11th

The outside marketing yesterday was fun. Camarillo is beautiful. I wasn't really sure where to go. Sharon just said, "Go out." I think she thinks I know what I'm doing more than I actually do. I didn't want to tell her that I have no idea how to do this grassroots sales stuff. I'm used to writing advertising proposals and doing presentations to new clients. Anyway, I went into a few doctor's offices with brochures. They were busy and didn't want to talk to me. So, I went to the Senior Center. The lady there let me put a brochure stand in the lobby. I told Sharon about my day and she seemed happy with it. Whatever. I'll just keep plugging away and do the best I can.

Dave finally arrived last night. I'm glad he's here. I was missing him and the trailer was getting lonely. I made enchiladas and rice for dinner tonight and we walked around the neighborhood. I love how peaceful it is here.

Ojai feels like the kind of place where nothing bad could ever happen. It just might be that kind of place, actually. I went to the police station to get fingerprinted because Sharon said they have to do a criminal background check on anyone who works with seniors. Technically, I was supposed to do it before I started working, but she figured I would pass.

I asked the cop about crime in Ojai and he replied, "We have no violent crime." I asked him, "What do you mean you have no violent crime?" and he said, "We had a murder about 15 years ago, but it was a fluke. The only crimes we have really are financial ones, like someone stealing a checkbook off the front seat of your car." Wow. Nice change from the city.

June 20th

I had lunch today with this lady, Francine Lange. She's 94 and lives in her own home here in Ojai. It is up on a hill and overlooks the whole Ojai Valley. I picked her up to take her to lunch because she's thinking of moving to The Gables. Her house was immaculate. So were her clothes and hair. She's soft spoken and intelligent. She seems like the kind of woman who chooses her words carefully—very gracious.

We went to Suzanne's, a nice restaurant in town, and Francine told me what it was like taking one of the first transcontinental flights back in 1949. She was 40 years old and married to a wealthy doctor. The night before their flight, the airline called and asked her how she wanted her steak cooked. The next morning, she got dressed up, hat and gloves, the whole nine yards. They called each passenger by name to board the plane one by one. Everyone watched as you boarded. I thought of the trip I took to Africa a few years ago. I wore sweatpants on the plane and, even though I was in Business Class, the staff could care less that I was boarding. We were herded on like cattle.

July 4th

I had to work today. I missed the barbecue with Dave's family. That really bummed me out. It's a big downside of this job. I've never had a job where I worked holidays. Sharon called me from home and chirped, "We're open 365 days a year," and I wanted to retort, "Then why the hell aren't you here?!"

Glenn, the activity director, and I baked cookies and sat on the front porch with residents, drinking lemonade and watching the floats come back after the parade. All the residents were decked out in red, white and blue. They're really patriotic. We had this Cabaret show last week and when Glenn sang "God Bless America," several residents stood up to sing along. They had tears streaming down their cheeks. The emotion was palpable and the looks on their faces showed a real love of this country. Watching them cry got me choked up. I couldn't imagine people of my generation crying like that over "God Bless America."

July 6th

I met a woman named Gloria Armstrong today. It was her 99th birthday and someone sent her flowers, so I took them from the office up to her apartment in independent living. This woman is amazing. My conversation with her felt the same as those I have with people my own age. She asked me to stay for a glass of iced tea, and I felt pretty caught up on my paperwork, so I accepted her invitation. We talked about politics and George Bush. Gloria is a lefty like me. She's also physically fit. She walked easily around her apartment, serving the iced tea, tidying pillows, showing me her paintings. And she still drives! Sharon says that Gloria drives better than some of the 80-year-olds.

I didn't think it was even possible to be that active at 99. After our visit she left to meet a friend for shopping and lunch.

July 12th

A guy farted on a tour today. I felt bad for him. I don't think he even realized he farted. His daughter and I did. I felt embarrassed for him and uncomfortable with the whole situation. He obviously doesn't have much control anymore. What a bummer getting old. I don't really like this part of the job. I like the outside marketing better, where I network with people my own age.

September 13th

I did outside marketing yesterday. I went to a networking luncheon in Santa Barbara. It was at a beautiful golf course. The drive was relaxing and it took me about an hour to get there. I met people who work in different businesses related to healthcare and assisted living. Mainly marketing people. Young people! So fun! After lunch I toured one of our competitors, Redwoods Santa Barbara. I'm amazed at how friendly my competitors are to me—so different from the advertising field. Everyone really supports one another in this industry. It's refreshing.

Robin, the marketing director, gave me a tour of her place. Then we strolled back to her office, which was <u>beautiful!</u> She has this immense cherry-wood desk, vases of silk flowers everywhere, Rembrandt replicas on the wall, and a gorgeous antique couch and coffee table. She sits there when she talks with families about moving in. What is up with <u>my</u> dumpy office?!

Anyway, the outside marketing is fun and it's starting to pay off. Our phone is ringing at The Gables and I feel good about that. I was starting to feel like I was spinning my wheels with this networking. But we're suddenly getting a lot of inquiries. Woohoo!

November 3rd

There is a resident named Katherine Conway. I just love her. She's kind and really interesting. She's an artist and an intellectual, but also down-to-earth. I love spending time with Katherine. It's funny, but somehow, I feel "lighter" after hanging out with her. I can't put my finger on it or completely figure out why.

Katherine Conway was my first move-in, a little over a month after I started at The Gables. She had been living alone in a condominium in Nevada after her husband's death and she sank into depression. It had been three years since her husband passed away and Katherine was growing more isolated. She also had Parkinson's disease, but her medications were working and she was still able to drive and function quite well. Her kids, one son and one daughter, lived in California and both adored her. When I met with them, they were actually *fighting* over which town Katherine would live in: Long Beach, which was closest to her daughter, or Ojai, closest to her son.

The day Katherine toured with her kids, she seemed low energy, but not overtly melancholy. She mentioned she was an artist but had not painted since her husband's death. I thought, *how sweet, a cute little old lady who paints*. I pictured amateur oil paintings: a house nestled in rolling hills, a bowl of fruit with bright red apples and a yellow pear. "Do you ever sell your paintings?"

"No, they're just for me and my family. I'd like to see something with plenty of natural light, so I can set up my studio."

I showed them apartment number 65, a one-bedroom with a large bay window. Natural light poured in and there was a tree, which gave it some privacy. "I'll think about it," Katherine said.

She went back to Nevada. I sent her a thank-you note then made a few follow-up calls to her and her kids. A month later, Katherine called and said, "I feel like I could be happy there, Liz. I feel like I could start living again. I'll take the apartment with the large bay window." She sent me a check for the deposit that day.

When Katherine moved in, she dedicated her entire living room as a painting studio. I dropped by the first week to see how she was faring and saw that every bookshelf was lined with brushes and paints. *She's serious about this painting hobby*, I thought. She then began to hang up her work. I looked at the paintings then back at this sweet little 83-year-old lady and thought, *was she dropping acid when she painted these?*

They were psychedelic, colorful, spiritual, and unlike anything I had seen. One had red swirls which melted into orange and black with obscurely interwoven shapes. I must have looked at that painting 20 times over the course of the next five months before I noticed the distinct shape of a brown penis in the upper right-hand corner. When we had a resident art show, Dave came and was blown away by Katherine's paintings. At my urging, Katherine finally agreed to make and sell prints of her work and I was her first customer.

A few months later, her Parkinson's accelerated and her hands started shaking so much that she couldn't paint. She was also having hallucinations from her medications. I had been marketing to a top-notch neurologist in Oxnard, an hour away from Ojai. I put Katherine in touch with him and he got her on the right combination of medications and she was able to continue painting.

Katherine intrigued me. She spent whole afternoons discussing Shakespeare with another resident named Frank Edwards. Sometimes they would let me join in. I loved my Tuesday through Saturday workweek because once in a while, Saturdays were quiet and I could sneak away to visit residents like these who had become my friends. One day, I went by Katherine's apartment. Sitting on her sofa sipping a cup of tea, I looked up at one of my favorite pieces and asked her how she started painting.

"I was in my mid-30s," she explained. "And I experienced my first bout with depression. It was severe and progressed to the point where I couldn't move or get out of bed."

"Wow. What brought that on?"

"I have no idea. But my husband tried every form of help to get me to snap out it. Finally, he took me to the Mayo Clinic. I can't remember exactly how or when, but at some point during my stay there, I started painting. I created my own process where I put water on the paper and then floated acrylic paint in various shapes onto the page. It was the only thing that worked. I started to feel better and I could function again. Medication and therapy were useless. Painting was the key and my doctors told me to keep doing it."

"That's amazing," I said, scanning the room full of powerful paintings. "And you kept at it from then on?"

"Yes, for the next 45 years, until the day my husband died. When I met you, I had not picked up a brush in three years."

"I'm sorry, Katherine."

"It's all right," she said, "I started painting again the day I moved in here. I just love this place. And I want to thank you for convincing me to move in. You were really the catalyst. You took your time, showed me several apartments, followed-up with me until I was ready to make the decision. You made me feel safe."

"Don't mention it," I said and winked at her, "I wanted the commission check."

Estelle Collins was another resident I grew to love. She was a Christian Scientist who one day drank a glass of her own urine instead of iced tea with our lunch, "because it boosts the immune system." That was a little creepy, but besides that, she was quite normal. She was 96 and had lived at The Gables for 16 years. Everything was wonderful to Estelle. The day she fell and broke both hips, she just said over and over, "I'm so lucky. I'm the luckiest lady in the world. Look at these two handsome men carrying me away!"

Breaking a hip is one of the most painful experiences there is. Breaking *two* hips had to be excruciating. Yet Estelle found the silver lining. That was her way. I never once saw that lady cranky.

Of course, the residents weren't *all* fascinating and delightful. There was Eloise Hersch, who severely got on my nerves. Eloise bitched about everything in a whiny, sing-songy voice. If there was an activity on the calendar and it didn't happen, Eloise let us know. It didn't matter that she wasn't interested in participating in the art class. It didn't matter that Glenn had to cancel because he had broken his foot and was at the hospital. Eloise was the self-appointed "Calendar Police" and, by God, if something was on that calendar, it better be happening. Eloise complained about the food, the weather, the housekeepers, the phone, the heater, the air conditioner, even the gardens, which were immaculate. If it was the first day of Fall and a leaf had found its way to the brick patio outside the dining room door, Eloise would be in the office saying to Mary, "The gardener had better sweep up those leaves. They're a fall hazard, you know." She had scrunched lips and bright red hair like a Raggedy Ann doll.

I found Eloise annoying not because she was old but because she was annoying.

Once, I was scheduled to drive the van for a field trip because we were short-staffed in the Activities Department and Glenn needed a hand. I was happy to pitch in. It was a welcome break from the phone calls and paperwork. The day before the field trip, I went to the office and asked Mary for the list of residents who had signed up. I was even more excited when I saw the names on the list: Abigail Hayes, Valorie Branson, Harry Minassian and Estelle Collins, some of my favorite people. *This will be a fun day!*

The next morning, I checked in with Mary before loading up the van. I took the list so I could check off names as the residents arrived. Glancing down, Eloise's name leaped out at me.

"*Bummer,*" I said to Mary. "When did Eloise sign up? Damn, she's such a pain in the ass."

"I thought you'd like that," Mary chuckled. "She came in this morning before breakfast and asked if there was still room."

"Well, why didn't you tell her there *wasn't* room?" I asked.

Mary laughed. "Liz, you crack me up. She'll be fine."

"She's going to ruin our day."

"Better you than me," Mary said. "I get to enjoy half a day without hearing her complain."

"Thanks," I smiled at Mary, "I'm going to make a recording and hide it somewhere in this office where you'll never find it. It will just play over and over, day after day."

"Enjoy," Mary said with a sincere smile as I walked out of the office towards the parking lot. It was a sunny, warm day, we were heading to the beach for lunch and now Eloise had gone and ruined it.

I climbed into the driver's seat and watched Eloise walk towards the van. Harry was already seated in the back and we were waiting for the others to arrive. Eloise demanded, "Where are we going for lunch?"

"Eric Ericsson's at the pier," I said.

"Well, I hope they don't have fish there, because I don't like fish."

I turned to look at Eloise's head, with its shockingly bright red locks, and thought, *there* had *to be another shade of red available at the salon.*

"It's a *seafood* place, Eloise. If you don't like fish, I don't know if this is the right field trip for you."

"Oh, that's fine, I'll just order something else. I'm sure they have burgers and things."

On the way to the restaurant, we stopped by Harry's old house. He wanted to say hi to his neighbor, Arnie. At first, he went to the wrong house and we all watched him have an awkward exchange with the woman who answered the door. When she closed the door, Harry turned around, walked back down the steps, stopping to spit in the bushes, and went to the next house, which was in fact Arnie's. Arnie didn't invite him in. I sat there, watching Harry talking to this man who had been his friend for 40 years. Their conversation was brief and their body language awkward.

I thought, *they seem so distant. I wonder if Kayleigh and I will be like that one day.* My best friend, Kayleigh, lived many miles away in San Francisco, but we immediately connected whenever we talked on the phone or visited in person. We understood each other. I couldn't imagine us ever growing apart and not feeling that closeness anymore.

Harry was quiet when he got back in the car. Eloise began rambling on about something in her high-pitched voice. Harry, sitting next to her, turned and asked, "Are you talking?" and I burst out laughing and almost hit the car in front of me. He had turned off his hearing aid . . . lucky guy.

We arrived at the pier and found parking close to the restaurant's entrance. The salty ocean air smelled refreshing. The seagulls sang overhead. Harry, Valorie, and Eloise got out of the van on their own. I retrieved Estelle and Abigail's walkers from the back and opened them up, checking that the brakes were set before helping each of the ladies onto the street, pleased with myself at how adept I had become at handling walkers and old ladies.

We asked a passerby to take our photo in front of the restaurant's entryway. Noon on a Tuesday meant the place was quiet, so we easily got a table with a full ocean view. I took one for the team and sat next to Eloise. Our waitress was a sweet young girl who didn't seem to mind repeating the specials four times. Eloise ordered a chicken sandwich and the rest of us ordered seafood. I had halibut and chips, which was cooked perfectly. We drank cokes and Abigail described her modeling days in New York. Estelle smiled and laughed a lot. Harry turned his hearing aid back on and listened intently. Eloise even gave Abigail a compliment, "You *do* always dress nice. I could see how you would have been a model."

We watched the waves and took our time with lunch. Harry talked about the RV trip he had taken cross country with his wife 15 years earlier. "She was so friendly, my Annie. Got along with everyone we met along the way. And the scenery was beautiful. We had a great time on the trip. I am thinking of taking my grandkids on the same route next summer."

"Oh, wouldn't that be lovely," Estelle said.

Harry and Valorie ordered ice cream and coffee for dessert. When the bill came, I looked at my watch and realized we had been there two hours. It had been a great day, so nice even Eloise couldn't ruin it.

In early December of my first year at The Gables, I was sitting in the office with John. He was working on budgets as I wrote notes and sent invitations for our Christmas dinner to hot and warm prospects. A group of kids from the elementary school down the street had stopped by and sung carols earlier that day. The songs ran through my head as I stuffed envelopes. Even our dingy office was festive, with a gold garland on the wall. Turning my chair to face John, I asked, "So, what're you guys doing for Christmas?"

"You know, staying home, going by Jennifer's parents with the kids on Christmas Eve."

"How fun to have little ones around on Christmas morning."

"Yeah, fun except for all the money it costs. How 'bout you guys, what are you up to?"

"Well, we got a cute little tree for our trailer. We're going to decorate it tonight."

Sharon came and stood in our doorway.

"What are you two quibbling about now?"

"We're actually playing nice today," I said.

"The Resident Christmas Tea is about to start. Are you guys coming?"

I sealed a couple more envelopes, made a quick call to one of my hot prospects, then made my way to the lounge.

The lounge was decorated with garlands, wreaths, ribbons, and a large tree in the center adorned with ornaments and twinkling lights. About 40 residents and 20 staff members sat or milled about the room. They were drinking tea and champagne, nibbling on appetizers and cookies, laughing and exchanging hugs. Almost everyone was dressed in festive red, green or gold. The ladies wore their nicest jewelry, their hair done up. The scene looked like a Norman Rockwell painting. I took the seat next to my friend, Katherine Conway, who smiled and gave me a hug. "Merry Christmas, Katherine," I said, a warmth washing over me.

"Merry Christmas, Liz." One of the ladies was playing the piano while Glenn, dressed as Santa, led us in singing "Joy to the World." I felt so happy—it dawned on me that I was now in my element when surrounded by elders.

By January I was feeling on solid ground at The Gables. Things had gelled. Life in Ojai was peaceful. Things were even harmonious, for the most part, with Dave and me. All was well in my world.

January 10th

I'm finally in a groove with this job. I feel like I have the flow down with tours, phone calls, thank you notes, outside marketing, all the things I need to do to get move-ins. I also like everyone I work with. John and I have our moments of conflict, but it feels like a family here, with Sharon being the "Mama Bear."

The only downside is the owner, Sofia Flores. Not a nice woman. She is really full of herself and rude to me and everyone else when she comes to The Gables. All she does is put pressure on people. There's no appreciation.

February 10th

Working with old people makes me wonder what would be worse, to lose my mind or my body? I've seen both here. People with dementia who stay very physically healthy yet deteriorate mentally. Others have heart problems, osteoporosis, or arthritis yet their brain still fires on all cylinders. Actually, either way would be a bummer. I want to be active and healthy until the end like Gloria, Estelle, and Gertrude.

June 8th

Dr. Baker has problems with his prostate and he lost control in the dining room today. He was leaking feces on the floor and didn't realize it. And there was Sharon, the boss, walking behind him with a rag and paper towels cleaning it up and trying to be sly about it so he and others wouldn't notice. That woman is amazing.

As the days and months at The Gables passed, I found myself spending more mornings and afternoons in the dining room, talking and breaking bread with folks in their 80s and 90s. Somewhere about a year into my job, it dawned on me that I was becoming less aware of their physical limitations, dentures, walkers, wheelchairs, and hearing aids.

I became fascinated by this generation of people born between 1900 and 1930, known as the "Greatest Generation." I got to hear what it was like to be in New York in 1942, serving in the Navy, meeting your sweetheart at the Officer's Club, driving her home and getting to know her mom that same night. "You couldn't waste time back then; there were not a lot of women to go around," Milton Foster told me.

"People got married quick. We were going off to war and there wasn't time for a lengthy courtship. I got to know my wife through letters. I was stationed in Italy; she was back home in New York, living with her mom. I knew her a month before we got married." He pulled out a picture of his wife that he carried in his wallet. "This is my Edith on our wedding day. We spent that first year and a half of marriage on separate continents. She was so happy I had made it home alive that things like taking out the garbage or other stuff you young folks fight about seemed trivial."

Over meals of pot roast and vegetables or chicken and mashed potatoes, I asked them to tell me about life back then. One lady, Margie, spoke about the Great Depression. I had not truly grasped how painful a time that was. "My two uncles moved in with us," she remembered, "and I felt the tension constantly. Dad didn't want them there and they sure didn't want to have to be there. My uncles were grown men, humiliated by having to depend on their sister and her husband. They even had to share a room. One was a skilled carpenter. The other had earned his college degree."

"Even as an eight-year-old child, I remember feeling sad for them.

We kept thinking things would get better, that the economy would turn around. This was the United States of America. But it dragged on and on. My uncles lived with us for six years. A lot of times there wasn't enough food on the dinner table, so we all ate a little bit and went to bed hungry."

Residents spoke of being adults the first time they saw television and for most of them, it was "The Milton Berle Show." I heard reminiscences of having one phone in the house and how they would pick up the receiver and say "Operator, could you please connect me with 1744-J?" If it was long distance, they could only speak for a minute or less and had to yell to be heard.

The Greatest Generation lived through Prohibition, women's suffrage, the invention of the automobile, the television, *and* the airplane. Some of the women I met were among the first to ever vote in this country. What must that have *felt* like? They saw their friends and siblings die in World War II and Korea and watched their kids die in Vietnam. They pulled together to win World War II, a war which affected *everyone* in the United States, not just soldiers and their families. Everyone back home felt its impact, from food rations to making bombs in plants. They created the greatest industrial and economic boom in history. They went from horse-and-buggy days to men on the moon, often struggling to meet basic human needs. Through all of this they developed amazing coping skills, which eventually helped them to deal with the challenge of getting old.

I remember one day overhearing a table of residents talking about their first time eating in a restaurant. "Do any of you remember the first time you went out and actually paid for a meal?" Emma Thompson asked.

"I remember," Bob Jameson said. "I was seven years old and my dad took me to this place that had a buffet. I couldn't believe we were someplace other than our house and we were paying someone to cook a meal for us. I filled my plate with baked chicken and it was delicious. I'll never forget it."

"My aunt took me," Zelda Derrickson said, "and I ordered a baked potato with butter, sour cream, and chives. It was piping hot and every bite just melted on my tongue. That was 80 years ago and I can still taste that baked potato."

Everyone went around the table and described their first restaurant experience. I sat there eavesdropping, realizing all the things I take for granted. Reproductive rights were another thing I have enjoyed my whole life, but not so for these ladies.

One day at lunch, Eileen Fisher said to the group at our table, "I remember when the Pill came out in 1960. I was 25 and my friends and I were all so happy! That Pill was the best thing that ever happened to women." The thought of living in a world without birth control pills is inconceivable to me.

On the whole Starbucks phenomenon, Filomena Meyer commented, "I just don't get it. When I was growing up, we paid 10 cents for a cup of coffee. I can't understand why someone would pay four dollars for one of those things." She recalled standing in soup lines during the Great Depression, then added, "I have to admit, though, I did go over there one day to try one of those lattes. I had to see what all the fuss was about. And, actually, it *was* delicious. But I won't do it again."

This generation saw philanthropy and service as a way of life. They grew up long before the 1970s "Me Generation." They didn't complain about giving time and money to others; they just did it because it was the right thing to do. They valued dedication, loyalty, duty, delayed gratification, hard work, and respect for authority. A person's word was gold. They bought things with cash, almost never on credit, and a 13-percent mortgage was considered a steal. They said "Please" and "Thank You." They sent notes on nice stationery.

I began to revere the WWII Generation. My generation looked like wimps compared to these guys. Then one day, over lunch, Ralph Blumenthal asked me, "So, what's it like living in San Francisco with all those queers?"

"Excuse me?" I replied, as I tried to swallow the piece of meatloaf caught in my throat.

"The fairies. Isn't San Francisco crawling with them? And now I hear they want to get *married!*"

"Ralph, I don't think you want to have this conversation with me." I took a drink of my iced tea and thought to myself before proceeding into the minefield. *Be respectful, Liz. Ralph grew up in a different time and you're not going to change his 82-year-old mind.*

"I just think we may see this situation a little differently," I said.

"It's perverse and immoral. They ought to be ashamed of themselves," he retorted.

"Ralph, gay men and women are born that way. Do you think they wake up one day and say 'I think I would like to be a homosexual'? Do you think anyone would willingly put themselves through the pain of trying to fit into a heterosexual world when they aren't heterosexual? I seriously doubt it."

"Geez, I didn't realize you felt so strongly about the issue," he said. "I'm sorry, I just think it's wrong. It says so in the Bible."

"Really? Where does it say so in the Bible? Everyone is always referring to that, but no one has actually *shown* me the passage. I have as strong a faith in God as the next person and if I remember correctly, Jesus said, 'Love your neighbor as you love yourself and judge not lest you be judged.'"

We sat quietly for a moment and then I went on. "Do you think Matthew Shepard, the young man who was brutally murdered and hung on a fence in Wyoming, *chose* his fate? No, Ralph, he was just being himself and he got killed for it. Thank God places like San Francisco exist, where there is a bit of love and acceptance. Gay rights issues are *civil* rights issues." We chewed our food for several long minutes.

"And as for gay marriage," I asked, "would you prefer that a gay man marry *your* daughter and secretly have affairs with men on the side? Anyway, how does it affect you if two men get married? They're not telling you that you can't be straight or marry a woman."

He looked at me with his mouth slightly open. I took a bite of my potatoes and stared angrily out the window.

Then Ralph said, "I suppose we probably shouldn't talk about the unemployed Negroes."

"Definitely not, Ralph. And FYI, people don't use that word anymore."

Getting to know these elders was an adventure and living in Ojai was a pleasure. Summer was my favorite time of year. Some people complained about the heat, but I loved it. Having lived all those chilly years in

San Francisco, wearing flip flops and shorts was a treat. There was something about warm weather that made everything more relaxing, even work.

June 30th

I started teaching the water aerobics class on Saturdays. It's really fun! Ojai is HOT in the summer, so it's a nice break to put on my swimsuit at noon and jump into the pool with the ladies. Sharon says we're all "Universal Workers." No one at The Gables says, "That's not my job." It's part of what makes the place so special. The Activities Department helps me with marketing; I help them with activities; caregivers help Housekeeping. So, when Glenn said he couldn't do the Saturday water aerobics class, I raised my hand.

I watched a DVD from the Arthritis Association and it showed me all the moves. I also brought my boom box and played some disco music. The ladies loved the music and moved nicely in the water. It was a joy to watch them scooping their arms and lifting their legs, building on whatever strength they had. I liked doing the exercises slowly, really being in the moment rather than rushing through like I often do at the gym. It felt good to cheer my students on from the front of the pool. Everyone said they got a good workout. At the end of the class, Miriam Lewis, said to me, "My dear, you have a lovely figure." She's such a sweetheart.

July 6th

General Braswell came by my office today and said, "I hear you're teaching water aerobics topless, so I'm going to sign up." What is he <u>thinking</u>! The guy is 94 years old. I told him, "No, I'm not teaching it <u>topless</u>!"

July 8th

Filomena Meyer intrigues me. She's 87, super political, and an accomplished writer. Her husband died 20 years ago and Filomena has kept plugging along. She wrote a book about her husband's illness and what it was like to slowly lose him.

Filomena wears hats a lot, mostly to shield the sun, and she loves art. She still drives. I can't believe how many of these seniors still drive! I like talking with Filomena. The other day she said to me, "George Bush is an asshole. How the hell did that guy get elected?"

One day, about a year and a half into my job at The Gables, a woman named Jessica Smith came to visit her grandmother, whom we called "Miss Golda." Actually, Jessica came to spend a month in Ojai to be near her grandmother, who had raised her. I had met Jessica several times and heard the whole history of how wonderful Miss Golda had been to her and her siblings following their mother's premature death. Miss Golda was now 92 and had lived at The Gables for 7 years. From a distance, I watched Jessica walk up to her. Jessica was 42, a triathlete, trim, and toned. She looked sleek in her black skirt and top. She leaned down to hug Golda in her wheelchair and handed her a bouquet of spring flowers.

Watching the scene, I felt an unexpected lump well up in my throat. I had witnessed many granddaughters visiting their grandmas at The Gables, but it didn't hit me until that moment that I missed *my* grandmother. I longed for her terribly. I did not think about my grandma often. It was too painful to remember, so I locked the memories of her away and rarely brought them out. Standing there, watching Jessica and Miss Golda, it occurred to me that my grandma was born around the same time as many of The Gables' residents.

My grandmother's name was Ruth and she was born in 1921. Our nickname for her was Nanny, which we always called her. She was the only grandparent I ever knew. All the others had died before I was born. Nanny wore White Shoulders perfume, which smelled like powder and came in a pink box with a silhouette of a woman on it. She loved that perfume. Every year, we saved our money to buy her a bottle at Christmas and she beamed when she opened it. It didn't take much to make Nanny happy. She always seemed delighted when we were around.

Nanny died in 1980 at age 59. On that day, Halloween 1980, my childhood came to an abrupt end. I was 10 years old. There would be no more making potions and burying them in the backyard. Whenever Nanny cleaned out her kitchen, she would give us old boxes of rice and crackers from the cupboards, all the canned foods, bottles of juice, and fruits, vegetables, and eggs that had gone bad in the refrigerator. These she would hand to us along with a large pot and say, "Here, go make up a witches' potion over a fire in the backyard. Cast some spells then bury the potion."

What fun we had with those marching orders!

There would be no more of that, and no more corn roasts or handmade costumes on Halloween, either. There would be no more sleepovers at Nanny's house, filling her living room with tents made out of sheets that smelled like fresh air because they had dried on the clothesline in her garden.

Everything was an adventure with Nanny. One of my earliest memories is being three years old on a trip to Minnesota with her. We were out in a field, singing and picking blueberries. Nanny wore a large, wide-brimmed straw hat. I have a photograph of myself on that day: I am wearing a green-and-white striped shirt and my hair is tied in pigtails. I had my bucket, filling it away with fresh blueberries, all the while, looking over my shoulder for bears because Nanny told me they loved blueberries and we needed to get the hell out of there if they came along and wanted some. The blueberries were forbidden fruit we were stealing from the bears, and somehow, the threat of that impending danger made the adventure even more fun.

When I was four years old, my mom, brother, sister, and I moved to Wisconsin because my mom was trying to reconcile her marriage with my stepfather, a stocky, violent man with black hair like a helmet and a face that rarely smiled. When Christmas rolled around, Nanny sent us huge boxes of gifts. I'll never forget the day those three boxes arrived, one for each of us. I was a tiny child and those boxes were a message of joy and light piercing through the darkness of fear in which we all lived, my mother most of all.

After six months, we fled Wisconsin one night and drove two days straight until we arrived at Nanny's house in California. I felt like Dorothy arriving in Oz. Nanny had prepared for our arrival by placing yellow smiley-face stickers on drawers, cabinets, and closets throughout her ranch-style home. Behind each smiley face was a present. It was like an Easter egg hunt in May. I don't remember what the presents were, only the yellow and black smiley-face stickers all over Nanny's house and how good it was to finally feel happy and safe.

After my mom escaped her husband, we stayed in San Diego and my mom bought a house one block from Nanny's. I was six years old and having my grandma nearby was heaven. I would wake up in the morning and she was there making her special pancakes, thin, like crepes: a taste sensation of warm, soft, melted butter and sugar rolled up in a succulent pastry. Eating those, I felt loved. I still eat my pancakes rolled up with butter and sugar and friends often look at me funny in restaurants. After school, Nanny would be there with fresh watermelon and Kool-Aid, which I would devour while I did my homework. She also taught me to crochet and we spent afternoons crocheting and watching "The Carol Burnett Show," both of us laughing hysterically.

On our birthdays every year, Nanny brought us breakfast in bed. The breakfast consisted of *anything* we wanted. The year I turned seven, I asked for an all-chocolate breakfast: chocolate doughnuts, hot chocolate, and a chocolate candy bar. And that is exactly what she brought me, served on her finest china, on a tray with a linen doily, a crystal bud vase holding a single red rose, and a bell I could ring if I needed anything else. I was "Queen for a Day." Snuggled into my warm, cozy bed at Nanny's house, I felt special, spoiled, and glorious.

When Nanny was 40, before I was born, her sister had cancer, which led to a double mastectomy. I don't think reconstructive surgery existed then, because Aunt Ruby had these cone-shaped hard plastic fake boobs. Whenever Aunt Ruby visited, Nanny would borrow those cones and put them on her head, her back, her underarms, her knees, anywhere she could think of to make us kids reel with laughter. We never knew where those fake breasts were going to pop up.

Many days, Nanny would pick me up from school and we would run errands. We drove to the bank, the dry cleaner, and the grocery store. On days when I was really good and patient, we would end our day at a thrift store. I was allowed one purchase and it was usually a pair of size-five high-heel shoes, or a new ball gown for my dress-up collection. Thanks to my grandma, I had the coolest dress-up trunk in town, full of taffeta and silk frocks. My girlfriends loved to come over. We smoked toothpicks, wore high heels, carried beaded evening bags, and sipped fake cocktails.

Nanny wasn't perfect. I suspect she was a far better grandma than she was a mother. While my mom, an only child, was growing up, Nanny was more interested in men than she was in child rearing. My mom still talks about the pain of those years, how she rarely saw her mom, how they were always moving to a different house. I think she never got over the revolving door of men. I inherited Nanny's love of men, sometimes to my own detriment. One time, consumed with thoughts of a lover, I forgot I was pumping gas and brought the hose and tank with me as I drove away.

I was eight when Nanny got cancer in her leg. She had a bump on her upper thigh and convinced herself it was a bruise from running into something. By the time she got it checked, the cancer had advanced to the bone and the surgeries and chemotherapy began. She sewed me a nurse's outfit, tailored to fit my four-foot frame, complete with a hat. I had charts to keep track of her medications. It was my turn to serve her breakfast in bed. I gave her a bell to ring. I told her to ring the bell if she needed anything at all. Sometimes she needed a glass of water, sometimes a game of Gin Rummy, which we always played for money. Usually, she just needed a hug.

Obstacles did not exist to Nanny. When the doctors told her she would never walk again, she embarked on her own plan of physical therapy: leg exercises she invented, secret attempts at getting up with the walker, attempts at walking a few steps. Finally, after six rigorous months, Nanny surprised us all and walked again. Every morning, she hobbled the quarter-mile down the sidewalk, from her house to ours, to make us pancakes before we went to school.

Her leg was in a brace and she could not bend at the knee, yet somehow, she managed to get to all my softball games and practices. She watched the game from a horizontal position on a nearby hill. I played left field and frequently looked over at Nanny, lying in the ice plant, wearing floral print pants, and a big straw hat.

The last time I saw Nanny was at Mercy Hospital in San Diego. Hallucinating from morphine, she mumbled a lot that night. She grabbed my mom's hand and swatted at the air, yelling, "There are bugs everywhere." My grandma, this rock of a woman, was terrified and that frightened me. My mom told her I was there and Nanny took my hand in hers and stared off into space. She didn't look at me, but for a moment she seemed lucid and present, conscious that I was there. "My Beth," she repeated over and over, "My Beth." I felt her calm down. I felt connected to her. Three days later, she was gone.

Nanny made everything fun and being with her felt like having a part in a movie, so fun that it didn't seem real. When she died, the movie ended and reality crashed in on us. Afternoons were now spent with a series of horrible babysitters. My mom was a single mom with three children, wracked with guilt. She couldn't be home with us—she was too busy trying to survive. I saw the sadness in her eyes, the longing to do fun, carefree, childhood things with us. I felt an incredible longing to bring Nanny back and fix this sad situation.

On field-trip days, my mom got up extra early and went to the local deli so that I would have a special sandwich to take with me. On Valentine's Day, we awoke to dainty gifts wrapped in pink paper, next to purple African Violet plants and heart-shaped candy treats. Mom created her own version of magic in Nanny's absence, but nothing could fill the void left by Nanny's death.

At The Gables, 23 years later, I felt sad for my mom and missed my grandma, with bittersweet memories flooding back. There, perhaps, was the root of some of the animosity I had felt towards seniors: they lived and Nanny didn't.

Why did Eloise, Filomena, Estelle, and Katherine get to live, yet Nanny didn't? It wasn't that I did not want them here; it was just that I wanted her here, too. *What would she be like now? What would she look like? Would she still be as funny? I bet she'd be even funnier and sassier. Would she still have her mind? Would she be physically fit, driving and dancing like a maniac? How would she spend her days? Would we play cards for nickels and pennies the way we did when I was seven? God, what I wouldn't give to hug her one more time, in the flesh.*

I imagined somewhere among the ladies at The Gables there were grandmas who had spoiled their grandkids the way Nanny spoiled us. On some level, without even being conscious of it, I decided rather than disliking them, I would love my grandma through them.

I began taking a little more time with Estelle instead of rushing off to the next task on my to-do list. I started buying flowers, stationery, and other small gifts for Abigail, Gertrude, and especially Violet, who had no children or grandchildren. I spent afternoons with Beverly looking at her Irish linens and hearing about the trips to Europe where she bought them. I even started being nicer to Eloise Hersch.

September 8th

I took pictures of Gertrude today with her cat. She loves that cat. Sophie has a gorgeous gray coat. The pictures will be Gertrude's Christmas card this year. She is so excited to send it to all her friends and family.

We often tell Gertrude not to let the cat out at night because of the coyotes. But she'll have none of it. "Cats are supposed to be free," she says. "They need to get out. It's unnatural to keep them cooped up inside!"

November 30th

Dave's grandma, Goma, may be moving to The Gables. She lives in Salinas and Dave brought her here for Thanksgiving. She loved Ojai and wants more social connection. She spends too much time alone and she's tired of cooking. We didn't realize how lonely she was until she and Dave started talking on the drive down. She started opening up to him about her feelings.

I took a tour of The Gables with Goma and Dave's mom, Yvonne. Yvonne said she doesn't like the idea of her mom living so far away and wants to see her more. We had lunch with Gertrude who raved about living there. Gertrude told Goma the place had great food, interesting company, a lot of activities. She really sold her on the place and I didn't have to say a word! Yvonne made fun of me for taking them into the conference room after lunch. She called it the "closing room." It's not about making a sale, though, with Goma or with the other families I meet. I really do think they would be happier here than sitting alone at home.

January 13th

Goma moved into The Gables yesterday. She got a great studio with an awesome view. I'm so glad it was available. Dave helped the maintenance team remodel it. They put in a new bathroom, new paint and molding. It looks beautiful! Goma seems excited about her new home. I went with her to her first doctor's appointment. Dr. Lazer was amazed at how vibrant she is for someone who's 90. During the endurance test, she jammed around that parking lot with her walker. He could barely keep up with her! I think she's going to have fun here. And it will be great for the family to have her close by.

January 23rd

Sofia Flores came by this afternoon. She met with Sharon and gave me a dirty look on her way into the office. I don't know <u>what</u> that woman's issue is with me. After she left, Sharon came in and said, "She wants you to write 'asked for referrals' on your activity report next to the doctor visits. I know that's what you're doing in the field but she wants to see it on your report."

I snapped at Sharon, "Tell her she can kiss my ass. We're full with a waiting list."

Sharon said I was right.

I feel bad for Sharon being caught between me and her boss, but give me a break! This woman is unbelievable. She's got the nerve to complain about my <u>activity report?</u> I liked it better when her husband was managing our property.

February 13th

We are finally ready to move from the trailer into the house and now Dave wants to sell the house. The house is almost finished but he doesn't like living next door to his brother. I'm not digging it anymore either. There has been major conflict over this whole property deal. Big mistake to mix family and money!

Maybe we'll go back to San Francisco. I don't know. Dave said it's my decision since it was his choice to come to Ojai. Now I <u>love</u> Ojai. I'm not sure what I want to do.

February 26th

I had a relaxing morning with Goma in her apartment. She loves her life here! She said she feels like The Gables is "two steps away from heaven." She played Mozart for me on the piano and we ate Pepperidge Farm cookies and drank tea. It's really nice to have a family member at The Gables.

I made a lot of friends while working at The Gables: residents, coworkers and colleagues, at places in Ojai, Santa Barbara, and Ventura. One of the best friends I made was Claire, an Irish woman with four kids, a full-time job, a great sense of humor, and a huge heart. Claire was the executive director of a 50-bed dementia care home in Oak View, the town right next to Ojai. It was a 10-minute drive for me and sometimes Claire and I had lunch or went out marketing together. We often saw each other at networking events and open houses. We supported each other and referred prospects back and forth. If I hosted a party or art show at The Gables, Claire always came and brought her residents. I did the same when she had an event. Three years into my job at The Gables, Claire called me about an opportunity.

April 3rd

Claire called today. Some people from Irvine bought her place and they are looking for a marketing director. I agreed to meet them next week to talk about the job. I'm not sure if Dave and I are going to stay in Ojai long-term or go back to S.F. One thing I am sure of, though, is that I'm ready to move on from The Gables. I've learned how to do this job well and I want more money. I love Sharon, but I'm pretty tired of working for Sofia Flores. I've made that woman bank and gotten NO appreciation.

April 12th

Dinner was great tonight. I loved the woman from the Irvine company! I felt like I had known her for years. She said she wants me to meet the CEO next week.

This job might be a great move. Oak View is close by <u>and</u> I would get to work with my buddy, Claire! The place is all dementia care, which would be easier than selling three different products. Plus, I already have tons of contacts and referral sources. And it's a bigger company with more opportunity.

The Gables is full with a waiting list and not only do I feel underappreciated, I'm actually kind of bored.

May 12th

We sold our house back to Steve and put down a deposit on a rental. I can't wait to move and get away from this family drama. I thought <u>my</u> family was bad!

The rental house is nice. It's still in Ojai, but at least we won't be right next door to Steve. I'm glad Dave will have a break. He has been working night and day on this house for three years. He's exhausted.

The opportunity with Claire's place, Sunset Oaks, fell into my lap. I loved the residents and staff at The Gables, loved the magical feel the place had. But it was time to go, so I accepted the new position. It paid a lot more and I connected with every one of the people at the new company, from the top down. It just felt right and it *was* right. I got to work with a dear friend and I learned a lot more about dementia care.

Dave and I now lived in the rental house and I worked as marketing director for Sunset Oaks. I loved doing outside marketing three days a week and spending two days at the building. My life felt balanced and I even had time to stay in touch and visit friends at The Gables. Then Dave unexpectedly got an offer to work for a friend who was doing a large condominium development in Mazatlán. I had only been at Sunset Oaks six months and it was the best job I had ever had, but still I decided to quit. I had been going hard for years, simultaneously working and going to school during high school and college, putting in 15-hour days at many of the jobs I had since then, and generally burning my candle at both ends. I was tired. The chance to lie on the beach and do nothing for a while sounded nice.

We left Ojai in December and spent four wonderful months in Mexico, cutting our trip short when we both received unsolicited job offers during the same week. Dave was offered a remodel project and I was offered a marketing director position at a 130-bed assisted living and Alzheimer's care property three miles from our house in San Francisco. Both opportunities were too good to pass up. We decided it was a sign to go home early, so we called our renters and told them they would need to move out.

We arrived back in San Francisco in April and I immediately started my job at Casa Amanecer. The place was a nonprofit and, like every retirement community where I had worked, it felt like home. I had only been there six months and was doing well when the owner of Sunset Oaks Ojai called and offered me an even better position, as regional director of sales and marketing, working from my home in San Francisco.

My fluke job in assisted living had turned into a career. I accepted the regional position and for the next two years I managed properties in California, Idaho, and Michigan.

Over the years, I worked for several different companies in many different capacities. At times I was in charge of filling one building; at other times I was responsible for as many as 22 buildings in three different states. I spent a total of eight years in the industry:

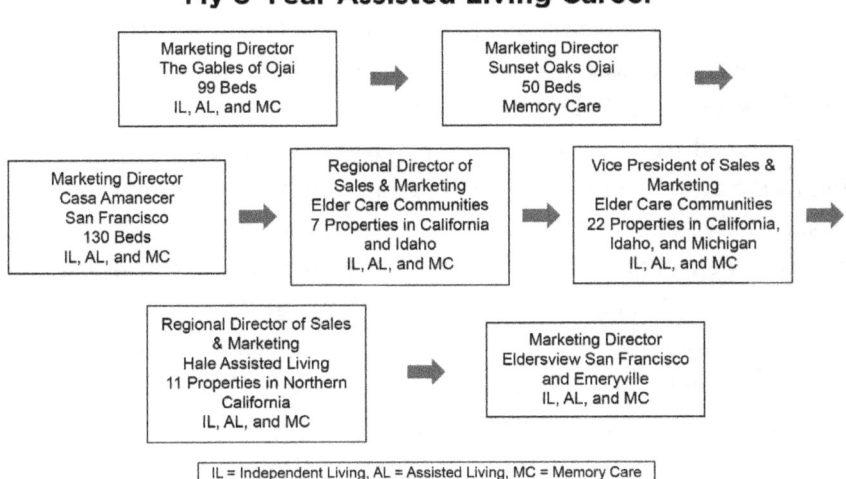

During those years, I met hundreds of seniors, and I visited numerous hospitals, assisted living communities, and nursing homes. I participated in conferences and training sessions on aging, Alzheimer's and marketing to seniors and their families. I attended networking luncheons with speakers talking about everything from macular degeneration to hospice to choosing the right walker.

When I began at The Gables and Sharon asked me to write a letter and send a brochure, I had no idea what assisted living was. The Assisted Living Federation of America (ALFA) described it as, "A special combination of housing, personalized supportive services and health care designed to meet the needs—both scheduled and unscheduled—of those who need help with activities of daily living."

But the assisted living world is so much more than that. Every day, I experienced a sense of community. I saw people of all ages and backgrounds interacting and sharing a commitment to one another's well-being. I also met cranky, racist, and homophobic elders. I witnessed both the fulfilling and painful sides of aging. My work was challenging at times but never boring.

I thought that moving to Ojai meant giving up my career. Ironically, it turned out to be the best career move of my life. I made great money doing work I loved in a nearly recession-proof industry: despite the economy, there always seems to be *a lot* of old people.

I learned from assisted living residents about things like marriage, family dynamics, dementia, death, aging, friendship, and life. In my mid-20s, I briefly dated a guy named Dan who was also in his 20s. My nickname for him when talking with friends was "Geriatric Guy" because he was editor of a senior's magazine and had obtained his degree in Gerontology. He wrote about seniors and about subjects that elders found relevant. I just didn't get it. "What could you possibly find intriguing about old people?" I asked Dan on our second date. "They seem so *boring* to me."

"Not at all," he said. "You're missing out. They are full of wisdom and resilience. We have so much to learn from them, if we will just take the time."

Chapter Three

Falling Apart

Old age ain't no place for sissies.

— Bette Davis

Dan was right. Wisdom and resilience surrounded me during my years in assisted living. It was an ever-present well that I could tap into, learn from, and from which I derived much joy. My career gave me a unique opportunity to pull up a chair next to elders and see what being old was going to be like when and if I arrived at that phase of life. To that end, the rest of my account of these years is thematic rather than chronological, sharing experiences I had with various people at different communities and different times. These people showed me and told me what it felt like to get old:

"I feel like an old sock with holes in it."

"There are a lot of hard knocks in life and the hardest ones come at the end."

"I feel like I am falling apart. Every day, everything hurts."

"Getting old sucks."

"It is really, really hard, letting go of your home, your family and friends, the life you knew."

"I look in the mirror and I don't see me. I look at old photos when I was young and *those* look like me. Then I look back at the mirror and I see this wrinkled old lady . . . and it's not me."

I once went to a marketing training for people new to the senior care industry. The speaker asked us to make a list of the 10 most important things in our life, things we needed in order to live and be happy. These were my 10:

1. Ability to breathe
2. Food
3. Family
4. Dave
5. Sleep
6. Friends
7. My home
8. Career and a sense of purpose
9. Ability to walk
10. Books and reading/vision

The speaker then told us to cross off five things from the list. "Imagine you have no choice but to live without five of these," he said. "Now choose which five you are going to live without." I crossed off: home, career, books, walking and sleep. This was a hypothetical list and it still felt stressful crossing them off. He then told us to cross off two more and I couldn't do it. Even though it was just an exercise, I couldn't bring myself to lose anything else. I started resenting the speaker.

Then he said, "Seniors lose almost everything that is precious and life-sustaining. They sometimes even lose the ability to eat or breathe without devices to help them. Many have feeding tubes or oxygen tanks they have to carry with them 24 hours a day. The difference between this exercise and what elders go through," he said, "is that you got to choose which items you crossed off."

After the man's presentation, someone stood up to talk about seniors cutting pills in half because they couldn't afford their prescriptions and eating dog food because they couldn't afford a meal. I sat there thinking of how it would feel to be 80 years old, with no means of generating income: cast out, eating dog food because I was too proud to ask for help, or even worse, maybe because there was no one I *could* ask.

A few weeks after the training, I went through my pile of mail and found a letter from Meals on Wheels that said:

Dear Friend,

- *Imagine not being able to cook because your hands are so impaired by arthritis that you can't even use a can opener.*
- *Imagine looking down dark or narrow stairs. Imagine your fear of falling if you have poor eyesight and osteoporosis.*
- *Imagine the terror of venturing out onto wet, foggy, and dangerous streets in the winter, when a fall can have devastating consequences.*
- *Imagine saving milk and bread from Friday's lunch just to have something to eat on Saturday.*

I couldn't imagine. I sent a donation.

A few months later, I went to a networking luncheon and the speaker had us wear glasses to simulate different types of vision loss which happen with old age: glaucoma, macular degeneration, and cataracts. Some of the glasses simulated all three, and soon I felt dizzy and nauseous wearing them. I couldn't even stomach my lunch.

I thought of General Braswell, in independent living back at The Gables. He had macular degeneration and chose not to participate in the Memory Enhancement Class we offered because of his vision problems. He was afraid there would be things to read out loud and he didn't want to draw attention to himself and his vision problem. I loved General Braswell. He was funny and intelligent, a tough yet endearing guy. He had spent several years at the Pentagon and was full of political stories. He took life in stride. When I started having success and getting move-ins, he said to me, "Be careful, kid, you're going to fill this place up and work your way out of a job."

Violet York was another resident with vision problems. She had macular degeneration, cataracts, and glaucoma. Violet loved three things: traveling, reading, and playing bridge. She was 93 years old when I met her and still able to read and play bridge. Although no longer able to travel, she derived joy from looking at the photos of her overseas trips. Within a year, Violet's vision deteriorated to the point where she could no longer do any of the things she loved. Six months after that, Violet's lungs filled with fluid and she was diagnosed with lung cancer. But she kept living, barely.

Violet had no family. Her one sibling and two ex-husbands had died. There were no children, no nieces or nephews. She was also running very low on money and that worried her. Where would she go? Maybe to a nursing home that took Medi-Cal? She had made great friends in her 10 years at The Gables. These friends had become her family. The thought of having to live someplace else, without them, filled her with despair. One day, with the help of an outside caregiver, Violet tried to kill herself. She took a very large amount of different pills. When she didn't show up for lunch, two staff members went to her apartment where they found her, semi-conscious, and rushed her to the emergency room.

Violet was petite and feisty with round eyes and curly, permed hair that she dyed brown. The day she discharged from the hospital and returned to The Gables, she pushed our caregiver away when she tried to help Violet into bed. "Go away," she said, "just leave me here. I hate you people." I went to visit her the next day. Her apartment was dark, with the curtains closed tight. It was a gorgeous, warm summer day and I opened them a bit to let some light in.

"No," she said. "Close the blinds, Liz, please. I can only see shapes and things, but still the light hurts my eyes. Close them." I did as she asked, then sat on the bed next to her. Violet's breathing was labored. The sound of it filled the room. The oxygen tank next to her bed was large and made of cold metal that touched my bare leg below my skirt.

I looked at the night stand full of pills then back at Violet. Her eyes were closed and there was drool running down the side of her mouth, snot coming from her nose that was hard to look at. Violet's tiny frail hand clutched mine. Purple veins with thin, pale skin. We sat silently and I thought of how this was the closest I had ever come to someone dying. I felt strangely calm.

We talked about Violet's life, her marriages, her travels, and friends. She was refreshingly honest and didn't mince words, especially when talking about her ex-husbands. I loved that about her. Finally, she asked, "Why the hell did you guys take me to the hospital?"

"We had to, Violet. You know that. We have a legal obligation to protect you, even from yourself."

"Protect me?! Protect me from ending my *suffering*? For God's sake, I'm 94 years old. If I want to die, let me die."

"I know. I'm not saying I agree with it."

"I have no quality of life. None. I can't even look at the pictures from my travels," she said, full of defeat. "They're in the living room. Will you go get them and look at them for me?" I brought an album and sat on her bed again, listening to the oxygen tank and flipping through the photos. Violet asked about my life and travels. We had gone to many of the same places in South America and Europe. I stopped at pictures of Arequipa, a small mountain town in Peru.

"I went here, too," I said excitedly. "Did you visit that convent? The one where the nuns have been silent for centuries?"

"Yes. Wasn't that neat?"

"Totally. I can't believe those nuns live their entire life there and never leave or speak. Did you chew coca leaves for the altitude?" I asked.

"No, but I drank the mate de coca tea," she replied.

"Me too. I hiked the Inca Trail up to Machu Picchu with a Quechua guide."

Violet seemed to be dozing off, so I decided it would be a good time to get ready for my one o'clock tour. "I've got a tour coming in half an hour," I said, "I have to go, Violet."

"Please don't leave."

"I'll come back afterwards," I whispered as I let go of her hand. "Get some rest."

I walked out of the room and saw a redwood tree with a blue jay sitting on it. Leaning on the railing, I stared at the blue jay, then the clouds, grateful I could see them. I took a deep breath, happy that I could do so without a machine. My appreciation for my youth and health made me think of how my friend, Elena, who works in a federal prison, appreciates her freedom. "These people can't even take a piss without getting permission," she once commented about the inmates. I thought of the day I whisked past Joe Cameron as he sat next to his walker and said to his wife, "I wish I could walk that fast."

My tour was quick, a 75-year-old looking for a place in the future. When it was done, I went back to Violet's apartment. For once, I didn't want to run away from the sickness and old age. I wanted to stay there and be with her. It felt sacred to be invited into such an intimate time in a person's life. She was dying and she wanted me there.

So, this is what I feared, ending up like Violet. *Will this one day be me? If so, I don't want it.*

It took Violet three more weeks to pass away from natural causes. I felt relieved when she was finally free.

One day, a few years after Violet died, I was sitting in the Tea Room of Casa Amanecer in San Francisco. It was a quiet day, only a few tours and one move-in. I had a lull in my schedule and decided to have a cup of tea and visit with whomever happened to meander in. Wilfred Jones appeared and I looked up at his lanky frame. Wilfred was a proud man and not one to show vulnerability, at least not in public, so I was surprised to see that he was crying. As usual, he was wearing a bold print vintage shirt. Wilfred was sweet and gentle, an accomplished artist and engineer.

I motioned for him to sit next to me, "What's up, Wilfred? Are you okay?"

"I don't want to talk about it." He was dressed up, so I figured there had been plans to go somewhere, plans that maybe got squashed. I sat quietly, sipped my tea, and waited until Wilfred finally spoke. If there was one thing I learned in assisted living, it was this: you don't rush seniors. You have to go on *their* clock. Trust me on this one.

"I don't like her," he said.

"Who?" I asked.

"That red-haired woman," he spat, referring to our activity director.

"What happened?"

"She wouldn't let me go on the field trip."

"Why?"

"Because it was uneven terrain and I didn't want to take my cane."

"Why didn't you want to take your cane?"

"Because it's out in public. Everyone here knows I use my cane, but out there is different—I'm embarrassed."

"So, you decided not to go."

"Yes, and I really wanted to go. They're going to the Legion of Honor museum to see the van Gogh exhibit." He cried a little more and I sat in silence. There was really no consoling him. There was no saying "Hey, cheer up, maybe you'll get younger tomorrow, maybe you won't need the cane."

"I felt demeaned," he said, "treated like a child."

"I'm sorry," I said. There was really nothing more to say.

Later that day, I attended the Resident Council meeting. Surveying the room, full of 80- and 90-year-olds slumped over walkers, I saw poor posture, hearing aids, and wrinkles everywhere. I thought of Millie, whom I had visited in the hospital the day before. She had suffered a massive stroke and had tubes coming out of every orifice. Like every other workday, there were people literally falling apart in front of my eyes. That night, I came home and said to Dave, "God, I hope I die young." Dave looked at me with the face he reserves for people who cut in front of him at Home Depot. I refer to it simply as "The Look."

"I hate when you say that," he responded.

"I hate when you look at me like that," I said.

"Then don't say you want to die young."

What I really wish on these days is that we'll both die *relatively* young. But it's not nice to tell your spouse that you wish he will die young. I didn't want to leave Dave behind without me, nor did I want him to go before me. Ideally, we would both die in our sleep, peacefully, on the same night, when we're around 75, still healthy, physically active, and mentally with it.

The average age of residents in assisted living is 87 years old. Naturally, by the time people reach that age, most are experiencing a plethora of physical problems. These physical limitations lead to a loss of independence and quite often that loss took the form of no more driving. I remember the day I got my driver's license: *freedom, independence at last!* Imagine enjoying that freedom for 70 years and then having it taken away.

Some people I met, like Gloria Armstrong, were great drivers despite their age. At 100, Gloria was a better driver than many of the 80-year-olds. She passed her road test when she was 98 and when she turned 100, her insurance company sent her a letter canceling the policy because of her age. Gloria marched down to the insurance office, claiming age discrimination. Much to our surprise, the insurance company wrote her a new policy and Gloria continued to drive.

Many seniors I met decided to give up driving on their own because they didn't want to hurt anyone. For others, usually men, the driving issue was probably the most emotionally charged one we came across in retirement communities. One would think that wearing adult diapers or having someone give you a shower would be the biggie. But, no, it was driving.

On one hot, relaxing day at The Gables, the phone rang and I heard the Ojai hospital on the line. One of our 85-year-old residents, Don Evans, had been in a car accident. Don's vision was terrible. His driving skills and reflexes were also horrible. On this day, he took out four parked cars. Luckily, he wasn't hurt badly and no one else was injured. Still, he was at the emergency room having his scratches and bruises examined. An irate emergency room nurse screamed at me through the receiver, "How could you let this man drive!"

"It's not *our* decision whether or not Mr. Evans drives," I retorted. "It is *his* decision and his family's decision. There's this thing called 'Resident Rights.' We do not have the right to take away a car or driving privileges from one of our residents, especially one in independent living."

The next day, Don's daughter spoke with him and asked him to stop driving. The conversation did not go well. So, she had someone sneak into the parking lot that night and disable his car. Don hired a mechanic to fix it the next morning. Next, his family had the car towed away. Don went out and paid cash for a brand-new vehicle. His daughter came to me exasperated. "Call the Department of Motor Vehicles anonymously," I told her. "The DMV can force the person to come in for a written and road test." Don's family did this. The DMV said it would be a while because they were backlogged.

The scenario was quite common. Families often find themselves at their wits' end with the driving issue. My heart aches for the senior who is losing his independence but then I think of the 86-year-old man who killed 10 people, including an infant, and injured 70 more at the Santa Monica Farmer's Market, and I don't feel so bad for seniors who lose their driving privileges.

A friend at a skilled nursing facility in San Francisco told me he's going to take up drinking and driving when he turns 80. He claims 80 is the age at which the body starts to shut down. "The end may still be a way off," he said, "but the decline starts then. In many countries, when people get old and frail, they die. That's it. It's ridiculous in the United States, the way we prolong life."

He had a point. It is not uncommon for people to move from independent living to assisted living, then to higher levels of care within assisted living, then to the hospital, and finally to a skilled nursing facility where they die. After they've gone through all that, their life ends in a nursing home or the intensive care unit.

Seeing lives dragged on spurred me to do things like set up a Living Trust and an Advanced Healthcare Directive. These things would not have crossed my mind until much later in life had I not worked in the industry. I made Dave do the same. We both agreed we didn't want to be vegetables and made a pact to pull the plug on one another. Attorneys usually advise people to never designate their parents as their healthcare agent. Parents, in 90 percent of cases, no matter how horrible their child's quality of life, will not pull the plug. It defies the laws of nature to kill one's own child, no matter how merciful that may be. So, I named Dave as my agent, and my best friend, Kayleigh, as my backup.

In 2004 I went to a seminar on Long Term Care insurance. In the class they told us some kids born today would live to be 140 years old. It seemed inconceivable, but the people who are 100 now were born during a time when the average life expectancy was 50. An article was all over the internet recently saying that average life expectancy for Americans is now 78 years old, the longest in U.S. history. Monaco, a tiny country on the Mediterranean Sea, has the longest life expectancy in the world at 89 years for women and 84 for men.

The loss of independence was unfortunate, the physical ailments were heartbreaking, but the harshest part of aging I saw was the loneliness. I had a tour once with a healthy, 92-year-old woman. "Why are you considering assisted living?" I asked her.

"I'm afraid I may forget how to talk," she responded.

"What do you mean?"

"I go weeks sometimes without seeing or talking to another human being. I don't drive anymore. I don't have much family. All my friends have died. Sometimes I get so lonely, I just sit in my house and cry. Sometimes when I'm out on my walk, looking at the beautiful scenery, I want to just walk off the cliff."

I met many people in their 80s and 90s who were longing to connect. Many older adults sometimes went months without being touched or hugged. It was as though old age were contagious and people were afraid to catch it, just as I was before working in assisted living. Now I make an effort to touch a person's arm or back when I talk to them. Sometimes, if I know the person well, I give them a hug or kiss on the cheek when I say "hello" or "goodbye." It is something seniors need but would never ask for. Elders often tell me they feel invisible. No one notices them when they walk into a room the way people did when they were young.

These were some of the many losses I witnessed which came with old age. Many people turned to their pets, faith, family, friends, community, and hobbies as a way to cope. These tools helped ease all of the losses except one. The loss of one's mind was perhaps the hardest.

Chapter Four

Dazed And Confused

*Last scene of all,
That ends this strange eventful history,
Is second childishness and mere oblivion;
Sans teeth, sans eyes, sans taste, sans everything.*

— William Shakespeare, *As You Like It*

When I think back to my beginning in assisted living, I remember a scene I witnessed on my second day at The Gables. Sharon had a new resident moving in and she wanted me to watch and listen while she went over the contract and paperwork with the new guy's wife. We walked into The Gardens, our memory care area, took a seat in the living room, and waited for them to arrive. Glenn, the activity director, was reading the newspaper to a group of seven ladies. Glenn was robust, in his late 50s, with grey hair and a beard, big eyes, lots of energy, and a deep voice. He looked a bit like Santa Claus and I later learned that he actually *was* Santa Claus for the town of Ojai every year.

Glenn was trying to get the group of ladies to discuss current events. I stared at one of the women with a vacant look in her eyes. I peered around the circle—all of them had the same hollow expression. It was a distinct look I had not seen before. The women spoke in clear voices but their words made no sense. A few had freshly coiffed hair and had obviously been to the beauty parlor recently. Most were wearing sweat suits, but one woman was dressed in a pink chiffon blouse, silk slacks, and wore a jeweled brooch over her heart. I felt odd, uncomfortable, and a little frightened by these women.

They did not care about current events or, if they had a moment of caring, it quickly evaporated. All they cared about was what day of the week it was. They were sharply divided on the issue. Half were certain it was Monday, the others adamant that it was Wednesday. "It's Monday," Glenn said for the third time. "Now can we talk about Robert Blake?" He held up the *Los Angeles Times* to show them. "Remember him, the guy who played Beretta on TV? Well, he has been charged with killing his wife."

"My goodness," one of the ladies said. The group mulled this over a bit then Glenn read the first paragraph of the article to them. Ten minutes later he took a break and came over to us. "Glenn," Sharon said, "I'd like you to meet Liz, our new marketing director."

Glenn, I soon learned, was a stage actor. He worked at The Gables to pay the bills, but his true passion was acting. Sharon told me he dressed in a different costume most days and the residents loved his ensembles. On this day, he wore a white ruffled pirate shirt tucked into apple-red knee-length pants. He looked like he'd just stepped out of a Shakespearean play.

I complimented him on his attire and turned to see the front door open. Our new resident and his wife had arrived. Mr. Charlie Hamilton was a tall man, 70 years old with a full head of silver hair. He was wearing navy-blue sweats and tennis shoes, trying desperately to maneuver the walker in front of him and getting more frustrated by the minute. The walker teetered and he shook it, lifted it slightly, and looked at the device as though he were trying to figure out what it was.

He looked at the ground then back at the walker. He took his hands off it and looked around at the strange faces surrounding him, his eyes asking for guidance. Mr. Hamilton's legs wobbled beneath him and I feared he would take a tumble right there in the middle of Glenn's current events circle. Out of nowhere, two female caregivers dressed in khaki pants and golf shirts appeared and held him up on each side. He looked at them with bewilderment and mumbled something that sounded like a baby's ramblings as they lead him to a couch where he lay down in the fetal position.

I was mesmerized by the scene. Out of the corner of my eye, I saw a look of fear and pain on Mrs. Hamilton's face. I knew nothing about dementia. I had heard the words "Alzheimer's" and "demented" before, and knew they were somehow related to memory loss, but that was the extent of my knowledge.

Mr. Hamilton's wife, Lynne, was a pretty woman who looked younger than her 73 years. Tears rolled down her face as she turned to Sharon, and said, "This is really hard," and then put her hand over her mouth. "I'm sorry to be falling apart like this." Sharon put her arm on Mrs. Hamilton's back.

"I know. You're doing the right thing. It's okay," Sharon guided Mrs. Hamilton to the dining room table, about 10 feet from the couch where Mr. Hamilton lay, and opened a file with the move-in contract and other papers to be signed. "While she arranged the paperwork, Sharon gestured for me to sit next to Mrs. Hamilton. "This is Liz," she said. "She's new and needs to learn about signing move-in paperwork, so I've asked her to join us today if that's all right with you?"

Mrs. Hamilton nodded, wiping tears away. "Nice to meet you." She looked over to her husband lying on the couch, "He taught high school English for 30 years. His students loved him. Now he can't even form a sentence."

"I'm sorry," I said. I wanted to ask how long they had been married, how many kids they had, what his students loved most about him. I also wanted to know how long he had been in his current state, but instead I sat quietly and waited for Sharon to guide the conversation. I knew she needed to take care of business and get Mrs. Hamilton's signature on the contract, emergency contact sheet, and a whole slew of other consent forms. Sharon had given me some background on this couple right before they arrived.

Sharon first met them two years earlier when Mr. Hamilton was forgetful but still able to talk and walk quite well. Mrs. Hamilton had toured The Gables and ate lunch while Mr. Hamilton watched television. At the end of the tour she told Sharon, "The place is lovely but I intend to keep him at home until I can't possibly care for him anymore."

Now here we were, that day had come, and Sharon couldn't believe how rapidly the man had declined. "He's really at the point of needing a nursing home," she told me before the Hamiltons arrived, "and I'm actually stretching the rules of our license by even accepting him. But I just feel for this poor woman and know how hard it is for her to place him somewhere. That's why she waited so long and now it's really too late for assisted living. I understand why she delayed: she has so much guilt and feels she is abandoning him and her marriage vows. I can't turn her away."

I watched Mrs. Hamilton sign the Consent for Delayed Egress, a form which explained that the area where Mr. Hamilton would be living was *secure*, not locked. "If you press on the door handle for 15 seconds, it will open but an alarm will go off," Sharon explained. "If you put the code in, the door will open with no alarm. This is to protect residents from wandering."

"So, he's essentially locked in here?"

"Yes."

Next, they signed the Guest Meal Policy, in which she agreed to pay five dollars per meal whenever she visited and ate with her husband. Then she signed the Consent for Emergency Medical Treatment and the Telecommunications Notice which explained that the phone company would provide a special device for the phone, free of charge, if Mr. Hamilton became hard of hearing. The stack of papers seemed endless and I could tell Mrs. Hamilton was getting tired. They stopped at several points so that she could cry and compose herself. "I'm sorry," Sharon said, "I wish we could postpone this but unfortunately our license requires me to get all this paperwork signed before someone stays here even one night."

"It's okay, I understand. Let's keep going." She looked over at Mr. Hamilton, who got up from the couch and nearly fell again, then sat back down. The last thing to sign was a 30-page rental contract and, by the time we got to it, we had already been at the table an hour. The contract explained the month-to-month rental agreement and included a billing sheet that spelled out the cost. Mrs. Hamilton signed these and then wrote Sharon a check for $7,500. This covered the charges for one month's rent and care.

"Now, I just need to borrow your husband's health insurance cards so I can make a copy for our file, then we are all done," Sharon said. She looked exhausted. I wanted to guide her to one of the resident rooms, bring her a cup of tea, and tell her to lie down and get some rest. Mrs. Hamilton I wanted to hug and say, "It will be all right," but I knew it wouldn't. I sat there wondering what I had gotten myself into.

I went back to my office and read the introduction to a book on Alzheimer's, then walked into Sharon's office. "That was really sad," I said.

"Yes, it's painful to watch."

"I felt so bad for her, having to move her husband here and also having to pay all that money. That was a big check she wrote."

"Yes, indeed. Pray you never get dementia, or at least just stay mildly confused, because the cost for Alzheimer's care is about double the cost of straight assisted living. The price of most memory care places averages about $7,000 a month right now. It will probably double in the next 15 years."

"What do families do if they can't afford that?"

"They stick it out at home and take shifts. Sometimes they get a little break for a couple hours by taking their loved one to an adult daycare that Medicare pays for. When it gets to be too much, they move them to a place that's not as nice as this one. Or to a nursing home which Medi-Cal pays for. But nursing homes are not the best environment for someone with dementia. The staff aren't trained and the residents are mixed with non-demented people, which causes them a lot of stress."

"Speaking of training," I asked, "what exactly *is* the difference between Alzheimer's and dementia?"

"Well, the terms are not synonymous, even though a lot of people think they are. The term 'dementia' is the umbrella term for short-term memory loss, mental decline, and confusion. Alzheimer's is just one form. People get them mixed up because the symptoms are the same but the causes are different. Alzheimer's is most likely genetic, and other forms of dementia can be caused by a stroke or Parkinson's."

"Does everyone lose their memory as they get older?"

"No. Dementia is actually not a natural part of aging. Many people stay clear-minded into very late age. Remember Gertrude whom you met the first time you toured? She's 99."

"That's *right*. She struck me as very sharp."

"Exactly. She does a fabulous job as our librarian. For those who do have a decline in brain functioning, the process takes many stages, from mildly confused to very advanced. Obviously, Mr. Hamilton is very advanced."

A month after he moved in, Mr. Hamilton died. His dementia weakened his immune system and he developed pneumonia, which was fatal. During those first few weeks and the following months and years of working in assisted living, I met a wide range of residents, from people like Mr. Hamilton, with late-stage dementia to those in the very early stages, known as Mild Cognitive Impairment or MCI. From these encounters, I learned about the progression of dementia through its many phases.

It was a crisp spring day at The Gables as I walked out of my office and began the half-mile trek up to Abigail's apartment in the assisted living Cottages. I needed to talk with her about a tour that was coming the following day. With the property 100-percent full, tours and prospects needed to be shown occupied apartments, and Abigail's was one of the most tastefully decorated and spacious we had. It was always a bit awkward asking people if I could bring strangers into their home for the purpose of sales. Fortunately, some like Abigail, actually loved showing off their apartments.

My high heels clicked on the pavement as my mind raced with the million and one things I needed to do before the end of the workday: *call Mrs. Branson back about the studio; fax the final ad to the Ojai Valley News; beg John for the THIRD time to finish painting apartment 16. Shoot, I forgot to ask Sharon about the lunch appointment with Joyce.* I looked at my watch. *Damn. It's already 3:30.* A typical day. It was also my 35th birthday and I was determined to leave work on time. Dave had made dinner reservations at The Ranch House, one of the two fine dining restaurants in Ojai.

I glanced at the rose garden as I hurtled past, never breaking my stride. The orange and red Perfect Moments were in full bloom, the afternoon sun glaring down on them. *I'll have to come back and snip some for Mrs. Collins,* I thought, *she's in the hospital recovering from her heart surgery.* The orange Double Delights, the crimson Oklahomas, the yellow Henry Fondas would all look nice with the ribbon I had bought at the craft store.

Through the screen door, Abigail sang out to me from her bedroom "Come in, dear. I'll be right there. Please help yourself to some chocolates." Sinking down into the velvet couch, I laid my head back, and felt it touch the soft fabric, and a large sigh escaped my chest. I listened to Abigail singing Irving Berlin's *Easter Parade: "In your Easter bonnet, with all the frills upon it, you'll be the grandest lady in the Easter parade."* Looking at the antiques in her living room, my phone calls, faxes, and the newspaper ad melted away.

I felt myself enter Abigail's delightful world and all of my awareness focused on that moment. Embroidered doilies and landscape paintings surrounded me as I picked up a framed photo of Abigail from her New York modeling days. In it, she wore a camel-colored cashmere pea coat and a matching hat. She looked to be in her late 20s when the photo was taken. Abigail hadn't changed much: so stylish, always looking like she was walking down a runway, or had just jumped off the pages of *Vogue*. Delicate porcelain figurines filled the teak table. Abigail had traveled all over the world and lived in her prior home for 40 years, bringing only her favorite things to this apartment.

Abigail was still singing when she entered the living room. She sat next to me on the sofa, our knees touching. "How *ARE* you, my dear?" she asked.

"I'm great," I said, "It's my birthday."

She gasped, "Oh, my!" Abigail was even more thrilled than I. "We *must* read your horoscope." She jumped up and flitted about the room, searching for the newspaper. "Oh, oh, here it is!" she exclaimed. "*Love is in the air. A special someone makes a grand entrance. Watch for signs of prosperity around the 28th.*"

"So," she continued, "what will you be doing tonight?"

"My husband, Dave, is taking me to dinner."

"Oh, how *lovely*. And, this man, this Dave, are you very fond of him? Is it serious?" I frowned and tilted my head, not sure how to respond. I had just said he was my husband. How much more serious could it be? "Well . . . yes, we're married."

"Oh, how WONDERFUL," she replied and jumped up to make tea. We drank chamomile tea and ate chocolates laced with hazelnut.

With Abigail, I realized that on most days, *everything* was wonderful. Ninety percent of the time, her dementia was of the pleasantly confused sort. But on rare days, she called the office terrified, insisting that her apartment was full of beetles. John and the other maintenance guys would go check and there were never any beetles. Eventually, she would believe them and calm down.

Abigail wrote poems. If we went on a field trip to a Mexican restaurant, she would come home and immediately jot down a verse about her pink paper placemat and how her fork had sat perfectly on it. If the field trip was a trolley ride, she wrote a poem about the trees out the window, and the mustard-colored blouse she wore that day. I often printed Abigail's poems in the newsletter. I did this partly because I secretly suspected that Abigail and I were from the same planet, in a faraway galaxy, and because of that, I *got* her poetry. I also printed them because it made Abigail so happy to see her poems in print. To be fully honest, though, I also did it to annoy Rosemary Emerson.

An agile 94-year-old, Rosemary was healthy, active, and smart. Her four kids visited regularly, although none of us could understand why. Rosemary walked about the property swinging her polka-dotted cane to and fro, twirling it around like Charlie Chaplin, pointing out trees or people, hardly ever using it to actually walk. She had a scrunched-up face and an opinion about everything. When we offered Qi Gong classes at five dollars each, Rosemary came to me saying, "I'm a millionaire, you know. Most people don't know that about me, but it's true."

"Really, Rosemary?"

"Yes, *really*. And I'll tell you something, I didn't get to be a millionaire by throwing my money away on silly things like Qi Gong classes.'"

"Okay, then don't take the Qi Gong classes."

"I don't *plan* on taking the Qi Gong classes. I just want to know why you are offering them if we have to pay for them."

"We are offering them because some people actually *like* them. And we're charging five dollars because the teacher is really good and, therefore expensive, and we need to supplement his cost."

"Well, I am not going to pay extra for a class when I already pay to live here," she huffed and then left my office.

The next day I saw her in the dining room, complaining to Magdala, the supervisor, about a few residents who were unsteady on their feet. As I prepared my salad, I watched Rosemary talking, one hand on her hip and another pointing to June Anderson, who was also trying to get a salad. June was having difficulty maneuvering both the salad bar and her walker. "This is INDEPENDENT living," Rosemary said indignantly to Magdala, loudly enough so that everyone could hear, including June. Magdala listened patiently and nodded. *I could not do Magdala's job,* I thought.

"They should move to *assisted* living if they need a walker," Rosemary continued. I walked by and smiled at Magdala.

"They're doing their best," Magdala responded, "not everyone is as strong as you, Rosemary."

"I'm going to talk with Sharon about this."

"I understand. Now, please, go sit and enjoy your lunch," Magdala said as she gracefully guided Rosemary to her table. "I'll get you some soup." I looked over at June, still struggling with a sad look on her face. I scowled at the back of Rosemary's head.

I knew on some level that living with herself was punishment enough for Rosemary, but once in a while, I just had to add an extra dash to the mix. So, I printed one of Abigail's poems in the newsletter, and just like clockwork, Rosemary charged into my office saying, "I have to talk to you."

"Sure, have a seat."

"I do not need or *want* to sit down."

"Okay, then don't sit."

"*Why* do you put these *ridiculous* poems of hers in the newsletter?"

"I think they're nice and we need to fill up the space." I tapped my pen on the desk, stared at Rosemary with my brows slightly raised and said, in my softest tone, "You *know* . . . you are more than welcome to submit a poem, too, Rosemary. I'd be happy to print that or anything else you would care to share. Maybe a recipe or a tidbit of information that might be helpful to others?"

"I don't *want* to write a poem. I want you to stop putting this crap in the newsletter. It doesn't make any sense."

"It's poetry," I said. "It's not supposed to make sense."

Rosemary's reaction to Abigail was actually common although not always as extreme. There was a fear of dementia among the independent and assisted living residents. In every community where I worked, they refused to visit the memory care area, even for a party. "Those people are sick," Janet Brown said to me one day. "Why would I want to go over there?"

"It's not contagious," I responded. The next week, when we brought the residents with dementia to a music performance in the assisted living parlor, the mentally alert people sat on the opposite side of the room. While the residents with dementia clapped and tried to sing along, I saw a few of the independent residents watching them, rolling their eyes, arms crossed over their chest. Holmer Smith said to Jim, sitting next to him, "Why even bring them here? They're not going to remember it in an hour!" and they both laughed.

Diane Norwood, who had a little early dementia herself, asked me "Aren't they usually locked up? I hear they can get combative and violent." I surmised that Diane was not really worried about them getting combative; she was terrified about being locked up with them. She knew on some level that the dementia unit was where she was eventually headed herself. She saw a police officer walk by and asked me if he was there to keep the dementia people in order. I assured her that he was there to visit his father, who lived in our assisted living apartments.

After about three years of working regularly with dementia, I began to understand the independent seniors' fear. There was just something about being around it day in and day out that made me start to worry—*What if I get Alzheimer's one day?* Sure, I forgot things, like words or where I left my keys, and I used poor judgment at times. I was only in my mid-30s, but were these signs that I was predisposed to develop dementia?

When people start to show signs of dementia, healthcare workers often do what is called a Mini-Mental State Exam (MMSE). When Abigail called for the third time about the beetles, Sharon figured it was time to do the test with her. Our nurse Joan and I met with Abigail in the tea room and Joan asked her the following questions:

"Abigail, we are here today to ask you a couple questions, just a standard test we do with everyone, to kind of gauge what kind of support you may need. Is that all right with you?"

"Oh, sure dear, of course. I'm more than happy to help."

"Great. So, I'm going to say a few common objects and then ask you to repeat them to me a few minutes into the test, okay?" She nodded her agreement.

"Horse, flower, penny," Joan said. "So, hold onto those and I'll ask you to repeat them in a few minutes. Now, can you tell me what year it is?"

"Two thousand." She was off by four years.

"Do you know what season we're in?"

Abigail looked out the window, then back at Joan and replied, "Spring."

"Excellent. Do you know what day of the week it is?"

"No."

I thought to myself, *well, lots of people who are retired don't know the day of the week and why should they? It's different when you don't have a schedule to keep. I often forgot what day it was when Dave and I spent that year in South America.*

"Okay, do you know the date?"

"April 10th?"

"Actually, it's March 16th, but that's fine. Now, can you tell me the objects I mentioned a few minutes ago?"

"Flower, penny and . . ."

"Take your time."

"I can't remember the last one."

"It was horse, but two is good."

"Now I would like you to count backward from 100 by 7s."

Oh my God, was she serious? I couldn't count backwards from 100 by 7s or probably even by 5s. I sat there trying to do it in my head while Abigail had a pained look on her face.

"100, 95, 89 . . . I can't do it."

"That's okay, we'll move on."

Joan then pointed to a plant in the corner of the room. "Can you tell me what that is I'm pointing at, Abigail?"

"It's a plant."

"Excellent."

"Can you tell me what state we are in?"

"California."

"How about the city?"

"Ojai."

"And do you know our street address here?"

"No."

"All right, now I'm going to draw two shapes and ask you to copy what I draw on a blank piece of paper." Joan drew two interlocking shapes and Abigail copied them perfectly.

"Beautiful, Abigail."

"Thanks. Are we almost done?" she asked, looking at Joan and then at me.

"Yes," Joan said, "This is the last question. I'd like you to take this piece of paper in your right hand, fold it in half, and place it on the floor." Abigail did the first two steps but did not place the paper on the floor. She simply hung onto it after she had folded it.

"That's it," Joan said, "We're done. Do you have any questions for me?"

"How did I do?"

"You did great."

"Good. I think I'd like to go home and rest now."

Abigail left and I followed Joan to her office. "So, how did she really do?" I asked.

"Well, the maximum score is 30 points. Twelve means pretty severe dementia. A person who scores 20 points or higher can usually live independently with a little bit of support. Abigail scored 17, which means she should move to a secure environment with more supervision." Seeing my facial reaction Joan said, "I know . . . it's disappointing."

"So, who is going to tell her?"

"I guess Sharon or I will have to. It's not like the move will happen overnight. But we need to start thinking about it."

"That's so sad. She loves her apartment."

"I know," Joan said.

Those were the most difficult situations: taking away freedoms from someone who still knew what was happening. In a way it was easier with people like Mr. Hamilton who didn't seem to understand. Yet even those who appeared completely gone to another world had moments of lucidity that shocked me. One night at Sunset Oaks, Harry Driscoll, a gentleman with late-stage Alzheimer's slipped out the front gate when a visitor was leaving. One of our caregivers found him frantically looking around in the trees, the bushes, and on the ground as though he were trying to find something very important.

The caregiver asked in a gentle voice, "Did you lose something, Mr. Driscoll?"

He replied, "Yes, my mind."

Vince Harris, who lived down the hall from Harry, was even more advanced in his dementia. The first time I met Vince, I thought back to an Alzheimer's convention where a neurologist showed us pictures of two brain PET scans. One was of an infant, the other a late-stage Alzheimer's patient. They looked identical. He explained that during the very last stages of dementia, people return to an infant-like state, losing the ability to walk, control their bladder and bowels, even to speak intelligible words. Vince had lost all these things.

When I talked with Vince's daughter, Susie, about visiting, she said, "I don't see the point. He doesn't talk, he stares at me blankly, he doesn't even know I'm here." It was true that her dad no longer spoke and he did stare into space. Yet when I walked by him one day after a rare visit from Susie, I sat down and asked, "Did your daughter visit today?" He looked ahead silently. I stared at the ground and when I looked back at Vince, there was a tear sliding down his face and he was nodding.

Despite their pain, residents still had many moments of joy. Seeing their families' pain was actually harder. It was an ache with no reprieve. It just got worse and their eyes got sadder. Some, like Susie, stopped coming altogether. Visiting a loved one with dementia is a lot to handle. I don't know if I could do it, even though I had worked in dementia care for years.

How would I handle my mom staring me in the face, not speaking to me, and not knowing my name? What would that feel like? Sometimes, I told family members to visit not for their loved ones, but for *themselves*.

"Even if there's no response, it can be healing for you to spend time with your dad."

"But," they sometimes said, "I don't know what to do when I visit him." I have seen families just sit and stare at their relative, feeling lost. Lily, our care manager, saw this, too, so she put together a list of things to do when visiting a friend or family member with dementia. It included ways to actually make the visit fun. People with dementia often still have their long-term memory, so they can do things like fix a car or bake chocolate chip cookies. Here is the list Lily wrote:

- Sing old songs
- Make cookies
- Read a book out loud
- Blow bubbles
- Have a tea party
- Dance
- Plant something in the earth
- Arrange fresh flowers
- Give a hand massage
- Feed the birds or horses
- Roll yarn into a ball
- Play with paints
- Fold a basket of clothes

Families appreciated the list and it felt uplifting to watch them spend more meaningful time together.

There were some family members, though, like Tracy Balinski, who had no trouble thinking up things to do when visiting her mom. Tracy, in her mid-50s with a stocky build and happy eyes, came to visit one Saturday when I was working. Tracy's mom loved butterflies. Tracy arrived that Saturday wearing brown cotton stretch pants with a brown top. Attached to her back were wings so large she had trouble getting through our front door. The wings were made of wire to which Tracy had attached lime-colored nylon decorated with pink, purple and silver glitter, along with assorted jewels and sequins. She stopped to say hi to Celeste and Marge, two residents who had become best friends and were sitting on their usual bench in the hallway. "What do you think?" she asked the ladies.

"Looks great," Celeste replied.

"Colorful," Marge said.

"Do you think my mom will like it?" Tracy asked.

"Oh, yes, I'm sure she will," Celeste said politely. As Tracy walked away, Celeste turned to Marge and said, "I think she's going to scare the *shit* out of her mother."

I laughed out loud, not expecting that from Celeste. She and Marge both had mid-stage Alzheimer's. Yet, like many of the residents, they had moments, sometimes entire days of lucidity. On another day, I walked by and overheard the two making plans for their day:

Celeste: "Let's go for a drive."

Marge: "Yes, we should. It's beautiful outside. Where should we go?"

Celeste: "How about the beach?"

Marge: "That's a great idea."

Celeste: "Or maybe we should go vote."

Marge: "Who are you going to vote for?"

Celeste: "Arnold Schwarzenegger."

I stopped in my tracks. The Governor's race *was*, in fact, happening and Schwarzenegger *was* in fact running. Most days, these two ladies had no idea where they were, what year or day it was, or what they'd had for breakfast.

The day which surprised me most, though, was the day I sat chatting with Claudette Halsey, a lady who usually had great difficulty following a coherent thought pattern, though her social graces were still very much intact. Claudette had been quite the hostess in her day, with invitations to her parties highly coveted. She had long sleek fingers and beautifully manicured nails. On this day, Claudette asked me, "So what have you been up to lately?"

"I just returned from a 10-day trip to Ireland with my best friend, Kayleigh. We went to Galway, the Cliffs of Moher and some little town by the beach. The ocean was freezing but we went in anyway. Afterwards we laid in hot seaweed baths, all slimy and warm. I had a fabulous time."

"That sounds lovely," Claudette replied. "Your last name is Irish, isn't it?" *Whoa! What did she just say?* My last name *is* Irish. On most days Claudette thought I was her younger sister who had died 40 years earlier.

I couldn't believe that all of a sudden, she knew who I was, and how on earth did she know my last name?

"Yes, Claudette, my last name is actually Irish. It's Breen, my married name." I sat there perplexed.

"So, how is work going?" she said. "Are you giving lots of tours?"

"Yes, lots of tours," I said slowly. *I didn't think she knew what my job entailed.*

All this time, Claudette had on some level been absorbing things around her, taking it all in, and now she was having a conversation with me as coherent as one I would have with one of my co-workers.

I could see how easy it would be for families to slip in and out of denial. When suddenly, one day, mom is completely cognizant of everyone and everything around her, it would make sense to think, *She doesn't have dementia, I've been imagining it. I need to get her out of this place.*

The next day, though, when I went to visit Claudette and take her some colored pencils and a sketch pad, she had gone back to thinking I was her sister. We drew pictures of flowers and I was, once again, dumbfounded by this disease.

Julia Eastwood was another lady who exhibited this stark contrast. A 93-year-old former Broadway actress and singer, Julia had perfect pitch and remembered the words to every song she had learned in the 1930s. She still loved to perform and often did shows for the other residents in our memory care neighborhood. Placed about Julia's room were pictures from her starlet days. There was one, a professional head shot, with her platinum blond hair in a silky shoulder-length upturn. Her skin was smooth and white like the petals of a calla lily, the ideal backdrop for her diamond tear-drop earrings. I was drawn to that picture whenever I visited. "You are so beautiful, Julia," I said as I held up the photo.

One day, while listening to Julia sing along with the piano player we had hired, a lightbulb went off in my mind. I threw my hands up and said out loud, "Oh my God, I've got it!" I walked quickly to my office and called the Alzheimer's Association. "Hi, this is Liz from The Gables and we have this resident who lives here. She's 93 and has an *incredible* voice. I was thinking, wouldn't it be great if she sang the national anthem at your Memory Walk fundraiser in Ventura next month?!" They were delighted at the idea and we agreed Julia would sing at the opening ceremonies, in front of 8,000 people.

There was a lot of excitement leading up to the event. The local newspaper did a write-up, The Gables' staff were pumped, the Alzheimer's Association thought it was grand. Julia's family were no longer involved much in her life, but her brother signed a release giving us permission for her to sing at the walk. The night before the event, I had a dream that made me bolt straight up in bed at 2:00 a.m. In the dream Julia was standing there frozen and overwhelmed by the crowd. *Oh my God*, I thought, *what have I done?* My motives for arranging the performance had been twofold: I thought it would be fun for Julia and I also thought it would be great marketing exposure for The Gables. Julia was a wonderful example of someone still engaged in life and sharing her gifts with the world, despite her Alzheimer's. Until two o'clock that morning, it had not crossed my mind that this event could turn disastrous.

We arrived at the Ventura Fairgrounds at 6:00 a.m.: Julia, Glenn, our activity director, Joan our nurse, and me. Julia turned to me and asked, "Are all these people here to see *me?*" Glenn and I looked at each other, wondering what to say, and I held my breath. We hadn't discussed this part of the plan. We rehearsed with Julia for weeks and told her every day leading up to the event that she would be singing the Star-Spangled Banner, but of course, she forgot. I said to myself silently, *What the hell were you thinking? This was a crazy idea.* A marketing director from another community walked up and hugged me. I had a worried look on my face and cut the conversation short, "Can I catch up with you later?" I asked. "I kind of have a situation to deal with here."

Julia asked again, "Where are we and who are all these people?" Surveying the crowd, she looked concerned. "Are they here to see me?" I raised my eyebrows at Glenn and held my hands open, mouthing the question, *What do we do?* He shrugged his shoulders with a look that said, *This was your brilliant idea.* Finally, Joan said to Julia, "Yes, dear, they sure are. They can't wait to hear you sing."

"Oh, how FABULOUS!" she exclaimed. She was back on Broadway, a chanteuse to the end. Twenty minutes later, Glenn and Joan escorted Julia to the stage where she strolled up to the microphone. My breath was short as I surveyed the huge crowd and then looked up at Julia, wondering what she would do. There was a brief pause and then, when the music started, she belted out a flawless performance of the Star-Spangled Banner, and my skin filled with goose bumps.

Glenn, Joan, and some spectators around me were crying. The performance went off without a hitch and for the next year and a half, Julia carried the podium sign around with her on her walker. The sign said "Julia Eastwood. National Anthem." She would ask us to explain what it meant and we would tell her about her spectacular performance, which always caused her to beam with joy.

Seeing people like Marge, Claudette, Julia, and others with dementia reminded me of the times in my 20s when I took psychedelic mushrooms. Some residents, like Celeste, Claudette, and Marge, were on a good trip most of the time. Others, like Joe, who often screamed "Where am I? They're going to kill us!" were on a bad trip. Joe had worked as an engineer for an oil company, was now in his 70s, and wore Wrangler jeans and a cowboy hat every day. His dementia was of the unpleasant sort where he was afraid much of the time and often had visions of people trying to kill him, possibly memories from his Korean War days.

When this happened, we calmed him by talking with him and assuring him all was well. It reminded me of being with my boyfriend, Larry, at Muir Woods 6 years earlier. An hour after eating magic mushrooms, I was staring at a brilliant turquoise centipede, having a fabulous time marveling at the contrast of its color against a green leaf, when Larry started to freak out. "Dude, there's people over there with guns. Shit, they're going to kill us!" Remaining calm, I said the same words to Larry that the caregivers were now saying to Joe, "It's all good, really, everything is okay. You're fine. You're safe." In dementia care it's called "re-directing." With mushrooms it's called "being a good trip guide."

Many residents, like Celeste didn't need re-directing. Whenever I walked by on a tour, Celeste told the visitors, "This is a really great hotel, but I'm biased because my daughter owns it." Then she would continue, "Everyone is so nice here. If you're hungry, they give you some food. If your room is a mess, they clean it up. I love this place!"

When Celeste passed away, her family gave me her 1930s boudoir chair. I had it re-upholstered in a lavender fabric. It sits in my room at home and I still think of Celeste when I look at it. I love how classy that chair is. Celeste was honest and witty, a self-made business woman who knew what she wanted and got it. Sitting in her chair each morning, I slip on my high heels, adjust my earrings, and head off to work as a business woman, just like Celeste did.

Brad was another friend I made. He lived at Sunset Oaks and was only 56 years old when I met him and very physically fit, six-foot tall, handsome, with broad shoulders. Brad was talented with set design, hair styling, and flower arranging. His was an odd case of dementia: brain damage from exposure to pyrotechnic chemicals while working on a Broadway show.

The first time I met Brad was the day I came to interview for the marketing director position. I was sitting in Claire's office and Brad came in, stared intently at me, and then looked back at Claire and said, "Walk." Claire told him, "Okay, we'll go in a few minutes." She then continued her conversation with me. Brad waited patiently, looked me up and down and again said, "Walk."

"Okay, Brad," Claire said, "I just need to finish talking to Liz and then we'll go." Turning to me she whispered, "Do you mind if we walk around the block with him? He gets agitated and needs exercise." As the three of us strolled down the street, Claire told me the word "walk" was the extent of Brad's vocabulary. It was true. In all the time I worked there, I never heard Brad utter any other word.

On my first day of work, I strode into my office and found Brad standing there, pointing to several tightly wrapped bouquets of pink hydrangeas perfectly placed around the room. They looked like bridesmaids' bouquets from a magazine. They were simple and elegantly arranged in square glass vases that Brad had confiscated from the kitchen storage room.

These were the only flowers growing within his reach, so Brad took what he had access to and made magic. My office looked stunning. I smiled broadly as I looked around the room. Brad stood there nodding at me. He hugged me and I said, "Thank you." Standing there, pleased with his work and my reaction, he hugged Claire when she came in, then gestured with his hand to the flowers and to me. "He's welcoming you," she said.

Brad did exquisite things with flowers, artfully arranging them just so. I often brought him a couple of ten-dollar bouquets from the grocery store and he would disassemble and rearrange them, making them into something much prettier.

One day, I decided to take Brad with me to the senior center in town. I figured he could share his flower-arranging gift with the people there and perhaps feel a sense of purpose again. When we arrived, Brad refused to get out of the car and I was left with a room full of senior citizens staring at me, waiting for some flower arranging. After a long, awkward silence, I jumped in and did my best while Claire tried to persuade Brad to get out of the car. Halfway through my debacle, as I was trying to distract people by talking about flowers so they couldn't see what a mess I was making, Brad arrived. He took over and began guiding the flowers, almost like he was painting, putting the right colors, shapes and sizes together. When he was done, the group applauded his creation.

Flowers were not Brad's only talent. He was also adept at hair styling. On my third day of work, I walked in with my hair styled as usual: a simple, shoulder-length bob that I blow-dried straight. Brad crossed his arms and shook his head back and forth. "What is he trying to say?" I asked Claire.

"I don't know," she responded, "disapproval of something . . . maybe your outfit?" I looked down at my clothes; they looked fine to me. Brad, as usual, was dressed impeccably in a crisp Oxford shirt and khakis. He kept shaking his head, arms crossed over his chest and then took my arm and directed me to the chair at my desk. He began tussling my hair. "Ooohh," Claire said, "is it her hair, Brad?" and he nodded an emphatic 'yes,' a stern, serious look on his face. My hair was apparently not acceptable in Brad's eyes. I handed him my brush and he opened the desk drawer and began taking out paperclips. He used them to assemble my hair into an elegant up-do. When Brad was done, every paper clip in my drawer was gone and I looked ready for the Academy Awards.

The hair styling became a regular ritual on the two-to-three days a week when I was on site at Sunset Oaks rather than out in the field. This was fine by me; my hair usually turned out far better than any job I could do on it. But the up-do was also a rather involved process which made phone calls and emailing difficult. I usually sat there making follow-up calls to family members and typing away on my computer while Brad pushed me around, telling me with non-verbal cues to "Sit still!"

Claire also got her hair done and for hers, Brad used a curling iron and comb. The two of us looked pretty fabulous most days. I never saw him smile, but when he was done styling our hair, he would stand back and nod in approval of his work, and I sensed in those moments that he was happy. After the hair styling was finished, he moved to the chair in front of my desk, sat, looked at me directly, and said, "Walk."

"All right, Brad. I just need to finish this email." Then we would walk. It was a welcome break from phone calls and paperwork. We walked arm in arm and looked at the trees and flowers, often stopping to feed carrots to the neighbor's horses. Other times I would sit at my desk and talk to Brad, even though he only responded with nods and tilts of his head.

Brad's sister visited every Saturday and told me those hairdos would have cost us a fortune if had we gotten them in Brad's New York salon days. She told us what Brad was like before the brain damage, how he had enjoyed a glamorous career in New York and Hollywood, hobnobbing with famous people, living in beautiful homes, going to posh parties.

One afternoon, we got to meet one of the famous people from his past. An actress from a 1980s television series came to visit and I remembered watching her on the show as a girl. Lily and I were star struck. The famous lady brought Brad a box of See's candy and tried to talk with him. They sat on the patio and Brad ate the chocolates one after the other while alternately staring into space then back at her. She talked to Brad and waited for a response, even though we had told her he no longer spoke. At one point, she started crying and Brad rubbed her arm to comfort her. It was heartbreaking watching her try to talk to him. The visit seemed harder on her than on Brad.

Brad understood a lot but there were things he couldn't comprehend, like why I would not answer my door sometimes when he knocked. One day, about four months into my job at Sunset Oaks, Brad was pounding at the back door to my office. He often pounded on my back door and I had learned to tune it out, not because I didn't care, but because some days, I simply *had* to finish the pile of paperwork on my desk.

This day, after about 20 minutes of pounding, the door came off its hinges and crashing down. It all happened so fast that I just screamed, hung up on the person I was talking to, and stared at Brad, who was standing on top of the flattened door. His lips were pursed and his fists clenched. Much to my shock, he lunged at me like the bad guy in a scary movie. I ran around my desk and out the door screaming as he chased me through the courtyard. I arrived at Claire's office and hid behind her. Claire was tiny. What did I think she was going to be able to do? Brad arrived and stopped in his tracks when he saw me behind Claire, who was laughing because the scene *was* rather comical. "What's going on, you two?" she asked.

"He literally knocked my door down because I didn't answer," I said, huddling behind her. The building was old and falling apart, so it wasn't surprising the hinges were loose.

"Oh, my," she mused. "Brad, it's all right. Are you upset with Liz?" He nodded, arms crossed over his chest, glaring at me. "Okay, let's all take a deep breath. Liz, say sorry to Brad."

"I'm sorry Brad. I didn't mean to upset you. I was just trying to get some work done." He nodded and his face softened.

Claire was still chuckling and I could feel the tension in the room dissipate. I came out from behind her and Brad stood there looking at me, his sweet self again, then walked over and hugged me. From that day on, I let him in my office, no matter how much work I had to do.

One morning a couple of weeks after the door incident, Dave and I had a huge fight before I left for work and I cried all the way to Sunset Oaks. The blow up had ended with Dave saying, "You're a bad wife. I want a divorce." When I arrived at work, I sat in my parked car before going in, trying to calm myself. I cleaned the mascara from under my eyes and put on some foundation and powder to cover the redness in my cheeks. I walked into the main living room of Sunset Oaks, said, "Good morning" to the residents and caregivers, then walked quickly to my office. Brad and Claire followed me.

When we got to my office, I turned around and said, "Hi, Brad," in a quiet voice, then told Claire about the argument with Dave. Brad listened, a concerned look on his face. Once again, I wondered if he understood everything I was saying. He walked over to me, put his arms around me, and hugged me. I hugged him back and broke down crying again.

I'm sure I added something to Brad's quality of life, but he added more to mine. I learned patience from Brad. I learned to slow down, to be present, to appreciate beauty, and to take a walk once in a while. I learned to shut up and listen from time to time instead of talking constantly.

Brad died at age 58, a year after I left Sunset Oaks. Claire told me his decline was bad. During his last few months, he sometimes defecated and rubbed it all over the walls of his room. I was glad I didn't see that. It's not how I want to remember him.

Brad's type of brain damage was something I rarely saw. Alzheimer's was the most common type I encountered. Alcohol dementia was the next most common example I saw, which is why it perplexed me that at all the conferences on aging and dementia, the subject was rarely, if ever, discussed. Doctors sometimes wrote "ETOH dementia" (which stands for ethanol, the alcohol made from distillation) on the physician's report instead of the word "alcohol." Why didn't they want to write the word? Sometimes they simply called it Alzheimer's when it wasn't. Some neurologists went so far as to claim that alcohol dementia didn't even exist.

Drew Robinson, a 75-year-old resident at Sunset Oaks, walked around most days wearing a leather Budweiser jacket. He was six-foot-four, with a drawl and a strut to go along with his ten-gallon hat. Each day when I arrived, I said, "Good morning, Drew, how are you?" He would touch his head and respond "Oh God, I feel awful. I really tied one on last night." I chuckled, since Drew hadn't had a drop of alcohol in over two years. He must have woken up, found himself locked up with a bunch of people who were not all there and thought: *my God, this is a bad hangover.* He was a happy guy, though, and I enjoyed him.

One time I asked him what he was drinking and he said, "Tequila. The cheap shit."

"Really?" I asked, "Let me smell that." I held the glass to my nose, discovered it was water, handed it back to him and said, "Yep, smells like the cheap shit to me, Drew."

The youngest case of alcohol dementia I encountered was a man named Larry. The day I met him I walked down the halls of Community Memorial hospital in Ventura, looking for Carrie, the Discharge Planner.

She had called me that morning about a possible admission. "He's a 53-year-old man with severe alcohol dementia," she said. "He's been here a month, his insurance days have run out, and he cannot afford our daily rate." The hospital apparently wanted him out because he wasn't old enough to qualify for Medicare and they were losing money on him. He had enough private funds to afford Sunset Oaks and I needed a move-in.

I brought a box of donuts as a small thank you for Carrie. I usually brought fruit platters, since every Discharge Planner I knew was on a diet. But on this day, I was in a hurry and Vons grocery store had Krispy Kremes ready to go. On top of the donut box lay the assessment form, which listed questions I would ask the hospital staff and Larry's family to determine if we could meet his needs. Marketing directors didn't normally do assessments, but it was halfway through the month and I had no move-ins. I was getting daily calls from corporate asking, "How many move-ins are you going to have this month?" "Zero" was not an acceptable answer.

Two months like that and I would be out of a job. I had called every hot, warm, and cold lead I had. I had visited nearly every referral source, and still, nothing, no prospects in sight. I was in the midst of planning an open house, trying to make *something* happen before the end of the month, when Carrie called and told me about Larry. My relief at the mere potential of a move-in was huge. Our nurse, who normally did the assessments, was out sick. Claire was next in line, but she was too swamped that day to drive to Ventura. I was going to do whatever it took to make this happen.

As I walked down the halls and inhaled the familiar scent of ammonia and bleach, I saw a woman in her 40s crying and hugging a man the same age outside a room. They stopped hugging and talked, looking towards the door of the patient room. I wondered what was going on, and again felt that strange contrast of feelings within me. On the one hand, I thought of this guy Larry, his damaged liver and brain, his family, his circumstances which I had read about on the chart Carrie faxed to me that morning. I truly wanted to help him, to somehow make his situation better. I felt somber at the thought that Larry's quality of life was pretty much over at such a young age. I pondered how difficult this must be for his family, thought of my own family and what it would be like to deal with something like this.

I needed to hold onto that caring voice inside me, which was real, yet also remember my objective for being at this hospital: get a move-in. I was there to do a job. It was an odd paradox, mixing emotions and business, melancholy and at the same time hope at the prospect of a move-in, a little pressure relieved.

Arriving on the fifth floor, I saw Carrie at the end of the hall.

"Hi, Liz," she said, "I'm totally swamped today so I'm going to take you straight to Larry's room and fill you in on the way. He's really sweet." She continued as we walked, "It's so sad. His liver is shot but the doctors say he could recover from that if he stops drinking permanently. The dementia is quite advanced. I know he's really young for your place, but I just don't know where else to send him at this point. Maybe a rehab, but he doesn't comprehend enough to participate in a recovery program. His sister is on her way. She can fill you in more on his history." She paused in front of room 537, "And here we are," she said and led me into his room.

"Mr. Davies, this is Liz. She's from an assisted living community and she's going to talk with you for a few minutes, okay?" Larry jumped out of his bed, got me a chair and urged me to sit down. He was gangly and had gray stubble on his chin that looked like it had been growing for a couple days. His hair was black and scraggly with gray bits woven in. His weathered face looked much older than 53 and his eyes were kind.

"Okay then," Carrie said, "I'll let you two get acquainted."

"Hi, Larry," I said, "How are you feeling today?"

"Fine, I guess." He shifted on the bed and shrugged.

"Do you have a few minutes to visit?"

"Sure, got no place else to go."

"Great. So, where are you from?"

"I'm from Hawaii and Virginia and New York. The ocean, you know. Warmth. I love warmth. Birds. My mom always thought it was funny but she didn't know. Anyway, it was that thing, you know the one you use to open cars. It was silly really." He chuckled, waved his hand, and threw his head back, as if he had just said something hilarious.

"So, you lived in Hawaii before coming here?"

"It's all crazy. My wife died when I was at the thing-a-ma-gig. Your sweater is beautiful. Can I get you some water? I can tell you're a nice lady."

"Thanks, Larry. I can tell you're nice too." I smiled and just looked at him for a while, not sure what else to say.

Larry's sister arrived a few minutes later and she and I talked out in the hallway. She was short like me and her lipstick was bright pink. I guessed she was about 60.

"He's the sweetest guy you'll ever meet," she said through tears, "wouldn't hurt a fly. But he was an alcoholic who married another alcoholic and moved to Hawaii with her. They drank together for 10 years until she died of cirrhosis last year. Now he has sort of landed in our lap."

I thought of Larry and his wife sipping Mai Tais on the beach in Maui. "Do you live in the area?"

"Yes, with my husband. We both work full-time and there's just no way we can take care of him. It's not safe to leave him alone. He could wander off or burn the house down, or drink himself to death. Do you think he can move to your place?"

"Most likely, yes."

We went back into the room, and as I sat talking with Larry, I recalled a television ad I had seen many times in high school. It showed a hand holding an egg. The voiceover said, "This is your brain." Then the hand cracked the egg into a frying pan and the voice said, "This is your brain on drugs. Any questions?" The phrase "This is your brain on drugs," became part of popular culture at the time, something we often laughed at in high school and college. I looked back at Larry and thought, *Alcohol is a drug, too. Am I drinking too much?*

Larry moved into our place and stayed three months. He stood out, being so much younger than the other residents who were in their 80s and 90s. The husband of one of our caregivers took him to Alcoholics Anonymous meetings, but I don't think he even understood where he was. One day, Larry's sister visited and said someone had stolen his cologne. "He drank it," Lily said, "no one stole it." Lily always knew exactly what was going on. He left our place and moved to an alcohol and drug rehab. They said it was probably too late for him, but they would give it a try. I never heard what happened to him after that.

I saw more substance-related dementia at Sunset Oaks as the months went on.

August 23rd

A man toured today looking for dementia care for his dad. His dad is a retired dentist, 71 years old. When he was in his 30s and 40s, the guy spent evenings sucking on nitrous oxide after all the patients and staff had left the office. Now he's got dementia and psychotic episodes because of it. Major brain damage. We couldn't even admit him because he was so physically combative. I think he's going to end up in a mental hospital. It's scary to see people in these situations.

November 14th

We had a meeting at the corporate office today focusing on occupancy in our memory care communities. The numbers are good, lots of move-ins. We're seeing more and more substance-related dementia. The CEO joked that even if they find a cure for Alzheimer's (which I hope they do), we'll always be able to fill our buildings. The Baby Boomers have done so much drinking and drugging that we've got a good 20 to 30 years of business in front of us. He chuckled and we laughed along. I felt a little bad laughing about it, but I also thought, he's right about the Baby Boomers: we are already seeing some of them come in—younger and younger cases. I remembered Camille Thompson at The Gables. She was only 72.

Camille Thompson was the wife of a famous musician. She moved into The Gables' memory care the second year I worked there. Years of substance abuse had brought Camille to our door. Her husband was fine, even though he had partied right alongside her. That always confused me. *Why did some people develop dementia from alcohol and drug abuse yet others didn't?* All of the doctors I asked didn't know the answer. It was a mystery, like why some drinkers develop cirrhosis of the liver and others don't.

Camille was agitated the first couple weeks after moving in and we could not figure out why. She yelled a lot and even punched the caregivers. We asked John, the maintenance director to try and calm her, thinking she might respond to a male figure. She attacked him with a broom. Eventually Camille's daughter came by, saw her hair in a ponytail, and told us she hated having her hair pulled back. When Camille was a child, her mom often pulled her hair back so tightly it would hurt her. Camille could only mumble unrecognizable words; thus, she could not tell us about the ponytail. When we took her hair down and let it flow, a gorgeous, thick, silver head of locks that went below her waist, she calmed and never again attacked anyone.

Camille was petite and waif thin. We called her the "ghost-walker," because she was quiet and graceful and could easily slip out the door unnoticed. She loved to wear her favorite powder-blue silk nightgown and matching robe all day. One day, Camille got out of The Gables and the police found her wandering the streets. The police figured they would go to each of the four dementia care places in town until they found the one where Camille lived. This was a benefit of living in a small town.

I stood in the main office and stared out the window at Camille emerging from the police car in her nightgown, her hair blowing wildly, a flat look in her eyes. I imagined going back in time 40 years, knocking on the door of her Hollywood mansion, and showing her a videotape of the scene I was now witnessing. *What would she do?* I wondered. Maybe Camille would say, "You know what? It's worth it; I am having a blast right now. I wouldn't change a thing." Maybe not, though. Maybe to actually see oneself in the future would be more powerful than saying, "This *could* be you." It would be saying, "This *is* you."

Watching Camille, as the police guided her in, I thought of my own drinking. I had lived a party lifestyle in San Francisco and concluded that was just normal for city life. I drank even more when we moved to Ojai, pretty much daily either with my sister-in-law or by myself. Staff in assisted living communities, doctors and nurses in hospitals often walk by people with emphysema, sucking on oxygen tanks, and still go out for their smoke break. Young people think they are never going to get old, get cancer, or suffer consequences from abusing their bodies. *It can't happen to me.*

May 7th

I was so hung over yesterday, it was hard to concentrate on work. Having a hangover is harder at 34 than it was at 24. I'm going to cut down, just drink on the weekends. God, I don't want to give it up completely—I love alcohol.

July 12th

I have been taking a few days off each week from drinking. It's hard, though. I really look forward to the day of the week when I can drink. Last night, I opened two bottles of white wine and drank half of each. I didn't want to admit to myself I was drinking an entire bottle of wine. Do normal drinkers do this kind of thing? Maybe I am overreacting. Everyone drinks to relax. I have never missed a day of work because of it.

January 8th

I feel melancholy sometimes when I drink. And Dave and I get into arguments. It's not as fun as it used to be, but I can't imagine giving it up. I'm having trouble thinking clearly after a night of drinking. And yoga and meditation were no fun at all after that night of tequila and cigarettes last week. I'm 37 years old. I wonder if I keep going like this, will I end up with alcohol dementia in my 60s or 70s?

Five years into my assisted living career, right after I left Sunset Oaks and hadn't yet started at Casa Amanecer, I gave up alcohol. Dave and I were in Mazatlán at the time. While making dinner, I polished off a bottle of wine, then moved on to tequila while baking chocolate chip cookies. As I swayed over the bowl of batter, Dave said to me, "Liz, you have been mixing that dough for 45 minutes—what is going on with you?" Then he looked at my face and said, "Oh my God, you're drunk. When did *that* happen?" This led to a fight, with Dave refusing to sleep in the same bed with me. I cried and looked at the bottle of wine, realizing in that moment, I loved it more than my husband. I did not want to lose him and the life we had built together. That was the last night I drank.

The amount of substance-related dementia I saw over the years was a big factor in my decision. If I live to a ripe old age, I do not want to lose my intellect because of choices I made. It is amazing how much the actions we take affect our propensity towards developing dementia. This was among the inspiring things I learned: there is so much we *can* do to prevent it.

I was working as vice president of sales and marketing for Elder Care, attending the annual California Association of Assisted Living Conference in Santa Clara, California. I sat in one of the lectures on "Brain Fitness,"

the hot topic that year at nearly every senior care conference. It was the first breakout session of the day and I hadn't had nearly enough coffee. I took a sip of my latte and a bite of cantaloupe, scanning the audience to see if I recognized anyone. I smiled and waved to a couple of familiar faces.

The moderator stepped up to the podium and got our attention. "Thank you, everyone, for joining us. We are going to be talking about brain fitness today: how to get it and how to avoid dementia." The speaker introduced the panel of experts. I was impressed with their credentials.

The first speaker, a neuroscientist, began talking about some studies they had done and the improvements they saw in people who stuck with a brain fitness program for six weeks. "Even people with the beginnings of dementia or mild cognitive impairment with a Mini-Mental score of 23, improved their memory and brain functioning," he said.

He went on to explain specifics of the program which included a variety of things: crossword puzzles, Bingo, painting, learning a foreign language, writing one's name each morning with the hand you don't normally use, eating blueberries and spinach. Blueberries, it turns out, are about as high as a food can get in antioxidants. Even two teaspoons of curry a month could delay the onset of dementia, and fish really *is* brain food.

The presenter said that one study from Tufts University found that people with the highest concentration of DHA in their blood (a fatty acid found in wild Alaskan salmon, herring, and mackerel), had an almost 50-percent reduction in their risk of developing Alzheimer's disease.

It was inspiring to hear how certain this guy was that this stuff really *works*. I was thinking of the implications for myself, our employees and our residents. Of course, I was also thinking of the marketing opportunities, the classes and events we could design around this to attract seniors to our communities. *We could do a class with eating curry while simultaneously doing pottery and learning Italian. How fun would that be?*

The second speaker on the panel explained that what is possible and what scientists are learning about brain science is changing on a monthly basis. "We can barely keep up with all the advances and changes," she said. She went on to talk about neuroplasticity, which is the brain's ability to adapt and change. "Scientists used to think we had a lot of plasticity in younger years and that later the brain got hardwired. Then they discovered there is lifelong plasticity." She told us about neurogenesis, a concept discovered in 1998, which holds that we can actually grow new brain cells. She handed us an article that said:

> *Scientists used to believe that cognitive decline was an unavoidable consequence of an old machine wearing down. They believed there was nothing we could do to resurrect cognitive skills that have been lost. At any age the brain can revise its processing machinery in response to stimuli and activities. Just as it can deteriorate, it can also grow.*

I was excitedly writing notes now, inspired by all the things the speaker was saying. "With training and practice we can increase memory and the speed with which our brain processes information." She went on to explain that we naturally gain and increase wisdom and vocabulary throughout our lifespan. She handed us another article that said:

> *Our sophisticated thinking and reasoning improves. At around age 50, our physical brain structure even changes, with the left and right hemispheres merging and beginning to talk to each other. The brain may not work faster, but it works better, and our brains are at their creative peak from age 50 to 90.*

The bottom line of the talk was this: *use it or lose it.* But, here's the catch—we cannot use it doing things that are comfortable or familiar. We have to do something *new*. The activities must require careful attention and focus, like juggling or playing ping pong to increase the brain's visual, tactile, and hand-eye coordination responses. "Take up knitting and try to get better and faster at it," she said.

Just as with training for a marathon, we have to continually raise the bar in our brain fitness regimen, i.e., do more difficult crossword puzzles or switch to Sudoku. We need to take it up a notch, do things that require paying close attention, make it demanding so that we re-engage the brain's learning machinery. Challenging the brain even hurts sometimes, like when I got a headache playing chess with Dave. *It is the same as how lifting weights makes my muscles sore.* This sharpens neural pathways and speeds up connections. Activities that are rewarding or surprising are especially good at increasing the production of key brain chemicals associated with intelligence, such as N-acetylaspartate and choline.

The last speaker on the panel concluded by saying, "Even in old age, the brain can rewire itself, and some areas of the brain actually add new cells in response to stimulation. The key to brain health is to protect neurons from damage and promote their vitality."

I left the conference determined to maintain as much of my mental vitality as possible for as long as possible. To begin with, I needed to do the same things for a healthy brain that I would do for a healthy heart, like exercise. I also needed to reduce my stress level, challenge myself with things like playing chess, and stay connected with friends and family.

When people don't engage socially, they decline rapidly. There was a study in Sweden that linked loneliness to dementia. I read another study about nuns who had died and when they did autopsies, it showed the advanced plaques and tangles of Alzheimer's. Yet these nuns had not shown any symptoms of dementia when they were alive because they were so engaged socially.

I was surprised to learn that stress was a major factor in developing dementia. Dave laughed at me for practicing what he called my "Radical Self-Care." It is true, I do a lot for my spiritual and emotional fitness and it is something I have always done, even before working in assisted living. The conference speakers said that older adults with a high level of psychological distress have twice the risk of cognitive impairment. *Twice the risk!* That's huge. One article I read said that high levels of stress hormones actually *kill* brain cells. Another article quoted Dr. Gary Small, a leader in the field of brain vitality as saying, "Constant stress literally shrinks a key memory center."

We must work to eliminate stressors that can be eliminated. But sometimes we cannot avoid stress, so we need to find effective coping mechanisms to deal with it because it's really our body's "stress reaction" and the chemicals released that do the damage.

The stress reduction tip I found most difficult to implement was meditation. I had been working on it for years and still did not get *how* to do it. I preferred guided meditation tapes because it was hard to turn my brain off; somehow having an outside voice guiding me helped. I also started following this simple "How To" that the speakers gave us:

How to Meditate

The best time to meditate is in the morning, before breakfast. Choose a place where you will not be disturbed by anyone, not even a pet. Sit for 10 to 20 minutes on the couch or floor and use this simple breathing meditation. Breathe naturally, preferably through the nostrils, without attempting to control your breath. Try to become aware of the sensation of the breath as it enters and leaves the nostrils. Concentrate on it to the exclusion of everything else. Thoughts will eventually creep up. When you become aware of them, simply re-focus your attention on breathing.

Sounds simple enough, but it is really hard. Many times, I wanted to give up because my mind kept wandering to the tomato bisque I was planning to make for dinner or the emails I needed to send for work.

At home I did whatever I could to stave off developing dementia. At work, I tried to be as supportive and compassionate as I could to those who had it. The best dementia-care communities provide ongoing training to foster this compassion, realizing that caring for people with dementia is both a skill and an art that we can't properly do if we don't at least try to grasp what they're feeling.

In one training, we did an exercise where the instructor had us partner up and spoon-feed each other apple sauce, so we could experience a level of vulnerability similar to what our residents felt. I felt demeaned as my training partner placed the food in my mouth. I wanted to say, "I've got the concept. Can we stop now?" Imagine a training where we give each other a bath or have to experience someone wiping our butt. Now that would be a *real* lesson in feeling the level of humiliation seniors feel when receiving personal care. They are adults, just like me, who have been doing these things for themselves their whole lives.

Much of the knowledge about caring for dementia residents is also gleaned through day-to-day experience of trial and error. I learned that aromatherapy works (lavender in the air *does* actually relax people). Studies have found that when researchers infuse lavender oil in Alzheimer's facilities, agitated Alzheimer's sufferers become significantly calmer. I thought, *if lavender spray works for agitated Alzheimer's residents, imagine what it could do for me on my stressed-out days.* I started keeping a bottle in my top drawer and spraying it in the afternoon to calm me.

When Sunset Oaks was first built in Ojai, in the 1970s, there were very few secure dementia-care places in the United States. This was the only one within a 50-mile radius. Some of our caregivers had worked there for 15 to 20 years and knew more about dementia than many neurologists. They lived and breathed it every day. Lily, who had been working with dementia residents for 18 years, taught the staff how to care for people with love and patience, not medication. She learned the history of every resident so she could tap into experiences that made them happy. Lily was so in tune to the people who lived at Sunset Oaks that she knew how to anticipate their behavior before it even happened. She put together a list of caring dos and don'ts:

Do:

- Keep everything as simple as possible
- Hug
- Remember, they will follow you and want to know where you are going
- Hold their hand
- Maintain your sense of humor

Don't:

- Expect accurate answers to your questions
- Get irritated when he/she asks the same question over and over
- Take his/her behavior personally
- Ask him/her to choose between peas and carrots—it can be too confusing and stressful
- Tease or make fun of her/him

The list helped us to make each day as enjoyable as possible. We also found fun things to do so that days weren't focused entirely on caring for people's disease. We took the residents on walks to the ranch next door where they fed carrots and apples to the horses. We were like kids again, laughing as the horses devoured the treats and let us pet them. We put on classical music and painted ceramics. We took field trips to the park. These elders with memory loss helped me to be in the moment and actually enjoy it. The more I learned from them and let myself relax into their universe, the more I realized its potential to be uplifting.

Not everyone found the environment of dementia-care uplifting. Dave, for instance, found it upsetting. He never stepped foot in the Gables' dementia-care area. When I went to work for Sunset Oaks, which was *all* dementia care, he figured there was no getting around it, so he came to visit one day. He was met with a drooling man, pants down to his knees, mumbling incoherently and grabbing Dave's hand. I watched through my window as Dave graciously extricated himself and made his way to my office. He never came back to Sunset Oaks. I felt compassion for his discomfort and relieved that over time, I had developed an ability to immerse myself in this world and find the beauty there.

For me, the world of memory care had become at times disturbing and at times inspiring. The enriching aspects included things like the art I saw residents create. When people lose the ability to follow a logical story line or communicate verbally, they often tap into other parts of their brain, parts they never knew they had. I have seen paintings by Alzheimer's patients that could be in a museum. There was one guy I met, Steve, who had been an engineer and was diagnosed with early onset Alzheimer's at age 47. His was the youngest case I saw. Steve had never been artistic, yet while in assisted living, he started to paint watercolors.

I ran into his wife, Sherry, at an Alzheimer's conference two years after I had met them. Sherry told me his disease had progressed rapidly to the point where he could barely communicate verbally. "He no longer has access to nouns," she said, "except when he is painting. When he sits with me and paints, he can communicate again." Steve, who had once been a brilliant and accomplished man, now spent his days staring into space, not saying a coherent word. Sherry said it was always a shock when she arrived for a visit and saw him there with all the 80- and 90-year-olds. The contrast was stark.

"So, I go and grab the paints and brushes," she said, "and Steve and I sit at the table and paint. He'll paint a mountain or a tree and then while naming the painting, he'll form complete sentences and have an almost normal conversation with me." She went on to tell me about moving him to the memory-care community. "It was the hardest decision I have ever had to make. I just couldn't do it at home anymore. I was worried about him wandering off. I had to keep my job. I couldn't leave him alone in the bathroom or kitchen or anywhere, really."

Luckily, Steve had given Sherry Power of Attorney before his decline, so she was able to make these decisions for him and her. Sometimes families struggle at home for years, trying to care for a loved one who has become completely unable to live on his or her own. They finally agree to move mom to an assisted living community, but they can't do it because mom did not give them Power of Attorney prior to becoming incapacitated. They cannot place mom in dementia care against her will and they cannot access the funds which are needed to pay for her care. Their only option now is to go through the courts to gain conservatorship: take away mom's rights without her consent.

If mom is having a "good day" when she goes before the judge, chances are conservatorship is not going to happen. If mom "wins," and demonstrates that she is still mentally competent, the kids have to pay legal fees and mom is still at home on her own, not taking her medication, isolated, at risk of wandering, perhaps even still driving and putting others at risk. It often takes a tragedy, like a burned-down house, in order for the court to see the reality of the situation. In dementia care, I told families, "Do not wait for a crisis," but some families have no choice but to wait for a crisis.

With the majority of families, though, it isn't lack of paperwork but rather a mixture of denial, grief, and love that stopped them from making the move to a community. One woman named Jan came to tour with me because her husband, who was only 62 years old, wandered off into the mountains surrounding Ojai. Jan was panic stricken for 14 hours before the helicopters found him. She came to tour with me the next day.

"People have been telling me for years that I need to look into a care home, but I just couldn't bring myself to even consider the possibility. My husband is 12 years older than me. We lived in Chicago for years. He was a very successful writer. We moved to Ojai to retire, enjoy the good life. This is not how I imagined it."

"I'm sorry," I said, then took a deep breath and let it out. I did not know what to say to Jan. She looked out the window at the mountains and put her fist over her mouth.

"When we found out he had Alzheimer's," Jan continued, "we even started working on a book to capture the process, his journey through the disease. But now he has progressed so rapidly that he cannot keep a coherent train of thought. This book won't get finished. I don't even feel like I have a husband. I feel like I have a child. Yesterday when he wandered off, I felt the fear of a parent whose child has run away. I've already raised three kids."

"Thank goodness you found him."

"Yes, thank goodness. So here I am. Everyone in town says this place gives the best care."

"We do. Our caregivers know what they're doing. Lily, our care manager, knows the people who live here so well that she can tell when someone has a urinary tract infection just by changes in their mood or behavior. It's a good thing, too, because many of our residents would not be able to communicate verbally that they were in pain. I'll introduce you to Lily when we tour. Do you have any questions about the place before we look around?" She shook her head and I led her out onto the patio.

It was a warm day and Blanca, one of our caregivers, was playing Bingo with a small group. We stopped at the table and I introduced Jan to Blanca and Mr. Driscoll, who had lived at Sunset Oaks for five years. He shook Jan's hand and smiled. We made our way to the dining room and saw Lily spoon-feeding Ruby. Jan stopped and watched them, a look of discomfort on her face. She stared for a few minutes then asked, "How is the food?"

"Really good, actually. I eat here on the days when I'm not out in the field. Rosalind has been our chef for 10 years." We continued walking and I pointed out the activity calendar and photos of our recent Fourth of July barbecue. "We had a band. It was really fun."

"Everyone looks a lot older than my husband," she said, staring at one of the group photos.

"We have a few people in their 60s, but most are in their 80s or 90s." I let her sit with that for a moment. It was true that most of our residents were much older than her husband and I did not want to sugarcoat this. It was a fact she would have to live with if he moved to Sunset Oaks or any memory care community.

When we arrived at the model room I said, "This room is $5,500 a month. That includes meals, housekeeping, laundry, help with bathing, dressing, medications—basically all of his care. There are no extra charges."

"That seems reasonable compared to the place I toured in Santa Barbara."

We headed back to my office and drank tea at my desk. "I'm 50 years old. Do you have any other young wives like me with husbands here?" Jan asked.

"Yes, actually, Lisa Jones. She is a nice lady. I am sure she would be happy to talk with you. Would you like me to give her a call and see if I can set something up?"

"Yes, I'd like that. My friends say I should get a lover. It's not like Paul would even know the difference. But I am so tired from taking care of him at the end of the day, the last thing on my mind is sex. It's weird because I wouldn't even feel like I am cheating on him. He's so far gone."

"Nancy Reagan called Alzheimer's the 'long goodbye,'" I said. "I think that is a pretty accurate description. I am so sorry you're having to go through this. You mentioned having support from friends. Are you getting additional support from groups or a counselor?"

"I am seeing a therapist and that's helping somewhat. My family has also been wonderful. And I read a lot, mostly mystery novels."

"Good. It is important to take care of yourself, do things you enjoy. This is a tough road you're on."

"Thank you for listening and being supportive," she said hugging me.

The next day, I sent Jan a thank you note. I called her the following week with the phone number of Lisa, the young wife whose husband lived at our place. I left a message and Jan did not return my call. A week after our tour, the crisis was now a distant memory. I never heard from Jan again. In fact, she wouldn't return any of my calls. Eventually, I gave up, but I wondered how she and her husband were doing. I didn't need a move-in. We were full with a waiting list. I just wanted to know how they were.

The scenario I experienced with Jan was common. I often called people after a tour and said nothing more than, "How are you?" and they practically hung up on me. These were people who had poured their hearts out to me sharing intimate details of their lives. The thing I learned about denial is that people get really annoyed when someone tries to break through it. A mere phone call or thank you note can be a reality check that causes them to practically scream, "Look, I am back in denial again; leave me alone. I wanted to talk to you for that brief moment when I was out of denial, but now you are a real pain in the ass." Six months later, another crisis would hit and they were calling me four times a day to see if I had a room available. "If you don't have a room for him," they said, "I'm going somewhere else."

Denial can be dangerous. What usually happens is that mom is sliding downhill, progressing gradually in her confusion, and family members don't want to see it, so they put blinders on and ignore the warning signs. Then, one day, they have a moment where they say, "Oh my God." An event so unusual happens that they can no longer excuse or rationalize away mom's bizarre behavior.

Mom just called the police and said there were Nazis in her living room or went to the neighbor's house in her underwear and asked to borrow a cup of sugar. That was usually the point at which I met them. They came for a tour and faced reality for a few days. Then mom had a few lucid days and the family slipped back into denial.

People with dementia fall or leave the stove on. Some take the wrong medications and give themselves a stroke. One of the saddest cases I ever heard of was a woman with dementia who wandered off at the Dallas airport when her husband walked over to the drinking fountain to get some water. He turned around and she was gone. They never found her. The guilt that family must live with every day. So, when I was harsh with a family, it was not because I am mean-spirited and enjoyed giving people reality checks. It was because I knew the damage denial could do.

People wait for a crisis because their loved one is often helpless and cannot communicate anymore, so it feels like abandonment to place him in an assisted living community. Many times, though, dementia care is the safer choice. For a person with memory loss, living in a community that provides good care, medication management, and fun activities is often better than being at home, plopped in front of the television, having one's kids get continually frustrated because they have no real education in dementia care or the disease process.

My friend, Kris, was telling me one day about her 86-year-old mother-in-law who had always been a sharp lady and now had dementia. They were at a restaurant and Kris's mother-in-law wanted more coffee. She held her cup out and grunted "Ugh, ugh." Kris imitated her as she told me the story and the irritation in her voice was evident. Kris then explained how she snapped at her mother-in-law, saying, "Use your words or I am not giving you the coffee. I am not going to play these games with you." A chill went up my spine as I whispered, "Oh God, Kris, no. Tell me you didn't do that."

"Well, I'm *not* going to play games with her. She's acting like a child. She just wants attention."

"I don't think so," I said. "I think maybe she really *doesn't* know the word for 'coffee' anymore." People who are not informed about dementia take the person's behavior personally. They think the person is annoying them on purpose. They argue and try to reason with them, oblivious to how frightened and frustrated the demented person is, how much they would give anything to have the words necessary to express themselves.

"Kris," I explained, "people with dementia literally lose their vocabulary. They go in reverse. They lose their nouns, then they lose *all* their words. It's called aphasia."

So, being with trained staff is sometimes a more nurturing environment than being with family. Also, because of the secure delayed-egress door, the resident is safe from wandering off, for the most part. People do sometimes wander away from secure memory care facilities. We call it an "elopement," and I've heard of a few cases, such as the time a 71-year-old man wandered off because the door was broken and the community where he lived neglected to fix it. They never found him. He was presumed dead and his family, of course, sued the assisted living facility. The facility lost their license and I ended up working for the company that took over the property. I read about another case where a woman in Idaho wandered away from her assisted living community and was found dead in a river nearby.

I was at a luncheon with other marketing directors and the conversation turned to the subject of elopement. One woman shared about a resident at her place who was adept at getting out. The executive director called one day and asked, "Is Doris there in the facility?"

"Yes, of course," the caregiver responded.

"Are you sure?" the boss asked.

"Yes, she's here," the caregiver said.

"Really?" the executive director continued, "because I'm in Macy's accessory department and I'm looking at her. She's shopping for scarves!" Doris had gotten on a bus and gone to the mall. Luckily, they found her and it ended well.

No matter how attentive we are, no matter how good our doors are, things happen. Even in the most diligent communities, a fluke can happen and someone leaves.

It was a Tuesday afternoon at Sunset Oaks. I arrived after attending a networking lunch and Claire met me at the door with a panicked look on her face. "Jerry got out," she said. "He scaled the back wall and now he's missing. We have been trying to find him for an hour."

"Oh my God," I said.

"Lily is driving up Burnham Road and Luis and Blanca are walking around the neighborhood looking for him." She was talking so fast I could hardly follow her.

I dropped my briefcase and headed for the door. "I'll go towards town," I yelled over my shoulder. Claire answered her cell phone, waving and nodding at me at the same time.

Jerry was 64 and had advanced Parkinson's Disease. Before moving to Sunset Oaks, he lived with his wife, Christine, at their home in Santa Barbara. Christine was 10 years younger than Jerry and still worked full-time at the law firm where they had met.

"He was such a powerful, yet kind man," Christine told me when she first came to look at our place, "and very funny. He still has his sense of humor. I am so glad Parkinson's didn't take that from him." Christine had adored her husband for 15 years and it was obvious the progression of his disease had not diminished her feelings. Jerry's incontinence and the side effects from all the drugs, especially the sexual acting out (grabbing women's breasts, exposing and touching himself in front of others), got to be too much for Christine and her daughters to handle at home. So, she moved him to our place.

Jerry understood on some level, and I sat with him and Christine as she explained that he would be staying at Sunset Oaks. He graciously agreed and wanted his wife to feel good about the decision. Christine visited every day and I loved watching them sit in the dining room or on the patio together, holding hands and laughing.

Jerry had declined rapidly in the three months since moving to Sunset Oaks. He needed more and more care and attention each day. Dementia brought on by Parkinson's was the most challenging type I saw. Residents often required more caregivers because of balance issues, incontinence, sexual behavior in public, hallucinations, and the constant body movements. Their legs, arms, and head moved continuously, which meant they burned a lot of calories, so we had to make sure they got enough nutrition and did not rapidly lose weight.

Jerry was in the late stages and unable to orient himself to time and place, yet he was still physically healthy and agile, another mystery of the disease. I was surprised, though, that he got over an eight-foot wall. I was 36 years old, did yoga three times a week, and *I* couldn't scale that wall.

As I drove up Burnham Road, I saw Blanca walking around the dry riverbed, calling Jerry's name. My breathing was quick and shallow, my face tingled with fear. My eyes darted back and forth from trees and side streets to the road in front of me. I had a fondness for all our residents, but Jerry was especially sweet and dear to me. I imagined his devoted Christine, how her face would look if we had to tell her something happened to Jerry. "Please, God," I said out loud, "please let him be safe. Please let us find him before he gets hurt, or ends up far away, or runs into someone unkind." I imagined how frightened and confused Jerry must be at that moment.

I drove around for an hour and then headed back to Sunset Oaks to regroup with the team. "It has been two hours since Jerry left," Claire said. "It's time to call the police." She called them to report Jerry's elopement and 15 minutes later, we heard the search helicopter flying overhead.

Claire, Lily, and I were sitting in the office, listening to the helicopter and looking at each other like worried parents. I fidgeted with a paper clip, bending it into all sorts of shapes. I paced around the office. It drove me crazy to not take some kind of action. *What if we don't find him? What if he's dead?* I couldn't bear the thought. All of the horror stories I had heard over the years flashed through my head, like the guy found dead of thirst next to a tree after wandering from his assisted living community. "I'm going to look again," I said and headed to my car. I circled the same area, this time trying different side streets. My cell phone rang. It was Claire calling.

"Come back," Claire said. "We found him." She hung up.

I walked into the dining room and saw Jerry laughing and drinking a cup of coffee. I smiled, let out a sigh, and put my arm around Claire, who had a relieved smile on her face. "He knocked on some guy's door about a half-mile from here. Jerry told the guy he was hungry so the guy invited him in and gave him a glass of milk and a peanut butter sandwich," she said and chuckled. "Halfway through their lunch the guy realized that something seemed off with Jerry, so he called the police."

"Thank God," I said, and walked over to Jerry and gave him a big hug.

"Am I in trouble?" he asked with a mischievous twinkle in his eye.

"No, not at all. We're just glad you're back."

Despite our amazing team of employees and our secure doors, Jerry still got out of Sunset Oaks that day. In the best memory care communities, staff are given continuous training on how to keep people safe and avoid scares like the one we had, but it still happens.

Employees are actually given training on working with *all* the nuances of memory loss and confusion. The training model we used at The Gables was the "Best Friends Approach"™ to Alzheimer's care, which gives staff members a goal of knowing 100 things about each resident. David Troxel, one of the authors of *The Best Friends Approach to Alzheimer's Care* says, "If you know one person with Alzheimer's, then you know <u>one</u> person with Alzheimer's." You cannot have a cookie-cutter approach to care. The Sunset Oaks' staff most definitely understood this. We had a nurse from another company visit one day and comment that it was the most wonderful dementia care place he had ever seen. "There is no separation between staff and residents here," he said. "They are truly like a family."

Sunset Oaks *was* extraordinary, especially when I think of the many places which simply gave residents the same things they would get at home: medication, television, a shower, three meals a day, and a bed to sleep in. "Three hots and a cot," as we say in the industry.

Eldersview in San Francisco was another place where I worked that gave excellent care. We never referred to residents as having "dementia." Instead, we said the residents had "forgetfulness." Eldersview's owners believed that rather than looking at these residents as helpless, we should ask ourselves what we could learn from them. The president of the company implemented an activity called "Photovoice," where staff members gave the elders cameras, had them take pictures and then asked them, "Tell me what you see in this photo you took." The company philosophy was to constantly strive to understand the world through *their* eyes rather than forcing them to live in our world.

Sunset Oaks, Eldersview, and another place I oversaw, Summer Gardens, were all exceptional.

I was working as regional director of sales and marketing for Hale Senior Living. My territory was Northern California and I was visiting Summer Gardens, a 60-bed memory care community I oversaw in Lodi, California. I walked into the cozy lobby that reminded me of a bed and breakfast. It smelled like coffee and fresh-baked scones. I loved how they had real china with little pink flowers in their hospitality station. From a distance, I saw Molly sitting in her wheelchair screaming and waving her arms, fists clenched. "They're coming to get me!" she yelled repeatedly. A caregiver walked over, got down to Molly's eye level, and held both of her hands. She spoke softly, "It's all right Molly, you're safe. Everything is good." Molly looked into the caregiver's eyes, calmed down, and stopped yelling.

I walked down the hall, past a group of third graders in Halloween costumes, singing with the residents. I stopped at a desk where Bob, a gentleman in the mid-stages of Alzheimer's, was working busily on some paperwork. He was using one of our Life Stations, a desk with pads of paper, a typewriter, pens, and an adding machine. "How's it going, Bob?" I asked, touching his shoulder.

"I'm making progress—someday this budget will get done."

Another resident named Julie was sitting with Alicia, who had worked at Summer Gardens for 10 years. They were looking through Julie's photo album of Greece. "That's the Aegean Sea," Julie said, pointing to the turquoise water. "I swam in it for hours and felt so at peace." Julie's daughter told us that the trips to Greece were the highlight of her mom's life.

I made some phone calls to prospects and then had lunch in the dining room, hot lasagna with salad and garlic bread. The residents had helped grow and pick the vegetables for the lasagna from the garden we had outside our kitchen. It tasted as delicious as a fine Italian restaurant in San Francisco. In the afternoon, the activity director worked with a group of residents on a community service project, baking and packaging dog biscuits to give to the local Humane Society. Another small group worked out on the patio with a resident's daughter, decorating pumpkins for Halloween.

It seemed like an idyllic scene, too good to be true, but it was actually a typical day for Summer Gardens. It was the way a memory care community was *supposed* to be. I saw residents engaged in a quality of life far better than what they would get at home. Most family caregivers are so busy trying to manage the basic activities of daily living that life enrichment falls by the wayside. It has to. There are only so many hours in a day—no time to decorate pumpkins or look at photo albums of Greece.

Summer Gardens, Sunset Oaks, Eldersview, and a few other places I experienced along the way kept their elders happy, safe, engaged in life, and productive. To do this requires very special people.

Chapter Five

Caregivers: Angels on Earth

Life's most persistent and urgent question is,
"What are you doing for others?"

— Dr. Martin Luther King, Jr.

When I met Blanca, on my first day at Sunset Oaks memory care, she had worked as a caregiver there for 10 years. Her olive skin and long, obsidian hair were the first things I noticed. Next, I saw her eyelashes, curled and long to the point of looking fake, but on closer inspection I saw they were real. Blanca was fit and slender, with hips that swung a little bit when she walked. Each day she wore hot pink or turquoise, form-fitting scrubs that showed off her figure. Her makeup was always done beautifully. She smiled, and bright teeth and dimples jumped out at me.

Blanca hugged, laughed, gave residents their meals and showers, changed their adult diapers, played Bingo, facilitated arts and crafts classes, sang, and danced. Using her own precious money, Blanca often went to the local drug store and bought blue eye shadow for Marge and red nail polish for Jane, who lived at Sunset Oaks. Blanca made sure Marge had that eye shadow on every morning because it made her feel pretty.

Three nights each week, when Blanca finished her eight-hour shift, she went to her second job, cleaning offices. After that she went home and took care of her three kids and husband. Blanca had not taken a vacation in nine years. She made ten dollars an hour. Over the years, I met hundreds just like her. They could make the same wage or more working at Starbucks or Macy's. Instead, they helped elders bathe, dress, and use the toilet. They strained their backs lifting people out of bed, they drained their energy giving love and emotional support. They rarely stopped to rest.

Diane, another caregiver, made a butterfly from cut-out cards for Mildred Balinski, because butterflies were Mildred's favorite thing in the world. During the winter months, Diane knit slippers for residents whose families had forgotten them. She also went home and took care of her own husband, who was bound to a wheelchair. The only time I heard Diane complain was one day when a co-worker didn't show up for her shift and Diane was left alone to care for 20 residents with dementia. It pushed her over the edge and I saw her have her one and only meltdown. The next day, she bounced back and kept giving and giving.

When I was working as vice president of sales for Elder Care Communities, I heard about a caregiver named Olga who worked at our Orange County memory care building. One Tuesday evening at midnight, Olga heard Marian, a petite 90-year-old lady with an Irish brogue, walking around and mumbling to herself. Olga worked the NOC Shift, 11:00 p.m. to 6:00 a.m., and it was not unusual to have a few residents up and awake, but Olga could tell Marian was agitated. So, she went to her, took her hand and asked, "Is everything all right, dear?"

"I'm hungry," Marian said.

"Did you not have dinner?"

Marian shook her head, "No."

At first Olga assumed Marian was confused and had simply forgotten about eating dinner at 6:00 with the other residents. So, she checked the log from the previous shift and sure enough, Marian had not eaten dinner because she was feeling restless. Unfortunately, the kitchen cabinets and refrigerator were sealed with large padlocks.

Corporate did not want caregivers stealing food and a recent accounting audit had revealed missing items from the pantry. It seemed the amount of food being purchased and consumed was increasing despite the same number of residents. The company controller assumed it was staff stealing food and mandated that the kitchen be locked at 5:00 p.m.

Olga went to the employee break room and pulled a plastic bag from the refrigerator. It contained a Russian dish of small minced meatballs covered with pastry. She heated this along with the tub of soup she had brought for dinner. There was only enough for one person—Olga had planned to eat the soup and meatballs during her 30-minute meal break at 3:00 a.m. Her work was physically strenuous and she was hungry by the time her lunch came around.

Olga arranged the food on a plate, then went outside and picked a daisy from the patio garden. She placed the flower in a vase and brought all of this on a tray to Marian in the dining room. For the next 20 minutes, Olga sat with Marian and talked, watching her devour every bite of the delicious homemade meal.

I heard about this happening with Olga because her co-workers sent a letter to the controller. "Olga is a good person," they wrote. "She willingly gave her dinner, knowing she would have nothing to eat when her break time came. We ask that you please leave the kitchen unlocked at night so that we can make the residents a sandwich if they are hungry." Reading the note, I knew it would not make a difference; almost all assisted living facilities locked their kitchens at night. I wondered how many other acts of kindness like this happened every day and we never heard about them.

Why, I wondered, do caregivers do this often-thankless job for meager wages? After a couple of years in assisted living, I began asking them, "Why do you do this work when you could make more serving lattes at a coffee shop? This is a hard job." The answer was simple for most of them, "I love the residents and I love taking care of them." Most caregivers I met knew, somewhere inside themselves, without a doubt, that they were put on this earth to do exactly what they were doing. There was a tenderness about their interactions with elders that was neither manufactured nor contrived. So many people in management, like the controller at Elder Care, took their altruism for granted.

The caregivers had bills to pay, just like the rest of us, yet they rarely made their voices heard or recognized their own value. At The Gables, it took five caregivers quitting in the same week to convince management to give them a 25 cent raise.

At Casa Amanecer, I brought my lunch and often ate in the break room with the caregivers and housekeepers. There I heard similar complaints to those I had heard at The Gables. The small room filled with the smell of Filipino, Ethiopian, and Mexican foods, delicacies the staff had brought from home. One day, as I munched on a lumpia eggroll that Daphne, one of the housekeepers, had given me, Vivian complained, "My husband never thanks me for cooking." Vivian was a 50-year-old Filipina lady with strong hands that were worn from so much work. "Yet that man wants sex every night. Are you kidding me?"

"Tell me about it," Daphne said and laughed. "My husband is the same, and he just sits there on his butt watching football while I take care of the kids. And never any appreciation for the money I bring home."

"It's true," Vivian said, "and we work so hard here because we're understaffed. The morning shift is so stressful, all of us running around trying to help people with their showers or toileting. There's not enough of us to go around. Can you help, Liz?"

"I know, Vivian. I hear you," I said. "It pisses me off, too. I feel so frustrated when you gals tell me this because when I try talking to the higher-ups, it falls on deaf ears. I wish there was something I could do but I'm just the marketing director. I don't make decisions about staffing or wages."

"But you're in *management*," she pleaded. "Surely you can do *something* about this. Can't you at least talk to them?"

By "them" she meant Nancy, the executive director. The woman was cold as ice.

"I'll see what I can do," I said. "I'll try again."

That afternoon I went to Nancy's office. "We need more caregivers on the morning shift, Nancy, and we need to pay them more. Our staff are struggling. This is an expensive city to live in."

"We're paying market rates," she said.

"Why do I get health insurance but the full-time caregivers and housekeepers don't?"

"We can't afford to give them health insurance. I've had this conversation with you before."

"Then what about the staffing ratios? We had seven new residents move in this month. The caregivers are overwhelmed with all the additional people."

"It's not going to happen. Don't you have some phone calls to make?"

I dropped it with Nancy but kept forcing the issue with people above her. Given any opportunity, I asked, "Why aren't we paying our caregivers a living wage?"

Every place where I worked, the responses were the same:

"Our workman's comp premiums were astronomical last year."

"These places cost a fortune to run."

"Our overhead is too high."

"We can't afford to pay them more."

"We have a responsibility to our investors to make a profit."

While there was some truth to these statements (these communities *do* cost a lot to run), the question that gnawed at me was this: if there is such a small profit margin in assisted living, why was there a new facility cropping up on a different corner practically every week? Most places where I worked were charging top dollar, paying low wages, and the building was completely full. *We must be making some money.* When I got the "we-can't-afford-to-pay-them-more" response at the nonprofit, I thought, *well then, why are all these for-profit places in business? It must be lucrative or they wouldn't be doing it.* We also gave the residents a rent increase every year, yet the staff hadn't had a pay raise in four years.

I researched two publicly owned assisted living companies. One was trading on the New York Stock Exchange for thirty-one dollars per share. The other was trading on the American Stock Exchange for forty-seven dollars per share. Plenty of money was being made. I went to a Human Resources training at Alma Via. They passed out a worksheet that showed how the company determined their pay scale. It was based on hourly wages for various positions in the San Francisco marketplace. It looked like this:

Job Title	Minimum	Midpoint	Maximum
Janitor, Housekeeper, Dishwasher, Hostess	$8.50	$9.65	$11.60
Caregiver, Receptionist, Activity Assistant	$9.00	$11.30	$13.55
Caregiver Lead, Dining Room Supervisor, Cook, Medications Technician	$9.70	$12.15	$14.55
Driver, Wellness Coordinator, Lead Cook, Maintenance Worker	$10.50	$13.15	$15.75
Food Service Supervisor	$12.25	$15.30	$18.35
Administrative Assistant	$13.20	$16.50	$19.80

The vice president of human resources, who was conducting the training, explained that this table determined what he paid his employees. *Heaven forbid he pay a little more than the market rate*, I thought.

The pay rate at Casa Amanecer was similar. As a marketing director, I made $80,000 to $85,000 per year, including my commission. The executive directors made from $90,000 to $100,000 per year. Yes, we had more responsibility and higher education levels. But the gap was *huge*.

At one meeting at Casa Amanecer, the quarterly gathering of department heads and senior management, I piped up, "But our residents pay an average of $4,000 to $5,000 a month to live in our building. That's $250,000 per month in revenue and our profit and loss statements show our costs are approximately $150,000 a month. That leaves $100,000 per month. Where is that money going?"

Silence.

"Well... we are working on a charitable fund for residents who run out of money," the vice president of operations said, clearly perturbed. He continued, "Liz, we've got a full day's agenda so we're going to move on."

"It's not right," I said.

"Well, the caregivers can go to school and improve their lot in life if they want to make more money."

"Why don't we just pay them a decent wage for the work they do *now?* If everyone goes to school and improves their lot in life, there won't be any caregivers left." I wanted to call or write to everyone who owned or operated an assisted living facility and say: you cannot keep abusing your staff then expect them to cheerfully take care of the residents. You must take better care of your employees. Period.

The truth was, most of the caregivers would continue giving great care, continue being exploited by their employers, and would never pursue higher education. Many were women of color and subjected to the systemic racism that meant they did not have the same access to higher education and they were paid less than their white counterparts. Mara, for example, did not finish high school, had children young, and couldn't find any other job. She was often sick, depressed, and in and out of physically abusive relationships with men. Whenever I saw Mara bending and lifting a lady onto the toilet, I was amazed at her physical strength and even more impressed by her finesse. Mara was tiny, yet she performed the task deftly, with such grace that the elder was able to maintain her privacy and dignity.

She was an amazing caregiver, yet did not have the confidence to ask for more money. Salespeople, on the other hand, tend to have pretty high opinions of themselves and rarely accept being underpaid.

I was working as vice president of sales and marketing and took a trip to Monterey, California, to do a market study. I was there to determine whether or not we should build a new property in Monterey. I gathered information on local prices, competition, and occupancy rates. My goal was to find out about the competition we were up against, figure out if the market was saturated, then make my recommendation to the CEO. I met some nice people, toured some beautiful buildings, then ate a delicious lunch at a cute bistro in downtown Carmel.

At the end of the day, I was sitting in my car, Mapquesting directions to my final stop while sipping a hot café mocha. The smell of it mixed with the Monterey Pines made me feel happy. These were the days I cherished my job. It had been a fun, productive day. As I savored my mocha, my cell phone rang. It was Mariana, my marketing director in Orange County. "My commission is wrong again," she declared.

"Oh," I said, "I'm so sorry. What happened? Who's missing from it?"

"Bill Jones. He died a week after he arrived, so I guess corporate felt they didn't have to pay me for the move-in. It's not my fault the guy died."

One would never guess from Mariana's tone that I was actually *her* boss. I took a deep breath, "Mariana, you know the resident has to live at our community for 30 days before commission is paid. That's the policy you agreed to when you took the job."

"I worked my ASS off for that move-in! I dealt with all of his screwed-up family members. I must have given them five tours. I deserve to be paid."

I looked across the street at the mini-mart and considered buying a pack of cigarettes even though I hadn't smoked in a year. I let out a deep sigh, "I'll see what I can do." I hung up the phone and called the payroll department. I did not want sales in Orange County to come to a screeching halt because of a pissed off marketing director. I got the controller to agree to pay Mariana commission on the Bill Jones move-in.

At seven o'clock that night, back home and getting ready for dinner, I opened my laptop to look at emails and there was one from Mariana. The subject line read: COMMISSION. She had copied the payroll department on the email, venting and stating her case for why she should get paid her $400 for the Bill Jones move-in. One line in particular jumped off my computer screen: "I am the reason everyone around here gets a paycheck."

Mariana was not completely off base. It was true that having a good marketer was an important factor in a property's success. I have seen sales skyrocket when a good one took over the territory, as with The Redwoods Santa Barbara, which kept all 135 rooms filled for the entire seven years that Krissy was their marketing director. Six months after Krissy went on an extended maternity leave, the building had 40 empty rooms. They begged Krissy to come back.

Still, Mariana's email annoyed me. So, I responded:

> Mariana, I have done your job and I could not disagree with you more. I think we should go to work every day and thank the <u>caregivers</u>, because without them, we would not have a product to sell. The <u>caregivers</u>, not you, are the reason everyone gets a paycheck.

Mariana wrote me an angry response. I confirmed that she would be paid her commission on Bill Jones and told her to drop it.

I thought back to a day when I had Mariana's position. I was sitting at a country club, attending a networking luncheon with others from the senior care industry. The building was a Spanish-style structure with large arches, terracotta tiled floors, and fresh-cut white lilies in every room. I remember looking around at the waiters dressed in tuxedos, the pale peach linens that matched the tulips at the center of each table. I stared out the floor-to-ceiling windows at the golf course that looked like green velvet, trying to decide if I should have wild salmon or grilled chicken on my Caesar salad. *What am I in the mood for today?*

I couldn't decide and asked the waiter to move onto the lady next to me, a blonde woman dressed in a raw silk suit. Taking a sip of my sparkling water and popping a bruschetta into my mouth, for some reason, I thought of Blanca, back at the ranch, doing her caregiving job. It dawned on me that I was making forty dollars an hour to sit there and chitchat while Blanca was making ten dollars an hour to lift a 200-pound woman off the toilet. It didn't seem fair because . . . well, it *wasn't* fair.

As I climbed the corporate ladder, I had less daily interaction with the staff and I lost touch even more with the reality of their lives. Many of them were single moms like my mother had been. One day, while working as vice president of sales, I gave a training on "The Caregivers' Role in Marketing." I started the class with one of my usual ice breakers, the one I used when doing trainings with marketing directors.

"Tell me your name, how long you've worked here, and the best vacation you ever had." Veronica was the first to introduce herself. She was Filipina, 35 years old, and looked tired. "I've worked here eight years. One time, about five years ago, I took my three kids camping up to Yosemite for a week. That was so much fun. That was the last vacation I've had. I still think about it."

Next Kim, a red-headed girl with pink nail polish said, "Well, I've never actually been on vacation. I work two jobs so there's no way they would both let me take off. But I do go to the park sometimes on Sundays with my kids and that is *really* relaxing." Cecilia, a woman in her mid-50s chimed in, "On weekends we go to the mall and walk around. We don't usually buy anything but it is still fun. I don't take vacations. I just take my vacation days and work those days so that I can pay my bills."

"I don't understand?" I was perplexed.

"Oh," Cecilia continued, "I take a vacation day and then work that same day so I get paid double." It turns out a lot of caregivers did this and consequently, many had not taken a vacation or even a three-day weekend, in over 10 years. They weren't being martyrs; they simply could not afford to take time off. They were part of the working poor, holding down two jobs, yet still unable to make ends meet.

A few weeks later, while staying the night at the property I managed in Sacramento, California, I crawled into bed at 10:00 p.m. in the studio apartment that had been set up as a model to show on tours. It had been a long day of work and the twin mattress was comfortable, the blankets so cozy, that I fell into a deep sleep almost immediately. At 3:00 a.m. I was awakened by bright lights and a woman's squeal. She was standing over me. "Aaaagh!" I yelled as I jumped out of bed wearing only my underwear and a t-shirt. We both gaped at each other and said nothing. Then she ran out of the room. After catching my breath, I deduced that the woman must have been a caregiver, coming to take a nap during her shift. I was too tired to bother going downstairs to talk with the night crew. So, I propped a chair under the doorknob and went back to sleep.

The next morning, everyone was talking about what had happened. The caregiver's name was Lupita and she called the maintenance director at 3:15 a.m. to tell him there was a homeless person in the model room and she was going to call the police. "No, no, don't," he said, "That's Liz Breen, she's from corporate. She likes to stay here instead of a hotel."

The maintenance director came to talk with me the next day at lunch. "Lupita is afraid she is going to be fired," he said, "because you found out she was taking naps on her shift. Lupita works two jobs, Liz. She's exhausted." I sat there remembering a trip I had taken two weeks earlier. Dave and I had flown from our ocean-front home in San Francisco to our ocean-front home in Mexico for a 10-day vacation. I thought of the argument Dave and I had at 36,000 feet when I told him I didn't want to fly first class anymore. "It's the most pretentious waste of money on the planet! I don't drink alcohol, I don't need the leg room, and I don't need a $600 Chinese chicken salad."

Like Lupita, I was tired, too, but I got an extravagant vacation to recharge my battery. "We are not going to fire Lupita," I said. "Please tell her not to worry."

A month later, I was in Irvine, meeting with the CEO and other senior management. We were going over profit and loss statements. I thought of Lupita and the tired caregivers with whom I had done the marketing training. I thought of Che Guevara and all the books I had read about him. I once made a pilgrimage to the house in Argentina where he was born. I walked the halls of the medical school he had attended. I admired this man, the quintessential revolutionary who had cast aside privilege and worked to free the poor from oppression. He could have stayed in Buenos Aires and enjoyed an aristocratic lifestyle. Instead, he devoted his life to balancing the scales. I even had a large painting of Che hanging in my house.

Now, here I was, sitting in a conference room in wealthy Orange County, fueling the engine of the capitalist machine. Being in upper management posed quite a quandary in terms of my political and spiritual beliefs. When the company cut the hours of our lowest paid staff to seven and a half per day, the executive directors had to deal with the backlash and low morale that ensued. The executive directors came to me to plead the case of their staff. "Liz, that half-hour difference in pay is a meal for some people and their kids."

I agreed with them, but didn't know what I could do. My responsibility as vice president of sales and marketing was to drive revenue. It would be inappropriate for me to bring up the cut in hours at our monthly management meetings. We were there to make a profit, not to save the world. I could get backlash and maybe even get fired if I brought it up too often. Would losing my job help the caregivers?

The CEO showed me a draft of a new brochure he was working on.

There was a line that said, our caregivers "gave sacrificially of themselves." He put the line in as a way to honor them, but it was a hard one for me to swallow from a sales perspective. To use our exploitation of caregivers as a key marketing message took things a little too far, so I changed the brochures.

The caregivers were the backbone of our community and we needed to highlight the value and wisdom they brought. So, when it came time to write content for our website, we asked them for tips to share with families. That seemed logical enough—it is amazing how much website content is written by people who have little or no interaction with the actual elders living in these buildings. Here are some of the gems our staff gave us:

Create a Focus That Calms

(contributed by Gracie)

When helping a resident with toileting, they may become agitated. I usually hold the resident's hands and engage them in conversation about family, or sing one of their favorite songs. The key is to have the resident focusing on something that calms and relaxes them. I also tell them something personal about myself, so they don't feel so vulnerable and exposed during this time.

Show Respect, Offer Dignity

(contributed by Angelica)

When I help a resident with something like getting dressed or brushing their teeth, something they used to do easily by themselves, I realize that they may feel embarrassed, feeble, frustrated, or even angry. To help them through their situation, I treat them with as much dignity as possible. For example, I'll show them choices of different clothing options and then let them choose what they want to wear. I also keep the interaction upbeat and let them enjoy dressing by laughing and joking while I'm doing it.

I have heard many accolades from upper management and owners of companies about how amazing caregivers are and how sad it is that they struggle financially. They talk about it as if they have *no connection whatsoever* to what caregivers make. These are the decision-makers, the people determining budgets and wages! Many of these company owners are good parents, friends, and spouses who do community service and treat others with respect. Yet there is a disconnect when it comes to the caregivers, an attitude of, *Well, this is just the way it is.*

When the topic of our hard-working caregivers, dining servers, and housekeepers came up at corporate meetings, the preferred method leadership chose to boost morale was a pizza party. The CEO would say, "Let's give the property $200 to have a pizza party." It happened at every company where I worked, as if a slice of pepperoni pizza and a Coke balanced the scales. "Let them eat pizza!"

We once had a conference call with the CEO of Hale where I worked as a regional sales director. The topic of the call was "Union Avoidance." As representatives of management, we were asked to write thank you notes to staff, tell them how much we appreciated them, and of course, have pizza parties. The next week he sent a memo to all of the regional managers and vice presidents telling us to brainstorm and submit our best ideas for "low cost" or "no cost" employee recognition.

The saddest part was how *grateful* the staff were for those damn pizza parties. If we had a drawing and someone won a twenty dollar gift card, it actually made a difference in the quality of their life that week. When one of my properties won a sales contest, the first-place prize was a barbecue for the staff, cooked by the regional team. Sally, the regional operations director, and I cooked hamburgers, hot dogs, and potato salad for the 62 employees at the property.

As Sally and I were cleaning up, Chad, a young boy about 17 years old who worked in housekeeping came up to me timidly. "Ma'am," he said, "if there is any left at the end, would it be all right if I had another burger?" I stopped putting away the buns and looked at him. The way he said it, so quietly, I could see he was hungry and a little ashamed. I sensed that he probably had many days where he didn't get enough to eat. I wanted to give this tall, skinny, lovely boy everything I had.

"Of course, you can have another," I said. "We have plenty. Take as much as you like, Chad."

It had been years since I experienced that feeling of fear and hunger.

I remembered when I first moved to San Francisco at age 23. I had no job, very little money, and rents were high. I was too proud to call my family for help, so I skipped meals. I ate Top Ramen or bought 69-cent hamburgers at McDonalds. Those days were so far from my reality now.

I asked myself what *could* I do? The truth was, I did care about the staff. I once saw a bumper sticker that said, "No one is free while others are oppressed," and I wholeheartedly agreed. I led a charmed life. Sure, I had worked hard, pushing myself in school, working long hours to get ahead in my career. But, I had also been born white, in the United States, with no physical handicaps. My parents paid for every dime of my university education. I married a man I loved who also happened to earn a great living.

The opportunities I received were by no means the norm. So, what was I to *do?* Donate money here and there? Volunteer? Run off and join the Peace Corps? Should we all shun our privilege the way Che did and hit the road spreading revolution? Or should we be part of the system, make our big salaries, and try to change things from within? I sponsored a woman in the Congo, I donated money to anti-war efforts and food banks. But was it enough? Is it *ever* enough? In college I spent my free time serving meals at homeless shelters and helping Central American refugees get political asylum. And now here I was, senior management for a corporation. I had become *"The Man."*

I didn't know what to do. So, I went along, making my salary and eating fancy salads at nice restaurants with the CEO. I treated the caregivers with respect, I went to bat and got people raises whenever I had the opportunity, and I held onto the memory of the day a resident named June moved into The Gables.

June was coming from a nursing home and on this day, there was no staff available to pick her up and bring her to our place. The skilled nursing facility said they were too busy to bring her over and her family wasn't available. So, I volunteered to pick up June. I don't let much get in the way of me and a move-in, yet it was unusual for me, as marketing director, to be doing this.

I am not sure when June had the bowel accident. All I know is that it happened and somewhere during helping June into my car, feces got all over June, me, and my passenger seat. The smell was strong and I wanted to retch as I helped June into the car. "Be careful," I said, guiding her head so she didn't hit it on the car door.

"Who are you?" she asked in a voice groggy from medications.

"I'm Liz," I said, looking at the mess on her pant leg and mine, while maneuvering her body. "I work at The Gables, the place where you're going to go stay for a while."

"Okay."

"How are you feeling, June?"

"Tired."

"All right, rest a bit. It's a short drive." I closed the door and walked around to the driver's side, got in and turned on the radio. I cracked all four windows in the car. When we arrived at The Gables, I walked around to help June out. "Look at that crepe myrtle in full bloom," I said, pointing up to the purple flowers. I didn't want June to look down and see the mess on the seat or her clothes. I walked with her up to her room in our assisted living area. "Can you help June with a shower?" I whispered to Betty, the supervisor. "She had an accident." Betty looked at me then at June and nodded.

I walked into the office smelling horribly and Peggy, one of our caregivers, saw me and burst out laughing, "Liz, you're covered in poop!"

"Thanks," I said, looking down at my soiled clothes and thinking, *I did not sign up for this. I am in marketing. I do not do shit. I do lunch. I do paperwork. I do welcome gifts. I do tours, thank you notes, parties, and phone calls.*

Then, in an instant, my energy shifted. Watching Peggy laugh at me, I felt an even deeper appreciation than I already had for the caregivers. It was good that I had a chance to walk in their shoes for a moment.

I went home to get cleaned up. It was noon and I was taking a shower at my house, thinking of how the caregivers did this work for eight hours every day. If they took a shower every time someone defecated, urinated, or bled on them, they would be bathing all day and never get their work done.

At the California Assisted Living Association Conference a few years later, they gave a "Caregiver of the Year" Award, honoring a person who exemplified the virtuous qualities I've seen in so many underpaid staff members. The woman, who had been a caregiver for 15 years, received a standing ovation from the room full of people who held much higher positions than hers. The presenter gave her a plaque and a check for $500. It was not enough and it certainly didn't make up for paying caregivers criminally low wages. Yet, acknowledging a caregiver publicly with an award at a conference, at least felt like something. It felt like a start. It was the first time I had seen an award like this given. These conferences were usually upper and middle management patting each other on the back. I looked around the room and thought, *it's about time.*

Of course, not all of the caregivers were saints. As with any profession, there were lazy and dishonest people. When I was in management and traveling to different communities, I liked to eat in the dining rooms and sleep in the buildings rather than in hotels. It gave me an opportunity to talk with the residents and get a feel for what was happening at the property. One night, at one of our properties in Idaho, I woke to an alarm beeping repeatedly at one o'clock in the morning. After 15 minutes, it didn't stop, so I went out in my pajamas to find a staff member. I found the night shift hanging out in the medication room, talking, laughing, and ignoring the loud alarm. "Oh, that's just a resident who needs help," they said when I asked about the beeping.

"Well, are you going to *help* them?"

"Yes, we'll get to it," they responded. "Who are you, anyway?"

"I'm the vice president of sales. I'm visiting from California."

Silence.

The next day, I told the executive director he needed to start doing surprise visits at night.

In addition to neglect and apathy, we also saw medication theft. At one building, we set up a sting operation with the police and caught a caregiver who was stealing Vicodin from residents. Vicodin apparently goes for twenty dollars a pill on the street.

When family members saw signs of bad care, they surprisingly often kept quiet about it. My mother-in-law once complained to me about the care her mother was getting at The Gables. The staff weren't bringing Goma her pills at the correct time. I no longer worked there, but I called to speak with the management on her behalf. "Don't make too many waves," Yvonne said, "I don't want them to be mean to her." This from the woman who ripped waiters to shreds when we had to wait an extra five minutes for our appetizer. I thought I was assertive until I met Yvonne.

"It's not that way," I told her emphatically. "If anything, it's more like the squeaky wheel gets oiled. Residents with strong family advocates get *better* treatment."

Yvonne's fear seemed preposterous to me, having worked behind the scenes. The employees I met would never dream of harming a resident and would immediately report anyone who did. Those of us who work in elder care are mandatory reporters of abuse and most take that role seriously. We were there to be protectors for the residents. Yet the media only focuses on negative cases. A sweet, kind caregiver knitting slippers for a senior abandoned by her family does not make for interesting news. I have seen the horror stories on television of employees beating or raping residents. Even one such incident is horrific. Yet, I never saw or even heard about any physical or sexual abuse during my eight years in assisted living. While I know elders sometimes do not report abuse, I also know the media paints a distorted picture which makes it seem more prevalent than the reality.

There was one type of abuse I did see happen pretty regularly, though. It is something we don't hear about on the news but it was pervasive. The abuse was overmedication. The most extreme example I saw was while working as regional director of sales and marketing for Hale.

I walked in the door of The Gardens at Roseville, a 40-bed dementia care community that the company had recently spent $400,000 to remodel. The building was 50-percent occupied, the worst performing property in my portfolio. The place had a bad reputation. I heard from sources in the community that some "things" happened in the past. Doctors, case managers, and other professionals would not recommend us to families because of these events, yet no one would tell me or my marketing director what exactly had happened. We faced an uphill battle trying to sell the rooms there.

The place was clean and smelled like flowers when I walked in. There were fresh carnations in vases throughout the hallways and activity room. The vintage wedding gown displayed on a bodice in the corner looked impeccable. I walked to the living room area in the back and my heart dropped immediately at the scene before me. As usual, the residents were plopped in front of the television in recliner chairs.

I had told the department heads a week earlier that I was going to visit on this day. Even when they *knew* I was coming, I still found this. I walked up to a resident named Mabel and knelt to her eye level. Mabel was 87 and had deep wrinkles on her pale skin. She was wearing a bulky wool sweater and a pink t-shirt which had some dried egg on it. *Is this from her breakfast this morning or are they not washing her clothes?* I looked up at the clock on the wall. It was almost 11:00 a.m. *Even if it is from this morning, they should have put a clean shirt on her by now.*

"Hi Mabel," I said and she didn't respond. Mabel's eyes were dilated and glazed over. She reminded me of the people in the movie "Awakenings" with Robert De Niro: comatose. I sobbed during that movie. I stood up and looked around. They all reminded me of people from "Awakenings." Mabel was drooling and showed little signs of life as I held her warm hands and talked with her. She stared straight at me but didn't appear to see me at all. This was not dementia. This was overmedication.

I walked back to the executive director's office and asked, "What's with the drugged residents, Jackie? They look like zombies." Jackie was in her late 50s but appeared closer 65. She had short, spikey hair, a petite frame, and bloodshot eyes. As usual, she had on way too much makeup, trying to cover the hangover I could smell on her breath.

"What do you mean?" she spat out. "They're fine."

"That's your definition of '*fine*'? They're all staring into space and I can barely get a response out of anyone."

"Maybe they're tired. They just had breakfast."

"Breakfast is at eight. It's eleven o'clock. And Mabel has dried food on her shirt."

"I don't need to be micromanaged."

"Apparently you do. It's no wonder this place is half-empty."

"We're doing the best we can. We have more work than we can handle."

"What are you talking about? Your staffing ratios are higher than any other property in my region. And you and I have talked many times about this issue of drugs and the lack of activities here. What exactly is your activity director doing with her time? And I want to see the medication logs."

"Again? You look at them every time you visit. You don't understand dementia," she retorted. Jackie sat straight up in her chair, poised for battle. "We have to give them medications or they will get combative."

My jaw tensed. "I don't understand *dementia?*" I asked. "I worked in a place where people threw chairs at windows and we didn't do what you're doing here. We made the residents feel safe; we met them where they were. We baked cupcakes and played Bingo with them. We did not pump them full of pills and plop them in chairs so that we wouldn't have to do our job."

Jackie brought the medication binders and dropped them on the table. I looked through them and discovered that my suspicions were correct. The number of PRN doses of Lorazepam, Xanax, Haldol and other antipsychotic and anti-anxiety drugs given that day and the preceding days were very high. Medicines that are taken "as needed" are known as "PRN" medications. Rather than prescribing the medication in a certain dose at a certain time of day, the doctor writes, "PRN," a Latin term that stands for *pro re nata,* which means "as the thing is needed." This is how the staff were able to over-drug people without breaking the law.

Seeing the numbers in the logs infuriated me. I was done with Jackie. When I drove away, I called my teammates, the regional nurse and regional operations director and told them what had happened. We fired Jackie the next week.

When I returned to the building two months later, I found the same thing. Jackie was gone and we had not hired her replacement yet. We had executive directors from nearby buildings filling in when they could and we put the nurse in charge of day-to-day management until we could find a permanent leader. At the morning stand-up meeting the caregivers who had worked there 10 to 12 years gave me the same blank stares as the over-medicated residents. *Are they taking the meds, too?* I wondered.

"These people did not move here so they could be drugged and neglected," I said to the group. "It's no wonder we aren't getting move-ins." I walked up to Marilee, who had worked there 10 years. "Would *you* move your mom here if you walked in and saw this?" She looked away and stayed silent.

"I didn't think so." My hands were on my hips. My face felt hot. "I know you're all looking at me thinking, *Oh, she'll be gone, just like all of the other management we've seen come and go over the years*. But I've got news for you. I'm not going anywhere. And if you aren't doing this work for the right reasons, if you don't actually *want* to care for these residents, then I suggest you get a job someplace else."

The place at Roseville was an unusual case. In most of the communities where I worked, I saw a genuine desire to care for elders, not just in the caregivers but also in people who worked in housekeeping, dining services, gardening, and other departments. Assisted living is a field which is a magnet for kind people. This posed a dilemma for me.

When I moved to Ojai, I had sworn to myself that I would not make friends. People say you can never have too many friends, but I actually *do* have too many friends, so many, in fact, that I rarely see many of them, even the ones I really want to see. My friends are loyal, kind, interesting, smart people and my relationships with them are genuine.

Yet, while I gleaned a lot of pleasure from these relationships, I also wanted time with my husband and time alone to plant roses and do yoga. I needed time to work, exercise, sleep, read, and cook. I definitely did not have room in my schedule for more friends. I had a plan: if I met people in Ojai and they approached me seeking friendship or a social outing, I would politely say, "You seem really nice, but my plate is actually full."

I had no idea that working in senior care I would meet people so dynamic, benevolent, and incredibly fun that I would end up breaking my vow and opening my life to make room for several new friends, some of whom became lifelong kindred spirits.

Camaraderie and relationships form among people in any workplace, but at assisted living properties, there is an even stronger sense of community. It reminded me of the small towns I read about in my high school history books. I had a feeling when I entered the building each morning, that I was literally walking into another world, a living, breathing universe of its own, something which seems to have been lost in today's technology-centered society.

Most places have an average of 60 to 100 employees and of course, with that many people, there were rivalries, power struggles, and romances that sprung up. I remember the day Peggy, a caregiver at The Gables, confessed to me that she had a crush on Pete, one of the maintenance guys. Pete was about 15 years older than Peggy. She flirted relentlessly with him for six months while he pretended not to notice.

"I'm going to ask him out," she told me as I assembled brochure packets at my desk.

"Cool, when?"

"Today. I gotta bite the bullet. Betty and Vivian dared me."

"Go for it. He's working on apartment 18 all day today—just so you know where to find him."

An hour later, Pete was in my office telling me what went down. Peggy had walked into apartment 18, and said, "Pete, would you like to go to the Ventura County Fair with me tonight?"

"Um, well, actually I can't tonight. I've got some other stuff going on. My grandson is coming over," he replied.

"Okay, how about tomorrow night? It goes on for a week," she insisted.

"Well, tomorrow night . . . actually that wouldn't . . . I don't know," he stammered.

"It's because I'm fat, isn't it?"

Pete told me he didn't know what to say. It wasn't because Peggy was overweight. He was just afraid of women and terrified of dating. After my talk with Pete, Peggy came back to process *her* feelings about it. I did not get much work done that day, but I felt touched to have a front row seat for the romantic action and to be there for Peggy and Pete, two of the many friends I made at The Gables.

Carlos, the chef at The Gables, was one of the dearest friends I made. I often ate lunch at the small table in the kitchen a few feet from the stove, while Carlos created sumptuous meals for our residents on a shoestring budget. We swapped stories about both of our travels through Mexico. We talked about work, our spouses, our dreams, our families, our faith. We swapped recipes. One day Carlos told me that if he and his wife, Delia, ever had a child, they wanted me to be the godmother. Two years after I left Ojai and moved back to San Francisco, Carlos called to tell me Delia was pregnant. "That's wonderful news!" I said, "I'm so happy for you two."

"And, of course, we want you to be the godmother." Carlos had made this offer way back when we saw each other on a daily basis, and now, I thought, he clearly felt obliged to follow through on his word. I had to let him off the hook.

"Carlos, that is so sweet of you, and I'm really honored. But you don't have to do this. I live in San Francisco now. I won't even see the baby very often."

"That's alright, we still want you to be the *madrina*."

"Honestly, Carlos, I am very touched but I won't be hurt at all if you have close friends or family there in Ojai who you would rather ask. I feel like I will let you down; I won't be a good godmother. I live six hours away. I'll miss birthday parties and first steps and things like that."

"We want you to be the godmother, Liz."

It went back and forth like this for 15 minutes until finally, Carlos, exasperated, said, "Listen, Liz. In our culture, when we choose a godparent it's our way of saying to God: 'We want our daughter to grow up to be like this person.' So, it doesn't really matter if you're in her life. God knows you are her godmother and that's all that counts." Well, how could I say no to *that?*

Chapter Six

Show Me the Money

*Sales takes a special kind of person . . .
someone who can wake up every day
and willingly hurl themselves at rejection.*

— Irving Stackpole

The day I arrived at Casa Amanecer, five years into my senior living career, the outgoing marketing director, Margot, a cute redhead in her early 50s, greeted me at the door of my office. "I am SO glad you're here! Thank *God* you're here!"

Wow, that's quite a welcome, I thought. Margot told me she was staying at Casa Amanecer but moving into the activity director position. She hugged me like a long-lost friend, even though I had only known her for 10 minutes. "Sales is just not me," she explained. "I don't enjoy slammin' heads into beds."

"Huh?"

"I'm not into slammin' heads into beds. Too stressful. It's just not me."

"I have never heard my job described that way," I mused.

It was an odd way to put it, but Margot was right—assisted living sales did boil down to filling beds with heads. In many ways, it was a cinch compared to my previous positions. In other ways, it was the hardest job I had ever done.

My first job was in sales, cold-calling for State Farm Insurance. I was 14 years old and the guy I babysat for, Jim Thornton, was an agent in San Diego. One night while driving me home after watching his kids, he asked how my day at school had been. It happened to be the day I was elected student body president.

"Wow—congratulations! And are your grades good?"

"Straight A's," I said.

I had known Mr. Thornton and his wife, Mandy, for over a year and I enjoyed watching their little ones.

"You seem like a sharp girl. How would you like to come work for me in my office instead of babysitting?"

"What would I be doing?"

"Calling people and asking about their insurance policy, trying to set up an appointment for me to meet with them."

Looking back on that night, I think Mr. Thornton's motive was twofold. He probably figured I could bring in some business for him. What cheaper labor was there than a 14-year-old? He was also a natural mentor and genuinely wanted to help me realize my potential. A year after I started working for him, he paid a large fee for me to attend a four-day positive-thinking seminar along with him and his three full-time employees.

After my parents got over the shock of my accepting a real job, they signed a special school work permit, since I was too young for a regular one. On Tuesdays, Wednesdays, and Fridays, I rode my bike to Mr. Thornton's office after school and sat at a desk with the Yellow Pages and White Pages, talking with people about auto, fire, and business insurance. From 3:30 to 5:00 p.m., I called businesses. From 5:30 to 8:00 p.m., I called homes:

Me: "Hi, I'm calling from State Farm and I was just wondering if your auto insurance is up for renewal?"

Them: "You're wondering if my auto insurance is up for renewal? I'm eating dinner!"

Me: "I'm sorry. I was just..."
Them: "I don't think you heard me—my dinner is on the table and you have the nerve to call me! Fuck off, phone maggot!" Click.

Damn, that was harsh. I dusted myself off and made the next call. Nine or ten people screamed at me and hung up. But then the 11th person would say the magic words:

Them: "Yes, my insurance *is* actually up for renewal. I am so glad you called."
Me: "*Really?* You're glad I called?"
Them: "Yes."
Me: "Do you want to book an appointment with my boss, Mr. Thornton?"
Them: "Yes."
Me: "*Seriously?!* How about next week? What does your schedule look like?"

I was hooked. On top of my minimum-wage salary, Mr. Thornton paid me a five-dollar commission for every appointment I booked. Psychologists call what I experienced "intermittent reinforcement." The psychologist, B.F. Skinner, said it is the most powerful way to motivate people. It is the reason people sit in front of slot machines for hours and the reason I have been in sales for most of my career since that first job at State Farm.

I have sold suits to business men, canned vegetables to Hispanic women ages 25 to 49, and environmental consulting to oil companies in South America. When I began working at The Gables, it seemed amazing to me that people actually called *us* and inquired about our product.

"You mean I don't have to call random people and try to get them interested in The Gables?" I asked Sharon.

"No," she said, "we get calls all the time from people looking into retirement living, usually for their parents. You just need to convince them to come in for a tour, then persuade them to move *here* instead of to the competitor."

With most sales jobs, I first had to create the need for what I was selling, then convince the customer to buy that product or service from my company. With The Gables, Sunset Oaks, Casa Amanecer, and all of the other places where I worked, the people calling already had the need for our services. No one wakes up one day and says, "It's really nice out, why don't we go tour some assisted living properties?" There was usually a crisis that took place, such as a fall, which prompted them to inquire. There was the rub. Dealing with that crisis and that family is what is known in the industry as "Inside Sales."

It was a typical day at Casa Amanecer in San Francisco. I had given three tours and received five calls from people wanting information about our place. Some days I received 10 of these inquiry calls, other days only 1 or 2. I was sitting in my office around three o'clock, having coffee and chocolate to give myself a little boost, when I received a call from a woman named Julie who was interested in finding a place for her mother:

Me: What made you start looking into communities for your mom?
Julie: She just seems depressed lately. A lot of her friends have died; she's lost interest in her hobbies; she's not eating well.
Me: How old is she?
Julie: Eighty.
Me: What kinds of hobbies did she do?

Julie told me how her mom used to bake pastries and make quilts. I asked for more details then asked about mom's health, work history, and current living situation, all the while jotting notes to myself on a yellow pad: *Living in own home, healthy and ambulatory, has help with housecleaning, still drives and cooks.*

Julie and I talked for 40 minutes. Our conversation consisted of me asking open-ended questions and Julie responding. (*The most successful salespeople listen 80 percent of the time and talk 20 percent.*) Once I felt Julie had gotten the majority of information off her chest, I began to tell her about Casa Amanecer:

Me: Well, Julie, let me tell you a little bit about our place. We are a

	nonprofit community. We have 130 apartments here, studios and one-bedrooms.
Julie:	How much do they cost?
Me:	The price ranges from $3,500 to $5,500 a month depending on the size of apartment and the amount of care the person needs. (*Most sales trainings teach <u>not</u> to give pricing up front, but I don't believe in skirting around this question. It just annoys people and wastes their time and mine.*) I would love to set up a time to meet you in person, show you our community, and answer any other questions you have.
Julie:	Okay.
Me:	I have Tuesday afternoon available or tomorrow morning at ten o'clock. (*Another sales technique: always give people two specific choices rather than saying, "When can you come in?" People almost always choose the second option.*)
Julie:	Tomorrow at 10:00 a.m. would be fine.

The next morning before Julie's arrival, I walked through the building, making sure everything looked right. I informed the department heads (maintenance, dining, housekeeping, caregivers) that a tour was coming. I checked the model rooms, fluffed the pillows on the beds, and spritzed lavender spray. I asked the kitchen to bake some chocolate chip cookies so that Julie would smell them when we toured the dining room.

I had learned that smell is the sense most closely tied to emotions. It is the reason realtors have bread baking in the oven when they do open houses: the smell of bread gives people a feeling of 'home.' People often buy on emotion and justify their purchase with logic and the scent of lavender, chocolate chip cookies, and oddly enough, grilled cheese sandwiches, all improved my sales. The inverse was true as well—unpleasant smells like urine evoked negative emotions.

Julie arrived right on time. "It's nice to meet you in person," I said, extending my hand. I led her to the small living room near my office. "Can I get you some coffee or tea? We also have fresh-baked cookies," I offered as we walked down the hall.

"No thanks, I'm fine."

Julie sat on the floral-print satin couch and I sat across from her in an oversized chair. There was a small, low coffee table between us on which I placed the brochure and price list. (*Another sales tenet: never have a large piece of furniture between you and the prospect. It creates an energetic block and impedes the flow of communication.*)

"So," I said, "when we spoke on the phone, you mentioned that your mom is living in her own home and feeling somewhat isolated. Could you tell me a little more about that?"

"Well, my father died 12 years ago. At the time my mom had a close group of girlfriends who really helped her through the loss. Of course, my sister, brother, and I were also there for her, but her friends were her rocks. Over the next several years, she went on a couple of cruises with her best friend, Bernice, to Hawaii and Europe. Mom, Bernice, and their other friends also went out to lunch, the movies, museums, things like that. Mom missed Dad, but she was also having a lot of fun.

Then, five years ago, Bernice passed away. My mom was devastated. I think it hit her harder than my dad's death. Then two more of her friends died and another one ended up in a nursing home, completely bedridden. Mom visits her from time to time, but it is really hard for her to see her friend in that state."

"Your mom has been through a lot."

"Yes, it has been *really* challenging for her, and it's not like she's going to make new friends at her age."

"Well . . . that's not entirely true. It *can* be difficult to meet new people later in life, but when seniors move into a community, they often do form new connections. They find the reason they haven't made friends was because they were not in situations where they could actually meet new people."

I asked Julie more questions about her mom's home, how long she had lived in it, her health, and hobbies. Julie elaborated and also gave me some new information related to mom's vision. She had problems with macular degeneration and the vision loss was affecting her ability to drive and manage her medications.

"All right," I said, while opening the brochure folder on the table, "I think I have a good idea of your mom's needs and interests and we can certainly help her with transportation and medication management. I would also like to introduce her to Mary Ellen Perry. She has traveled a lot and loves to quilt. I think they would hit it off."

I pulled out a drawing of the building. "Our apartments range in size from 200 to 650 square feet. The base rent includes meals, housekeeping, transportation, and 24-hour emergency response. We also have four levels of care, which cover things like help with bathing and dressing, medications, and getting to and from the dining room. Our nurse does an assessment to determine a person's care level before they move in. It sounds like your mom would be level one, because she just needs help with her medications." I reviewed the floor plans, activity calendar, and menus that were also in the folder.

"Do you have any questions before we take a look around?"

"No, I think you've covered everything. I would love to see some apartments."

Julie and I had been sitting in the living room for 45 minutes, which was how I handled most tours, using the basic formula for assisted living sales: Sit, Tour, Sit. We sit with the prospect, then we tour the building, then we sit again. The reasoning behind this approach is that most people don't really care what the place looks like. Ninety percent of retirement homes are elegantly decorated, clean, and have the same size apartments. People may *think* they care about the aesthetics of the place, but deep down they know that the color of the walls is irrelevant when making this decision for themselves or their parents. People show up thinking they want to look at the dining room when what they really want is to talk about the heart-wrenching losses that come with aging.

Julie and I walked and even though I had toured the building many times, I was always impressed with its loveliness. Casa Amanecer's walls were mauve and cream colored. Tiny Japanese maple trees, bonsai plants, and silk orchids were placed in just the right spots. The furniture was mostly made of cherrywood with pearl inlays. The art was original and modern, not the chain-store prints found at many of our competitors. Casa Amanecer had even won a design award from an architectural magazine.

I led Julie to the elevator and we got off at the second floor then walked to the model studio. The apartment was 200 square feet, with three windows looking out onto the courtyard. The twin bed was decorated with a sage-green satin comforter and several white throw pillows. On the night stand stood a framed picture of a family from a stock photo book. There was a small kitchenette with a microwave, two cabinets, a mini-fridge, and a sink. The bathroom had a walk-in shower, pink hand towels, and rose scented guest soaps in a dish next to the sink. In the closet were slippers, a robe, and a few dresses to make the room look authentic.

I could still smell a faint trace of the lavender I had sprayed an hour-and-a-half earlier. Julie liked the apartment but thought it would be too small for her mom. When we got to the one-bedroom, she loved it, especially the view of the eucalyptus trees outside the window. The apartment was almost double the size of the studio.

On our way to the dining room, we ran into Ludi, one of our caregivers, who was wheeling Leonard Jones down the hall. "Ludi, Mr. Jones," I said, "this is Julie. She's looking at Casa Amanecer for her mom."

"How's the food here?" Julie asked Mr. Jones.

"Pretty good. A little better than Meals on Wheels," he said. "What's really great here is the service. Nicest kids you'd ever meet working in that dining room."

I asked Ludi to tell Julie a bit about her role.

"I've been here 10 years," Ludi said. "I help people with getting dressed, taking a shower, getting to activities."

I waited, hoping she would say a little more. Like many of the caregivers, she was shy with visitors. Once someone moved in, they became like family but before that, it was difficult to get a word out of the staff. Julie and I continued our tour, stopping in the grand dining room. The wallpaper was pale pink silk, two sparkling chandeliers hung from the ceiling, and the tables were decorated with pressed linens and fresh-cut roses. The room looked immaculate. "Wow," Julie said, "gorgeous."

We moved on to the activity room, where I introduced her to Margot, the activity director who had held the marketing position before me. She was leading a discussion on U.S. foreign policy with Israel. The room had a television, a large sink filled with paints and brushes, and three round tables. These were cluttered with embroidery projects, scrapbooks, and chess, checkers, and dominoes games. It was February, so pink and red Valentine's Day decorations hung from the walls.

I introduced Julie to the five ladies and two men sitting in a circle, then Margot gave her 30-second spiel on field trips, entertainment, and other goings on at Casa Amanecer. "I would have to say the Giants games outings and Bob the accordion player are the most popular activities on our calendar," Margot concluded.

The tour was going better than I had planned. As we headed back to the living room to sit again, I saw Lucille, one of the more independent residents, heading our way. *Shit, this could go either way,* I thought. Lucille was feisty and unpredictable and running into her on a tour was a crapshoot.

"Lucille," I said as we approached. "I'd like to introduce Julie. She's looking into Casa Amanecer for her mom."

"My kids toured this place before bringing me, too," Lucille said dryly, her hands folded in front of her erect frame. "Then they dumped me here."

"What?" Julie asked, surprised.

Lucille had come to Casa Amanecer reluctantly. She was physically healthy when she moved in, but her memory was slipping, so her kids wanted her to live somewhere safe and closer to them.

"My family," Lucille said, "they dumped me here . . . against my will. They sold my house from under me, then they told me I was moving to Casa Amanecer."

For once, I was at a loss for words. *Great,* I thought, *all this time I've spent with Julie on the phone and in person, and now Lucille is going to blow it.*

"That's terrible," Julie said.

"And you know what," Lucille said, "I LOVE it! I absolutely love it here. The food is delicious. The museum trips are fun. I've made wonderful friends. The staff members are kind."

"Well, that's a relief," Julie said, as I smiled and Lucille winked at me. "I hope to meet your mom, dear," Lucille said to Julie and continued walking down the hall.

The narrative of "being dumped" was common. Many residents moped around and look depressed whenever their kids visited. They knew how to lay on the guilt trip for being "abandoned to a home." Yet, the minute their kids left the building, they sprung to life, socializing and enjoying activities, meals, and friendships with their peers.

When we got back to the living room, I poured Julie a cup of tea and asked, "What do you think?"

"It's great. I think my mom would be surprised. She has a different idea in her mind of assisted living: a hospital-like place similar to the ones in 1950s movies. An institution where she's locked up."

"A lot of people have that misconception. I had the same vision myself before I started working in this field. You know, Julie, we've talked a lot about your mom, but I'm wondering how *you* are doing with all this?" We sat silently for a few minutes and Julie started to cry.

"I've visited four places," she said, "and you're the first person to ask me that question. It has been really hard. My brother and sister are not much help at all. My sister is too busy traveling and obsessing about her boyfriend and my brother is focused on his own life, kids, and career. I have a life, too. They just expect me to do everything because I live close by. I've been the one responsible for my mom for the past 12 years."

"How would things be different for you if your mom lived in a retirement community?" I asked.

"Oh my God—it would be a huge relief. I wouldn't have to worry about her so much. I would know she was safe and around other people. I could focus on my job and husband again. Maybe I could even take a vacation!"

"I'd say you deserve one after 12 years of caregiving. So, the next step is to have your mom come in for a tour and lunch. Do you think next week would work?"

"I'll see what I can do. First, I have to tell her I've been touring these places."

The following Wednesday Julie brought her mom for lunch and a tour. Patricia Mancini was about five-foot-three inches tall and wore large clip on earrings and big, movie star sunglasses. Draped over her forearm was a powder-blue Chanel handbag. Patricia immediately began to complain about the arduous task of sorting through 44 years of belongings. "I have so many things, like my fur coat I never wear anymore. In my day, we wore fur coats. Now they throw rocks or paint at you!"

"They sure do," I said and chuckled. "Especially in San Francisco."

I asked Patricia about her quilting and baking. "What is important to you at this stage of your life, Patricia?"

"I want to enjoy myself as much as possible and I don't want to be a burden to my daughter. But that doesn't mean I want to give up all my freedom, my house, and my car and move to a nursing home."

"Why don't we take a look around?" I asked, "I think you'll see this place is very different from a nursing home."

We walked and I chatted with Patricia, remembering again what Sharon had taught me about a common mistake most marketers make: they talk with the adult child as if the mom or dad weren't there, forgetting that the ultimate decision maker in this equation is the senior, *not* their kids.

When we arrived at the activity room, we ran into Penelope Kent, who was working on a quilt she had started a few months earlier. "Penelope," I said, "I would like to introduce you to Patricia. She's looking at our community today and this is her daughter, Julie."

"Nice to meet you," Penelope said. "What do you think of it so far?"

"It's attractive," Patricia said. "I may move to a place like this when I get older."

"What do you mean?" she asked. Penelope was six years younger than Patricia and looked great for her age.

"You know," Patricia continued, "when my hair is gray like yours."

Penelope looked baffled, and responded, "Your hair *is* gray like mine."

"Well, you know, I'm just not ready," Patricia continued.

I interjected, "Penelope, your quilt looks great. It's really coming along nicely. I love all the bright colors. You're making it for your granddaughter, right?"

"Yes, it's for her 16th birthday."

"Patricia is a quilter, too," I said.

"Yes," Patricia said. "I just haven't had the motivation to quilt lately."

"We have a class here on Wednesdays or you could do like Penelope and work independently on a project. Let's keep going. We have more to see and we don't want to be late for lunch."

As we meandered down the hall, we passed two residents with walkers and the large activity calendar on the wall. Patricia perused it and said,

"You know, I'm not really into Bingo or movies."

"All of the activities are voluntary," I said. "People only participate in the ones that interest them."

"Everyone seems pleasant enough," she whispered, "but they're all so *old*."

"Mom," Julie sighed, "they're the same age as you. I'm sure many of them are still active and healthy like you, too."

This issue of living with "old people" often came up during tours. Sharon once told me that most people see themselves as 20 years younger than they actually are. I remembered one night when I joined Dave in watching the Miss America Pageant and I asked him if it was Miss Teen U.S.A. "No," he replied, "these girls are not teenagers, Liz, they're 22 to 25." I was 36 at the time and I thought the girls looked about 14. "We're getting older," Dave said.

A marketer from a nearby assisted living told me she gave a tour to a 99-year-old man. He stopped in his tracks outside the dining room, looked at the line of walkers, started sobbing uncontrollably and said, "This is *not* me. I am *not* as old as these people!" The tour had been going fine up until the row of walkers.

When we got to the apartments, Patricia liked the one-bedroom but said even the size of that would be a stretch.

"My home is 2,000 square feet and has 4 bedrooms."

"But how much of the house are you actually using these days?" I asked.

"You know," she pondered, "I really only spend time in the kitchen and my bedroom. Once in a while I watch TV in the living room. The other rooms are basically storage."

I looked at Julie and she smiled.

We made our way to the dining room where Mary Ellen Perry was waiting to have lunch with us. Whenever I had prospects come for lunch, I usually invited someone who lived at the community to join us so they could give their perspective of Casa Amanecer. At 98 years old, Mary Ellen was an artist who still sculpted and painted three times a week, drove herself to the grocery store to buy cat food, and whenever we served champagne, threatened to dance on the tables. She was charming and seemed younger than some of the 40-year-olds I knew.

As we approached the table, I noticed Mary Ellen's outfit. She was wearing turquoise pants with a matching sweater and a chunky gold and turquoise necklace and bracelet. The shoes were what really tied it all together: beaded red flats. *I bet she got those on one of her trips to India*, I thought. As usual, she was the hippest-dressed woman in the room.

Halfway through the baked chicken and french fries, our conversation turned to sports. "I'm a fanatic for the Los Angeles Dodgers," Mary Ellen said. "My apartment is full of memorabilia I can show you after lunch if you like."

"I love baseball." Patricia chimed in, "but I'm partial to the Giants since I'm a native San Franciscan. Where are you from originally, Mary Ellen?"

"New York."

"Mary Ellen was a singer and dancer on Broadway in the 1930s," I bragged.

"Wow, that's exciting," Julie said, "What was that like?"

"It was fun. Lots of fun!"

"I love looking at those pictures of you with the feather hats," I said, "and you went to Europe every summer to paint, right?"

"Yes, I did," Mary Ellen said, "for about a 20-year period. I have led a charmed life. I've had my struggles, of course, like we all do, but I've been pretty lucky over all."

I sat there thinking that one of the things I loved most about Mary Ellen was how down-to-earth she was. She was educated, well-traveled, and she had ample resources (each of her three husbands had given her a sizeable amount of money, either through divorce or death), but she wasn't a snob. Mary Ellen was someone most people enjoyed being around. Our lemon cake and coffee arrived when Mary Ellen asked Patricia, "So, do you think you will move to Casa Amanecer?"

"I'm not sure. This is my first visit. I think we're going to look at a few more places." She turned to Julie. "I don't want to give up my house, though."

"It's a big decision," Mary Ellen chuckled. "This is the end of the road, you know. You won't be moving out of *here*, that's for sure."

Oh God.

Mary Ellen continued, "This is the LAST stop on the train." Julie and Patricia looked askance, yet still laughed out loud.

I shook my head and raised my eyebrows at Mary Ellen, who shrugged. We finished our dessert and thanked our server. Julie and Patricia said goodbye to Mary Ellen and I guided them to the lobby. "Thanks again for coming," I said. "I'll touch base with you later in the week to follow-up on any questions you might have."

Walking back to my office, I felt annoyed by Mary Ellen's comment, but I also knew she was right. I remembered when I was struggling to close sales a year after I arrived at The Gables. I was irritated with the seniors who had called me in a panic, desperate for a tour. I felt perturbed that I had moved things around to accommodate them, often even going into work on my day off for a tour. Sometimes they would come back again to show The Gables to one of their kids, and again, I would drop everything and devote time and energy to them.

Then, when I called to follow-up on the tour or ask how they were doing, they ignored my messages. *Had they found another place?* That was fine by me, it was just that I was emotionally invested. I had gotten to know them and sincerely wanted to know what had happened. *Did she decide to stay at home? Did she have a health issue come up?* Other times, they returned my call and acted annoyed, like I was some kind of pushy sales person and why was I bothering them?

My frustration reached an all-time high with a prospective resident named Francine Lange. I had given Francine two tours. I followed up with her, visited her several times at her home, picked her up and brought her to parties at our place. Yet she wouldn't move in. She had given me a wait list deposit, but every apartment I showed her just wasn't quite right. I offered to return Francine's deposit but she didn't want her deposit back. She wanted to be able to tell her kids that she was on the wait list at a retirement community to get them off her back. I went to Sharon, exasperated. "I am done with this woman. She has sucked up so much of my time and I don't think she is *ever* going to move here! What is it with these people? If they don't want to move in, then why do they even bother visiting?"

"Assisted living is a tough sell, Liz. It is the final chapter in people's lives. You are essentially asking them to take a conscious step towards their own death."

"What?"

"They know this will be their last move. That is a hard pill to swallow."

So, Mary Ellen was right. Casa Amanecer was the last stop on the train. I just didn't appreciate her pointing it out during lunch.

Over the next five months, Patricia toured four more assisted living places and came back to Casa Amanecer two more times for events. I talked with her and Julie on the phone several times throughout this period. It was time to bring things to a resolution one way or the other. I called Julie and left a message, then I called Patricia.

Me:	Hi Patricia, I'm calling to check in, see how things are going?
Patricia:	I'm doing well, thank you.
Me:	How was your grandson's birthday party?
Patricia:	Oh, it was lots of fun, worth the trip to Los Angeles.
Me:	So, I am wondering, have you come to any decisions about moving to a retirement community?
Patricia:	I just can't decide about which place to move to. The place down the street has a choral group, you know. Do you have that?
Me:	No, we don't have a choral group. Are you a singer?
Patricia:	No, I just thought I might want to start singing maybe. Other places have choral groups. Do you have yoga at Casa Amanecer?
Me:	No, but we have Tai Chi. There is also a group of ladies who go to the local senior center every Wednesday for yoga. I didn't realize you did yoga.
Patricia:	I don't. I mostly do my chair exercise video.
Me:	Are you planning to start doing yoga?
Patricia:	No.
Me:	Hmmm... all right... I see.
Patricia:	You know, Liz, you are a very nice gal and your place is great, but one of the main issues I have is that it's foggy there.
Me:	It's foggy at your house, too, isn't it? I mean, your house is only a mile from here.

Patricia: Well... yes... that's true.

Me: You've lived in the fog for 44 years. The only way you're probably going to get away from it is by leaving San Francisco.

Patricia was looking for any excuse not to move into a retirement community, even though she realized on some level that she really needed to take the leap. She did not move to Casa Amanecer nor to any other senior home. She stayed in her house for another year, while her daughter continued taking care of her. Then one day, Patricia lost her balance on the front steps. She fell and broke her hip, had surgery, and spent the last six months of her life in a nursing home.

Patricia's scenario happened with a portion of the people I met. Others moved to a competitor facility. Others moved in with family. Some stayed home and hired caregivers to help them. Homecare agencies are one of the main competitors for retirement homes. Texas, Illinois, and Indiana are the only states which license these non-medical, attendant care providers. Most states have no regulations for home care and people sometimes ended up having a lot of problems when they went that route. Some people tried to save money and do it without an agency.

The caregiver they found through putting an ad in the paper sometimes abused or robbed the senior. Sometimes the caregiver staged a fall and sued them. Other times the government found out and nailed the senior with back taxes, workman's compensation, unemployment, and payroll fines. Many seniors had to have the 'caregiver at home' experiment fail miserably before they came back to our door. It was a process they needed to go through. For others, having help at home worked out beautifully. They found a gem of a caregiver who was honest and did a great job.

When someone did choose our community, we called it a "closed sale." Closing sales involved many factors: connecting with the person, understanding their needs, and having the right product that would be a fit for them. People want choice, and there are a lot of niche assisted living communities cropping up to meet that demand. There are places which are primarily Jewish, Catholic, Japanese, or LGBTQ. Older adults want options of when they eat, what they eat, how they get to the doctor and on which days, and how they spend their leisure time. They want freedom.

Providing choices was one way to improve the number of deals we sealed. Having a great marketing director was another way. The average closing ratio in assisted living is about 45 percent. That is, when a marketing director does her job, roughly 45 percent of the people who tour will write her a check and move-in. My closing ratio was around 60 percent, with the exception of one place where I worked. At Eldersview, it seemed I couldn't close a sale to save my life. I was working long hours, giving tour gifts, writing thank you notes, connecting genuinely with prospects, listening intently, and matching needs. Yet everything I knew about filling rooms in a retirement community wasn't working. I was failing miserably and couldn't figure out why. There were three of us marketers at Eldersview. The building had recently been built and had a lot of rooms to fill. My fellow marketer, Natasha, who had the office next to mine seemed to get lots of sales. She didn't like me. She had dark energy and I didn't like her either. She would say weird things to me in group meetings, often insulting me publicly for no apparent reason. Then, an hour later, she would ask me to go out to dinner. I did not want to be friends with this woman and I kept my distance. After three months of utter failure and very few sales, I decided to look around Natasha's office one day when she was on vacation, to see if I could find clues to her success. Instead, I found a possible clue to my failure. There in her desk drawer was a voodoo doll with my name on it! That's why I wasn't getting sales. That bitch was doing voodoo on me! I went to the third marketer, Hillary's office and said, "Hey, come here, I need to show you something." Hillary's jaw was agape as she stared at the doll. "Shit, it even has red hair like you!" Hillary and I got to work immediately throwing salt around my office, burning sage, saying chants to counter the voodoo. My sales and closing ratio improved slightly but I ultimately ended up leaving a few months later.

When I became a regional sales director, there was a guy who worked for me who consistently maintained an 80-percent closing ratio. Everyone who met this guy wanted to move into his building. He was kind, compassionate, a good listener, and excellent at follow-up. Hiring people like him was a key to my success because some things, like compassion and the ability to connect genuinely, cannot be taught.

When I worked for Elder Care as vice president of sales, I received an email with feedback from a tour my marketing director in Orange County had given. Her executive director forwarded it to me because she was so proud of the great job Paige was doing. The email, written by the son of 95-year-old parents, said this:

> *I was very impressed with the way you interacted with people as we walked through the building. The dancers were outgoing so you mirrored that, the smokers were perfectly content among themselves and you didn't intrude to include them in a "dog and pony show" to benefit your marketing at the expense of their privacy. When the woman was hesitant about going in to eat, you prompted her so she could make her own choice about what to do—you didn't make a show of trying to convince/manipulate her with how good the food was. You respected her hesitance, but gave her a thought for her to consider.*
>
> *Enough said. The layouts are great, but beyond the floor plans I perceived a planned approach to provide your residents with a home that will allow them respect as individuals and the care they may require not eroding that personal dignity. I am very alert to small details and manipulations vs. actual settings. I noticed you didn't talk a lot about how my parents would feel at home or "just like home." It will become their home when they make it their home in their own way. You had good instinct about relating with seniors and were able to recognize them for who they are at this stage of life and appreciate the past lives they've had before this point.*

That email summed up what it takes to be successful at inside sales. Paige had a 70-percent closing rate. This guy's parents, and the majority of the seniors who met Paige, ended up moving into her building. She understood, among other things, the importance of greeting residents on the tour. She also knew she had to have genuine connections and rapport with them; otherwise, don't bother saying hello on the tour. It would just look like she was using them as part of her sales pitch.

I read that email out loud at sales trainings, along with this additional guidance for marketing directors:

1. Slow your pace while walking with seniors. I have received actual notes from prospects thanking me and describing tours they had been given at other places: "The marketer rushed through the tour and walked two paces in front of me the whole time. You didn't do that—thank you."
2. Send a HANDWRITTEN thank you note. People from all generations appreciate this.
3. Have patience. Let people talk about whatever they want for as long as they wish. *Listen.* People need to be heard.
4. Follow-up, follow-up, follow-up.

Sometimes sales closed on the third or fifth tour and sometimes they closed on the first tour, like the one I had with Betty, a retired teacher. Her daughter, Tina, had come in the previous week. She visited eight places including ours, and narrowed her choice to the top three she wanted her mom to see. "She's not going to move to any of them," Tina said. "She doesn't want to move to assisted living. She's just touring places to appease me. She has seen the horror stories on television about abuse and she is afraid of losing her independence."

They arrived at the scheduled time and Tina guided Betty into the lobby in her wheelchair. Betty asked a few questions about the food and activities, but I could tell Tina was right, she had no intention of ever moving in. Her uninterested tone and her body language showed resistance from the onset. She was humoring me and her daughter.

We looked at the studio and one-bedroom model apartments. I went through the motions and did the best I could, all the while feeling like I was wasting my time. Then, on the way back to the dining room, we ran into Winnie, one of our sweetest caregivers. She was helping Perry Kahner to lunch, guiding him gently with his walker. I introduced them. Winnie smiled and shook hands with Tina, then knelt down in front of Betty and said, "Hi, how are you today?" Betty smiled brighter than I had seen on the entire tour.

"Okay, I suppose. I would rather be at home."

"This is a nice place," Winnie said. "We're like family here." She talked with Betty a little more while Tina and I chatted with Mr. Kahner. I was surprised that Winnie spent so much time talking with a visitor. I noticed how Betty and Winnie maintained eye contact the entire time they spoke. I don't know what transpired in their brief conversation, but clearly, they connected. After about 10 minutes, Winnie stood up and said, "I'm going to help Mr. Kahner to the dining room now for lunch. It was really nice to meet you, Betty. I hope you move in here."

Betty took Winnie's hands in hers and said, "Thank you."

As we continued down the hall, Betty pulled her checkbook out of her purse. "I want to take the studio," she said, looking up at me. "How much of a deposit do I have to leave?"

I was shocked. Tina was shocked. "Mom, are you sure? Don't you want to go home and think about it?" *Now you're talking her out of it?* I thought, glaring at Tina.

"That lady is going to take care of me," Betty said. "I saw it in her eyes. I know that woman is going to take care of me." Betty moved in three weeks later and loved her life at Casa Amanecer.

With other prospects, it was someone other than the senior blocking the move. I had a tour at Casa Amanecer with the family of Georgine, a 97-year-old woman with dementia. Georgine was physically healthy and living in her own home in San Francisco. After their third tour, the family decided to put a deposit down for a private room in our memory care.

Now, the only thing left to do was to give Georgine's in-home caregiver notice, a task they were dreading. The caregiver, Carla, was a registered nurse from Guatemala who spoke very little English. She had been watching after Georgine for two years and loved her dearly. She did an excellent job. It was just that Georgine's dementia had progressed. She had started to get combative and was now wandering. It wasn't safe for her to be left alone anymore and she could not afford to pay Carla around the clock.

The family told Carla about their plan to move Georgine to Casa Amanecer then scheduled a fourth tour with me. They wanted Carla to see the place. I had learned Spanish and became fluent at a young age, so I spoke directly with Carla throughout the tour, hoping that would smooth things over a bit. Instead, when Carla realized I spoke Spanish, the floodgates opened.

"In my country," she said, "we take care of our old. Here you cast them aside like dogs, like used animals. Actually, you treat your pets better than you treat your elders."

There was some truth to that statement. In Latin America, people do take care of their elders. They could not imagine putting a family member into a "home." She was also correct that people in the U.S. sometimes get a little obsessed with their pets.

"You are right in a way, but the thing is, Carla, it kind of runs both ways here. At age 18, we are shown the door with our bags. American culture is all about independence."

"This country is crazy."

"Carla," I said, "Georgine cannot be left alone anymore. That's the bottom line. I understand that you love her like a relative and her family is very happy with the care she is getting from you. But they cannot afford to pay you 24 hours a day, 7 days a week and that is what she needs at this point."

"Money!" she spat. "Money. That is all you white people care about is money." Another criticism with more than a grain of truth. Still, as much as Carla clearly cared deeply for Georgine, I wondered if money might be playing a role in her own indignation over this situation. Perhaps Carla was worried not just about Georgine's well-being, but also about losing her full-time gig.

The family kept looking at me with questioning eyes.

"What is she saying?" Georgine's nephew whispered.

"She doesn't want your aunt to move here," I responded, omitting the moral judgments.

After several more phone conversations with the family, Georgine moved to Casa Amanecer. Carla was spot on about a lot of things she said that day. She was wrong, though, about everyone in the United States abandoning their elders. Many families truly wanted to keep their loved ones at home.

One morning, I walked into Casa Amanecer at my usual time, 8:30 a.m., balancing my briefcase in one hand and my purse in the other. Before I could get the key into my office door, the receptionist, Eugenia, came up to me and said quietly, "There's a walk-in tour." *Damn*, I thought, *I*

haven't even had a cup of coffee yet. She tilted her head towards the lobby and I glanced at the 70-something gentleman sitting in a leather chair with an expectant look on his face. I mustered a smile in his direction. "Let me at least set my things down," I snapped at Eugenia. It wasn't her fault, but I sometimes have a tendency to shoot the messenger. Eugenia handed me the piece of paper the man had filled out with his contact information: John Severan, Crescent Drive, San Francisco, looking at places for his wife.

With my best phony smile (honed during my waitressing days in college) I looked at the paper and walked over to him, extending my hand, "Hello, John. I'm Liz, come right this way." John was wearing a white cotton golf shirt which barely contained his large belly. He had a full head of gray hair. I led him to our private dining room. "Can I get you a cup of coffee or some juice?" John declined and dove right into the reason for his visit. His 74-year-old wife, Karen, had Parkinson's and the in-home caregiver he hired a year ago had quit.

"She walked out yesterday," he said, "just hit the wall and couldn't do it anymore. She was a great caregiver... loving, kind, responsible. But Karen, my sweetheart of 53 years, has dementia and has become incontinent. I think it is time for me to start looking at these kinds of places. I don't want to be here."

"How did you meet your wife?"

"We met in grammar school. She put up with my drunkenness for the first 18 years of our marriage. I've been sober now for 35 years in Alcoholics Anonymous. Karen was a gourmet cook, a great mom, wife, homemaker. She did homework with the kids every night, volunteered at their school, and still had energy to make me laugh at the end of each day."

"She sounds amazing."

"She is amazing. Our third baby died of meningitis in her arms. Somehow she recovered from that and still managed to be there for me and the kids." He stared off into space, then pointing to the ceiling said, "I don't understand who's in charge up there." John covered his face and started to cry.

"You're right," I said. "It's not fair."

"It is so painful to watch her lose her dignity. She doesn't deserve this," he said, intimating that he, perhaps, *did* deserve this. John's face was still in his hands except now he was sobbing. I watched him intently.

Strangely, I didn't feel uncomfortable that a person I had just met was falling apart in front of me, nor did I feel the urge to say something to smooth over his sadness. This man needed someone to witness his pain, to just be there and see it, not to try and fix it. John looked up at me, saw I was still watching him, and continued to weep.

I didn't need John's business. I had a long list of people waiting to move into Casa Amanecer. It was also a nonprofit, which meant there was less pressure on me for sales than at the corporate-owned places where I had worked. I had taken a pay cut for the job and though I missed the extra money, it was nice to not feel so stressed about the numbers.

"The hardest part," John continued, wiping his nose and eyes with a handkerchief, "is that our grandkids never got to know the phenomenal woman I married. She started slipping away when they were very young. Anyway," he said, shrugging off this thought, "how much are the private rooms here?"

I gave John the prices then showed him the main dining room, living room, and lounge where I talked about the various entertainers who came in.

We took the elevator to the memory care area. I punched in the code and the door opened. I could see John was uncomfortable with this. "It's a secure door," I explained, "to prevent people with memory loss from wandering." We met Tanya, the memory care director as soon as we walked in. She was setting up a craft project with three women and two men. Others milled about. Some sat staring into space. I guided John down the hall and showed him the private and shared rooms.

"They're nice," he commented. "Clean and nice. Looks kind of like a hotel room."

"You could, of course, bring Karen's furniture, art, pictures, anything you like that might make the surroundings feel more familiar to her."

When we got back downstairs to the private dining room, we discussed care levels, availability, and the support group we hosted once a month for families. I looked at John's eyes welling again with tears then looked at the silk orchid on the credenza behind him. It was lemon-colored with little brown flecks and I got lost in my thoughts as I stared at it and listened to John cry some more. I felt so sad for him, for Karen, their kids and grandkids. I almost started to cry with him but, somehow, I kept my composure. We sat silently for a while after he stopped crying and then John said, "You're doing God's work, you know."

I never heard from John after that day, but I learned with him and many others like him that a marketing director in assisted living is more of a therapist than a sales person. This posed a conundrum for me because I am highly emotive. When people started sobbing during tours, I sometimes ended up crying with them. It was not very professional, I realize, but I couldn't help it. Sometimes these prospects were so surprised by *my* crying, it actually helped *them* to calm down.

For the most part, I felt a lot of compassion for family members, especially the spouses. With the adult children, I was filled with empathy much of the time, but not always. The kids sometimes bothered me, whereas spouses did not. The kids often plopped down in in my office and cathartically vomited up all their parent's problems, the stress they had been through with the doctor, a blow-by-blow account of dad's fall down the stairs, his tracheotomy and subsequent feeding tube, the medications, the walker, the bedside commode, the nurses, the nightmares with home health care. They had probably told bits and pieces to others, but I sensed that I was the first one to get the *entire* story.

They just needed to talk. So, I listened, then listened some more. It became exhausting. There was the caring side of me that truly wanted to help and be there for these families. I absorbed more of their feelings than I probably should have, then felt completely wiped out when I got home. There were days when I felt so emotionally spent that I considered committing job abandonment, like the days when I had three people moving in, five people calling for information, three more wanting to tour, all interspersed with numerous calls from discharge planners, geriatric case managers, and dysfunctional family members.

When I wasn't receiving calls, I was making them: to doctors, family members, co-workers, trying to keep it all together. Being busy was certainly better than having no business, but it sometimes got ridiculous.

On one of these days, Becky Aldridge called to inquire about care for her mother-in-law who had suffered a stroke, was unable to walk on her own and lived with Becky. Mom also needed help bathing and getting dressed. Becky was dealing with a lot of grief. Her own husband had died at the age of 43. He had gone in for a simple shoulder surgery and three weeks later died instantly from a post-operative blood clot. Becky's husband left her with three kids under age 12. That was a year ago.

After an hour on the phone, I knew Becky's life story and I was, once again, welled up with tears. Becky wasn't looking for sympathy; she was simply telling me, in a straightforward way, what had happened in her life in recent years. The fact that she was not on a pity party made me feel even more understanding and care for her. She went on to tell me her mother-in-law had two daughters. "But they're not involved," she explained. "She wasn't a loving mom when they were young. She favored my husband, so I can't really blame them. I'm caring for her because she has always been very kind to me, and because I loved my husband. I'm doing it as much for him as for her. But I can't do it much longer. I'm working full-time, taking care of three kids, caring for her, and still grieving the loss of my husband. Something's gotta give."

Stories like Becky's were downright tragic. Others were just mildly to moderately sad. I would often go home at the end of the day and the last thing I wanted to hear about was Dave's aching back or his work stress, or even what he had for lunch. I did not want to return phone calls to family and friends. I didn't really care how their lives were going. I had spent all day listening to people, depleting my emotional energy.

I started to resent Dave for simply wanting to talk to me. It got especially bad at Casa Amanecer, where I didn't do outside marketing. The phone rang off the hook from our great reputation and the few newspaper advertisements we ran. I didn't need to attend luncheons at country clubs or meet colleagues for drinks or coffee. No more networking. Now my days were spent holed up for eight hours in a beautiful building listening to people's troubles. I felt like an emotional prostitute, giving away all that nurturing for money. I did not want to get desensitized to what I was hearing, but six years into my assisted living career, it happened anyway. There were days when I found myself thinking, *I don't really care about your dad's heart surgery. I haven't had a decent conversation with my own mother in months.*

There is a word for what I had: *burnout.* Still, I rallied every day and showed up for my job at Casa Amanecer while on the side I began to explore management positions where I could travel and make more money.

Each morning before work, in spite of my dread, I prayed, *God, please show me how I can be of service today.*

At the height of my burnout, I met Annie Wong. It was a Saturday afternoon at 5:30, the end of my workday and my workweek. I was looking forward to cooking a batch of enchiladas suizas that night for Dave, one of his favorites. I still needed to stop by the grocery store to get sour cream. As I was packing up my things, Annie walked in and asked for a tour. It is an unspoken rule in assisted living: we do not say no to a walk-in tour. It's bad manners and bad business. So, even though I was tired, I invited Annie into my office. I did not have the energy to take her to the private dining room and do the whole tea and cookies bit.

Annie was Chinese-American, five feet tall, with pale skin and large eyes. She began to tell me about her mom's dementia and the strange behavior mom was exhibiting: putting jewelry in the cat box, forgetting to shower, talking about events from the 1940s like they happened yesterday. I had already done three tours that day, met with four family members of new residents, and talked with two more adult children on the phone.

Listening to Annie, though, I noticed something different from the other people with whom I usually met. I realized how difficult it was for Annie to share the family secret of her mom's illness and all its manifestations. I heard stories like hers every day. Annie's was no more bizarre than the countless others. Most people were usually quite happy to have a captive audience, but not Annie. She was reticent, proceeding through her tale with trepidation.

About 10 minutes into our conversation, something in me rose to the occasion and I found myself forgetting about the grocery store and the enchiladas and instead really being present with Annie. She felt it, too; I saw it on her face. Eventually, she opened her heart and cried and I cried too. "I can't believe I'm doing this," she said. "In my culture we don't cry in front of strangers."

Interactions with Annie, Becky, John, and others like them helped my burnout by reminding me how sacred it was that people were sharing their intimate struggles with me. It gave me a second wind to keep doing the work. Yet, not all of the family members I met touched my heart in a tender way.

Marianne Smith called Sunset Oaks on a Monday morning in a panic. Her mom was living in a mobile home park in Goleta, a town just north of Santa Barbara. Mom's dementia was progressing and Marianne could not leave her alone anymore. It was starting to take a toll on Marianne's life and her interior design business. "It sounds like you need to move pretty quickly," I said. "Could you come over today at 11:00 for a tour?"

I watched Marianne walk up the driveway. She was 50-ish, with coiffed platinum blond hair, impeccable posture, and subtle makeup. We spent about half an hour in my office before the tour, talking about her mom and how hard this was on Marianne. "I hate the thought of placing my mom in a home, but I know I have to do it. I can't spend 24/7 with her and I cannot afford round-the-clock care," Marianne said, seeming more annoyed than concerned. She spent 30 minutes complaining about what a nuisance it was to have to care for her mom. I searched for a sign, any sign of compassion, but found none.

We toured, walking through the dining room where lunch was being served, then around the outdoor patio area where I had carefully placed new hanging begonias and ferns in preparation for Marianne's visit. Tours in a memory care building were always interesting. We wanted to put our best foot forward, pop some popcorn so the place didn't smell like feces or disinfectant, set out fresh flowers, and avoid residents who might be screaming or urinating in a planter. The harsh reality of dementia was difficult for families to face, so we tried to avoid showing all sides of the disease on the first visit. People almost always thought their relative wasn't "that bad," so we planned to conveniently run into the very active, happy resident who still golfed once a week. But it didn't always work out that way.

The day of Marianne's tour was also the day we had a new resident moving in, a retired priest who swore like a truck driver. The hospital had promised to "prepare him" for the trip by giving him a sedative. Apparently, he refused the Haldol, so when we crossed Father Murphy's path during the tour, I greeted him cheerfully, "Welcome to Sunset Oaks, Father Murphy. How was your trip over today?" He began swinging his metal cane at me and screaming, "Where the fuck am I and who the fuck are you?"

Marianne stepped back a few feet, looking frightened.

"I'm Liz, Father Murphy. I work here. This is an assisted living place. Do you want to have some lunch?"

He looked at me with a sarcastic smile and fumed, "I just want to be left alone. Could you people just leave me the fuck alone for one moment?"

"Sure," I smiled and wrote on my clipboard: *avoid Father Murphy on tours.*

"That was disturbing," Marianne said as we walked across the patio. "That man is a *priest?*"

"Yes. Retired." I showed her the private room we had fixed up with fresh paint and Shabby Chic linens from Target. Our place was not the fanciest in town, but we did our best to make it look nice. We went back to my office and sat down. "So," I asked, "what do you think?"

"I think putting my mother here would be like putting her in HELL." I caught my breath, surprised by Marianne's bluntness. I noted her stern expression then looked down at her large breast implants and obnoxiously tight blouse. "I can't believe you people actually convinced someone to move their parent into this shit hole," she continued. I watched an anger rise in her that had nothing to do with our building.

I looked down again at her white cotton blouse. She had only clasped the two middle buttons and it was difficult not to stare at her cleavage. The buttons looked like they were about to fly off and hit me in the eye.

"You're right that our place doesn't look great," I retorted, "but our care is excellent." I agreed with her about the physical appearance of our community, not because I believe the customer is always right, but, because in this case, she actually *was* right. She could have been a little *nicer* about the way she said it, but Sunset Oaks was run down. The owners had hired me with the promise that they would do a complete remodel. That was six months earlier and not a single nail had gone in.

Then there was Father Murphy yelling, and the other residents whom Marianne had seen slumped over in their wheelchairs who were close to the end of their lives. Many of our competitors hid residents who were advanced in their dementia when a tour came in, locked them away in their rooms. We weren't willing to sink that low for a sale. We shouldn't have to. Our care *was* outstanding.

I bid Marianne farewell, then went into my office and sent an angry email to corporate about the remodel.

Marianne, of course, did not move her mom to Sunset Oaks. She likely found a place that looked nicer. The most common reason someone did not move their loved one to memory care was guilt. The reasons seniors didn't move to independent or assisted living were fear, denial, anger, and resistance to change. People who were considering the move to assisted living were filled with fear of not having enough money, not being accepted, not making friends, going somewhere to die, losing their independence, and going to live with "old people."

They were also in denial about the aging process, denial of their ability to care for themselves, and anger that they were getting older. I once called a 98-year-old woman who was on our waiting list for independent living, excitedly telling her, "Francesca, the studio you liked is available now!"

"Oh, I'm just not ready," she said, ". . . maybe down the road."

Down the road? I thought, *you're 98.*

Fear of death, as Suzanne had taught me, was by far the biggest obstacle. Mrs. Adele Williams-Morris, a woman who toured with me at The Gables, had more than her share of it. Mrs. Williams-Morris wore a St. John knit suit and looked petite next to her husband's six-foot frame. They had thick British accents and an acerbic wit. Mr. Williams-Morris was 87 and his wife was 67. They had been married 40 years and were touring The Gables because Mrs. Williams-Morris had been diagnosed with Parkinson's.

"She needs care," Mr. Williams-Morris said. She looked fine to me; *he* looked like the one who needed care. As we sat in the sunroom and talked before the tour, Mrs. Williams-Morris repeatedly said, "We are going to move in here and we're going to die."

"Well, actually people often thrive when they move into retirement communities," I told her (which is true). "They don't have to worry about cooking, cleaning, keeping up a house, or driving. It's like living in a resort. You can spend your time doing what you enjoy instead of what you have to do."

"So, about how many deaths on average do you have per month?" she asked.

"Well, I don't know actually. It varies from month-to-month." I thought about it for a minute. "Maybe two or three?"

"See," she said, turning to her husband, "they drop off like flies at these places."

We did have some deaths every month. The average age of our residents was 88. It was also true that assisted living *is* a life-affirming environment where people tend to live longer than they would at home. In an attempt to change the subject, I suggested we take a look around the property. We walked through the lounge, by the swimming pool, looked at a one-bedroom in independent living, passed the rose gardens, and made our way up to the Cottages assisted living. The Williams-Morris's weren't ready for assisted living, but they wanted to see it in case the need ever arose.

As we strolled up the hill, I pointed to a redwood tree and mentioned the variety of flora and fauna we had on the property. Then, out of the corner of my eye, I saw a stretcher coming out of Jean Meir's apartment with a purple body bag on it. The men carrying the stretcher wore black jackets with big yellow letters that read: CORONER. *Oh Shit,* I thought. *Shit! Really? Now?* I kept talking about the tree as the men headed straight towards us. There was no other way to go, actually. They walked down the winding path and passed us with the stretcher. We actually had to move out of the way to let them get by with Jean's body. We stood in silence as Mrs. Williams-Morris looked at me. The expression on her face said, *How do you explain that, miss people-don't-come-here-to-die?*

I shrugged my shoulders and muttered, "I don't even know what to say right now."

One place I toured was actually next to a cemetery. The large dining room with high-backed silk chairs had floor-to-ceiling windows that looked directly at a sloped, grassy hill covered in tombstones. "What was your architect *thinking* when he designed this?" I asked the marketing director.

"I have no idea," she said, "but let me tell you it is a huge challenge on tours. People stare out at that hill during lunch and think, *I'm here now, eating my soup, and that's where I'm going next.* And I am asking them to move in here and stare at that cemetery during every meal."

Eldersview, where I worked as marketing director, was actually next door to a crematorium. It was a busy one, too. They incinerated over 4,000 bodies a year. The crematorium shared a wall with us and we could hear the ovens firing up from our offices, usually around 3:00 p.m. each day. Our exercise pool often filled up with ash, which piqued visitors' curiosity. I told them it was from a family barbecue we had hosted over the weekend.

On the afternoons when we smelled fresh coffee, we knew our neighbors had received a shipment of bodies. The crematorium mixed coffee grounds in with the corpses to mask the smell of burning flesh and hair (which apparently smells *horrible*) and I appreciated the gesture. Internet blogs written by people living nearby started writing things like, "There's dead people on the side of that assisted living building," which was true. The side of our building was covered in ash. Even my car was covered with it. One morning when Dave walked me out to my car, he asked, "What's all this ash on your car? Did you go near a fire?"

"Oh, it's dead people," I told him, "from the place next door to my work. It's not helping my sales."

If fear of death was the biggest obstacle to move-ins, lack of funds was my next largest challenge. I often had to turn away people who had little or no money. There were so many of them. Few assisted living places exist between the high-end communities where I worked and the roach motels that cost the equivalent of a monthly Social Security check.

Dr. Ethel Andrus, the founder of AARP and The Gables, knew well about poverty among seniors. Dr. Andrus started The Gables because of an experience she had one day in the late 1940's when she went looking for a retired teacher whom a neighbor had said was in need of food and eyeglasses.

This particular lady's address was in a town on the outskirts of Los Angeles and when Dr. Andrus arrived at the house, she found the woman was actually living in an old chicken coop in the backyard. The retired Spanish teacher was in poor health and could not afford medical care. The scene of this woman emerging from the coop galvanized Dr. Andrus into action—this is why The Gables and later, AARP, were formed. Her first step was to purchase eight acres in Ojai where she built The Gables, a place where retired teachers could live and get medical care in their old age for a minimal cost.

Ethel Andrus' view on aging was, "Aging is not just a problem; it represents a real and thrilling challenge. It is one thing to recognize that older people represent the nation's greatest single human resource available, and it is quite another to do something about it."

I often thought of Dr. Andrus on days when I took two or three phone calls from seniors like the lady she found in the chicken coop. The lack of resources available to seniors shocked me. Here are some statistics from a letter I received from Meals on Wheels in San Francisco:

- *4.9 million older Americans worry about not having enough to eat.*
- *Half of all hospitalized seniors are suffering from malnutrition so severe that it either caused their illness or it prevents them from getting better.*
- *One in eight elderly people must regularly choose among paying the rent, buying medications and purchasing groceries.*

What could I tell someone who could not afford assisted living, yet needed and wanted it badly? Someone with no family or friends to help? I told them the truth, that if they had a moderate amount of money, they could go to a six-bed board and care. If they had little or no money, their only option was a nursing home, which would be covered by Medi-Cal. Many people who do not need medical care often end up living in nursing homes because they have no money, are not fully independent, and have no place else to go.

Slowly, this is changing. I have heard of a few independent and assisted living communities that offer a low-income choice for people. I read about a place called the Gardens at Osage Terrace in Bentonville, Arkansas. The article said:

> *The ... facility ... is one of the affordable assisted living residences developed under the Coming Home Program of the Robert Wood*

> Johnson Foundation and NCB Development Corp., a national nonprofit that assists low-income communities.
>
> Coming Home, working with nine states, has helped establish 30 affordable assisted living homes, with 59 more in development. The idea is that other nonprofits will learn from these homes and build more like them.

The residents are a mixture of secretaries, factory workers, and other low-income individuals. They pay for the room and board with their Social Security and Medicaid pays for the health and care services.

Another one mentioned in this article is a place in Livingston, Texas called Rainbow's End. It is in a campground and residents live in their motorhomes and pay $800 a month for meals, housekeeping, and personal care.

Many of the older adults I talked with were sad about their situation, others felt angry. Mildred Walker called Casa Amanecer to tell me she lived at a competitor facility down the road and was looking to move. The annual increase, she complained, was three percent last year. "That's pretty good," I told her. "Ours was five percent and we are a nonprofit. The place where you are living is a for-profit."

"I'm 90 years old," she spat. "What if I live to 95 and things continue to increase at a rate of three percent? How will I pay for it?"

"I don't know," I responded.

"This government we live under is criminal. They rob us through taxes."

"I agree with you 100 percent on that. I cannot stand the fact that I pay exorbitant taxes yet most of the money goes to buy bombs instead of providing healthcare, housing, and education."

"What kind of society do we live in?" she asked.

I thought to myself, *we live in a society where modern medicine has advanced at a far more rapid rate than our social model can handle and the government doesn't care about old people. We are not equipped to deal with people living this long, yet doctors are doing everything possible to keep seniors alive.*

"An unfair and greedy one, Mildred."

I tried to help Mildred and pointed her in the direction of some residential homes with six rooms, a few caregivers, and prices significantly lower than our place or the place where she was currently living.

"You're a thief," she said. *I'm a thief? I'm just trying to help here.* Mildred started yelling at me. The more I tried to help, the angrier she got. Our conversation ended with her hanging up on me.

Mildred's prospects were not good if she lived another 5 or 10 years. At a networking breakfast the following week, I heard about a 98-year-old woman who was being evicted from a large, for-profit retirement community in downtown San Francisco. The woman had lived there for four years and paid $7,000 per month. She paid her rent on-time every month, had no family, and had exhausted the proceeds from selling her home. Now all she had was her Social Security check. The retirement community gave her a 30-day notice to move out. She called a referral agent to help her find something in her price range. There was nothing. She called the ombudsman who intervened on her behalf and threatened to show up on the doorstep of the retirement community with news crews if they kicked her out.

The latest development in the saga, the networking group reported, was that the retirement community was actively looking for a Medi-Cal paid nursing home where this woman could live. I knew that is exactly where she would end up. There was no way the assisted living would take a financial loss on one of their apartments, even for a month or two, and even though they had already made a nice sum of money from her four-year stay at their place.

I was often the one communicating the financial realities of elder care to seniors and their families. Once, while on vacation with my friend, Kayleigh, I got a call from my assistant, Kristi, about a move-in. I was on the phone in our hotel room, directing all the arrangements, while Kayleigh sat next to me on the couch, sipping her coffee.

"Did you get the Physician's Report?" I asked Kristi. Yes. "Is the apartment cleaned and ready?" Affirmative. "What about the ripped screen? Did the maintenance department fix that?" They had. "Great. When is the family moving furniture in? Tomorrow? Okay, then they need to start paying rent tomorrow. What? No, no, no, they're going to have to bring their own hospital bed. I'm sorry. We are not providing a hospital bed, no way. How about mom's meds? Did they arrive from the pharmacy?" Yes, they had. "Thanks, Kristi. I'll check in with you tomorrow." I hung up the phone and looked over at Kayleigh, who was laughing.

"What?" I asked her.

"My God, you sound so harsh. '*She'll have to bring her own hospital bed. I'm sorry, no way.*'" Kayleigh repeated, mocking me.

"Well, it's a business. We can't be buying hospital beds for every person who moves into our place. We would go bankrupt."

It was not that I was without compassion. I simply had a job to do and that job was to fill rooms with people who had enough money to pay for them. In the midst of doing that, there were cases that really tore my heart apart, like Maria Fernandez who called from the county hospital looking for an assisted living community. I went to meet her in her room and quickly discovered there was no way she could afford Eldersview, where I was working as the marketing director.

Maria was a 74-year-old lady and was at the hospital because she had taken a fall. She was homeless. When I explained to the hospital case manager that we did not have even a shared room at Eldersview that was even remotely close to Maria's price range, she managed to find a single-room occupancy hotel for her on Sixth and Mission Streets, one of San Francisco's low-income neighborhoods. Sixth and Mission was actually skid row for San Francisco. Maria's Social Security check would cover the rent but there would be nothing left after that. Two days after she was discharged, she called me and asked me to come visit her at the hotel. She was lonely and cold.

I walked down Sixth Street through a group of prostitutes, stepped over homeless people, and watched a man openly shooting drugs into his arm on the sidewalk, before I arrived at the front desk of Maria's building. The man behind the metal bars said in a gruff voice, "I need your driver's license." After I showed it, he buzzed open the heavy, locked steel gate, and I walked through. I was carrying a bag with a sandwich, juice, blankets, and towels. He inspected my bag and said, "Number 233. Upstairs." There was no elevator in the building and I wondered how the hell Maria had made it up those stairs to her room.

I sat with Maria on her bed because there was nowhere else to sit. "How are you doing?" I asked. I could hear a man getting beaten up in the hallway. He was yelling as someone was punching him. No one came to break up the fight—it just went on as Maria and I continued talking on her bed.

"I'm okay," she said.

"Maria, how did you end up in this situation?" Then she told me her story. She had three kids with her abusive husband. She was in and out of the emergency room many times over the years. The last time she had a fractured skull because he had pummeled her so badly. She left him and struggled financially, living on welfare. When she lost the kids to foster care, the suicide attempts began.

"I am so sorry."

"It's fine, *mija*, I'll get by."

I took the blankets and towels I had bought out of the plastic bag. Maria was thrilled and hugged them as she slowly ate her sandwich. I forgot the thirty-two-dollar receipt in the bag and later Maria called and asked if she could get on a payment plan to repay me what I had spent. I could tell she was sincere about her offer. "No, Maria. Please do not worry about it." I visited her a few more times because she had no family or friends in her life. I didn't know what else to do to help her.

I saw an overwhelming number of cases like Maria's. There is indeed a crisis in the United States. Every day, 10,000 people turn 65 and this trend will continue for the next 20 years. There is more and more need for nursing homes and assisted living. Nursing homes, the last resort for seniors with no money, are closing at rapid rates due to government funding cuts. We need more geriatric doctors, yet fewer physicians are going into this field of medicine. It's not sexy and it doesn't pay as well as other specialties like orthopedic surgery.

I am afraid we will start seeing alarming numbers of elderly people with dementia and physical care needs literally living on the streets. I already see it happening in San Francisco. I have even seen a few cases where hospital case managers discharged seniors to a homeless shelter. These were elders who could not ambulate on their own and needed help with activities of daily living. The case managers had no other choice. The person's medical needs did not warrant living in the hospital and there was literally nowhere else to send them.

Money was a common obstacle to moving to an assisted living community, but certainly not the only one. Another road block I often encountered was when people had plenty of money, but mom had dementia and the family wanted her to live in independent living. "My mom is a little forgetful," they would say. *No, your mom is a lot forgetful*, I thought when I finally met mom and saw the glazed look in her eyes. Mom asked me five times during the tour, "How many residents do you have here? What are the meal times? How long has this place been here?"

When we sat down after the tour to discuss medications and care needs, the daughter told me mom was on Aricept. So, your mom is a *little* forgetful? People who are a *little* forgetful do not take Aricept. I have never had someone call me and say, "My mom is really demented." Everyone always had "a little bit of dementia." No one ever had a lot.

If we recognized signs of dementia when potential residents toured, we performed the Mini-Mental test and then reviewed their Physician's Report, a seven-page document which must be completed and signed by a doctor before someone can move into a community. The form has a section where the doctor writes the person's primary and secondary diagnoses. In California, if a resident has a primary diagnosis of dementia, our license required them to live in a secure area of the building. As marketing director, I had the unenviable task of breaking this news to families:

Me: So, with the results of your mom's Mini-Mental Exam and the doctor's report, it looks like she will need to live in our secure memory care area.

Son: My mom can't live there. You're talking about that place you showed me on the tour, right, where everyone was so out of it? No, I want her to have that nice one-bedroom apartment in independent living.

Me: The problem is, your mom scored 18 out of 33 on the Mini-Mental Exam and her doctor wrote "dementia" as the primary diagnosis on her Physician's Report. We can have people with mild cognitive impairment in independent living but we cannot have people with dementia live there. It violates our license.

Son: Then I will have the doctor change the diagnosis to mild cognitive impairment.

Me: I'm not sure the doctor would be willing to do that. Anyway, it wouldn't be ethical for me to accept the new Physician's Report.

Son: The place down the street said she could be in independent living, but I like your place better.

Me: The place down the street has the same licensing requirements we have. If they allow your mom to live in independent living, they are violating their license, too. It is also a matter of safety. She could wander off and we might never find her.

The obstacles to move-ins, like these, sometimes seemed endless. I tried my best to get every prospect to move in. Once I had done everything I could with the people who had toured, it was time to pound the pavement and generate more prospects for the top of the funnel. Outside sales was my favorite part of the job. It meant visits to networking groups, nursing homes, senior centers, and hospitals. These were our referral sources. When I was new to the industry, Sharon simply told me, "Go out." She was great at the inside sales training, but I was on my own for the outside networking. I had only a vague idea of where to go, but did not want her to see my lack of experience, so I went out and made the best of it.

Surprisingly, it was my competition who helped me the most. I started touring places because that was part of the job: get to know what we were up against, see the size of their rooms, try their food, look at their activity schedules. There was a general sense that the pie was big enough for everyone. Everyone knew everyone and we all toured each other's communities. Whenever I called to tour a competitor, I was honest. I told them that I worked in senior living and wanted to see their property. I am not good at lying, and I could always tell anyway when someone was shopping me, pretending to look for a supposed "family member." I could tell within three minutes into the tour that the person worked in elder care. It was transparent by the questions they asked, the terminology they used, and the fact that they clearly were not in the midst of a crisis.

During my competitor tours, people like Krissy, the marketing director at Redwoods Santa Barbara, gave me lists of doctors to visit. Lindsey, at Oakcrest Senior Living, told me how to succeed with senior centers. I was suspicious at first. I had come from the cutthroat world of advertising. I found help from the competition odd, but I desperately needed it, so I accepted. Later, when I was more established in the industry, I passed along the good will and helped other marketing directors.

Here are some of the tips I gave people in trainings on outside sales:

- Always have a reason to be there.
- When you go out, the phone rings. If you stop going out, the phone stops ringing.
- Build relationships; get to know your referral sources.
- Have a "What's-In-It-For-Them" attitude.
- If you want to see a 60-year-old doctor turn into a 5-year-old before your eyes, take a homemade birthday cake to his office.
- When taking thank you gifts, be specific. Call the front desk and ask what the person likes and then take him or her that thing. I once took a bottle of Bombay Sapphire gin (his favorite per the receptionist) to a doctor who had never spoken with me in person. He was so appreciative of my thoughtful gift, he spent an hour sitting in his office and talking with me that day.
- Take food. I have often heard pharmaceutical sales reps say they feel more like a caterer than a marketer. It's true and it is just a fact of the business we are in. If you want people in medical offices to talk with you, you need to bring breakfast or lunch.
- In California, if you want to have a full assisted living community, you had better align yourself with the Filipino and Russian communities. If you dig deep enough, you will find they are controlling the flow of seniors throughout the state.
- Caregivers are the gateway. I made friends with the caregivers, asked them to visit doctor's offices and hospitals with me. A simple look or nod of the head, a line exchanged in Tagalog, and next thing you know I had three more move-ins heading my way.

My friend, Jacqueline, who worked for a homecare agency, handed me a list of doctor's offices when I first started, "They're brutal," she said, "but there is no getting around them, so just dive in."

She was right. A year into my assisted living career, I walked into Dr. Granger's office and the office manager didn't even look up. "Can I help you?" she asked, while simultaneously opening mail and tossing it into piles.

"I'm Liz from The Gables," I said in my cheeriest voice. She didn't reply, so I continued, "We are an assisted living community about a mile from here. I notice that Dr. Granger is an Internal Medicine doctor. Does he see elderly patients?"

"Yes," she said coldly. "How can I help you?" She swiveled her chair so that her back was to me as she straightened a pile of envelopes.

"I was just wondering if maybe I could get on your lunch calendar," I asked the back of her head. "Do you have a favorite restaurant nearby? I could bring lunch from there and maybe talk with your team for 10 or 15 minutes, find out more about your patients, and see if we can help some of them?"

"Our lunch calendar is full."

"Maybe another time, then? Is it full all year?"

"Yes." She answered a phone call then flicked the back of her hand at me, actually shooing me away. She never did look up from the mail.

Encounters like this one made me hate my job. I am not a pushy salesperson. I give people their space. I realize they're busy and don't ask too much of their time. I was also offering a product that actually helps people. I left Dr. Granger's office full of indignation. *Why do I do this job?* I asked myself. It took me half a day to shake it off and get my mojo back so that I could do more visits.

Hospitals could be challenging too. Before working in the medical field, I thought a hospital was a hospital, with very little difference among them. I was wrong.

I walked into St. Agnus Hospital and looked down at the freshly shampooed cream-colored carpet. My heels did not make a sound as I walked down the hall. Every bed in the hospital was full, yet the halls were tranquil as a luxury spa. The staff spoke in whispers and walked slowly. This hospital was highly regarded for their hip and knee replacements. Most hospitals have a psychiatric ward, but not this one. It was too close to rich people's homes for that.

I went to the security desk to get my vendor badge. I was required to get one each time I visited and not allowed to enter patient floors without it. Getting registered for the badge took me three months. I had to get a Hepatitis B shot, take a bloodborne pathogen test, a HIPAA privacy test, and provide blood tests (titers) to prove I have had chicken pox and measles, mumps and rubella shots. I also had to submit a letter signed by my boss stating that I had been thoroughly trained in all the services my company offered. I had to get a chest x-ray showing that I did not have active tuberculosis. Lastly, I had to take a three-hour exam on hospital safety.

Even after all that, I could not just go up and visit the discharge planners—I had to have an appointment. I had to be *invited*. So, I called ahead and asked Kelly, the 10th-floor discharge planner, if I could please visit that day, and she said yes. I headed up to the 10th floor with a fresh-fruit platter that I had prepared myself the night before.

Kelly was at the nurse's station, dressed in pressed wool slacks and a green silk blouse. All of the nurses wore bright pink scrubs. I approached Kelly with a smile, "Hi!"

"Oh, thanks. Just put it over there," she replied flatly. *Oh, thanks? I worked on this thing until eleven o'clock last night.* "I would love to help some of your patients, Kelly. Do you have anyone discharging this week?" To get referrals, I had to deal with Kelly's rudeness.

"Nope," she said. "I don't. But thanks for the fruit platter." We stared at each other for a minute. I knew she was lying. She had patients leaving; she just didn't want to refer them to me. She had her friends at other assisted livings where she was sending the referrals. "Okay. Bye," I said. "Have a good day."

Next, I headed to the county hospital to visit a patient who was leaving the following day and needed assisted living. I got into the elevator and a man with tattoos on his face, holding a bandage over his bleeding neck, entered after me. He lifted his chin at me and asked, "'Sup?"

"Not much," I said. "How are you?" realizing immediately what a ridiculous question that was, given the bloody mess on his neck. The man had obviously just been stabbed or maybe even shot. He laughed and replied, "Just great, lady. I'm just great." I stared at the numbers lighting up on the panel above us. I stepped off on the fifth floor and walked towards room 17B. There was not a scrap of carpet in this hospital. This was the city's top trauma hospital and they did a damn fine job with gunshot wounds, stabbings, and car-crash victims. The place was buzzing with energy, and as usual, the halls seemed to have more police officers than doctors and nurses. This hospital did not require vendor badges so there was no need to go to the security desk first.

I stopped at the nurse's station, found the chart for my patient, then walked to the nearby Xerox machine. No one seemed to care that I was leafing through confidential files and making copies of medical records. The nurses at the station had no idea who I was. They just saw a woman with an assisted living nametag. I did have permission from the case manager to copy the files, but they didn't know that. The doctor walked up, a young resident who had just finished medical school. *Money buys privacy and students get to work on poor people.*

I went to meet my patient, a pleasant 85-year-old woman. She was one of the few people at the county hospital with money and good insurance. Her surgeon happened to be working at the hospital the week that she needed heart surgery, so that's where she had her procedure done. She was happy to be moving to Eldersview. I told her I would have her room ready when she discharged in a week.

On my way out, I passed several homeless people sleeping in the lobby. I stopped by the case manager's office, "Hey Leah, how's it going?"

"Hey sugar, it's great. How are you?"

"Good. I just met your patient. Thank you for the referral." I gave Leah a chocolate bar and she acted like I had just given her a dozen roses.

"Oh my gosh, thank you, Liz!"

"You're welcome. It's just a chocolate bar, Leah." I loved the county hospital. The staff were nice, appreciative, and very different than snobby St. Agnus.

A couple days later I was marketing at the Veteran's Hospital, where employees seemed highly stressed much of the time, but very committed to their patients. Masculine, military energy permeated the place. The case managers wore white lab coats and got six weeks paid vacation and every holiday imaginable off work. "Do you guys get Groundhog Day?" I asked the nurse I was visiting.

"No, silly!"

The patients received whatever care, surgeries, medication, and equipment they needed and that made me happy. Our country did right by veterans when it came to medical care, at least in San Francisco. This hospital had systems, formulas, and procedures for everything. They were efficient and I enjoyed working with them.

Later that day, I visited University Hospital, which was a cutting-edge research center. There was a vibe at this hospital, an energy that said: *important stuff is going on here.* Yet there was no ego. It was all about the work at University Hospital, one of the top 10 in the United States. If someone needed a new heart or kidney, this was the place to go. The case managers were concerned with one thing: taking care of people. They liked me because I followed through on what I said I was going to do. When they were too busy to talk, they let me know. When it was a slow day, we chatted. I stopped by Farrah's office on the 14th floor and she yelped with excitement at my new hairdo.

"Hey, girlfriend, I dig those hair extensions!"

"Thanks!" I beamed. "I got them last week."

"You want some of this tuna salad?"

"Yes, please. I haven't eaten all day." We talked for 20 minutes over tuna salad and crackers.

"This is delicious," I said.

"The guy downstairs made it. My buddy."

After we finished eating and catching up, Farrah gave me a referral, I went to meet the patient, then left the hospital happy.

Hospitals were definitely more fun to visit than doctor's offices. I also visited senior centers, the Alzheimer's Association, geriatric-care managers, adult daycare centers, anyone who worked with elders. My first six months in the industry, I thought I was spinning my wheels. I thought all this socializing mixed with sometimes getting doors slammed in my face, was a big waste of time. Then a prospect called and I asked, "How did you hear about us?"

"Where didn't I hear about you is the question. My doctor, my attorney, the senior center—everyone recommended your place." I was delighted; my pavement pounding was paying off.

Here is what I have learned about outside sales since my first week at The Gables, when Sharon told me to "go out":

- People will forget about you if they don't see you for a couple weeks.
- Integrity and follow-through are essential. Do what you say you are going to do.
- Positive energy is imperative.
- Clothes and jewelry matter.
- Lastly, and perhaps most importantly, people *love* cupcakes. When all else failed, I showed up with cupcakes and my phone started ringing.

One of my favorite things to do for outside marketing was to take flowers to seniors when they were in the hospital or nursing home. I did this whether they were prospects, current residents, or former residents with no hope of ever returning to our place. It gave me a reason to be at the hospital and it reminded me that my job was not a typical sales job. I wasn't selling widgets.

Mr. Williams-Morris, the man whose wife was obsessed with death, was one of those visits. He and Mrs. Williams-Morris had toured The Gables a few more times after that day we ran into the coroner. They came to a couple of our parties, but I knew they probably would never move in. Still, I stayed in touch because I liked them and I had grown attached.

One day I called their house and Mrs. Williams-Morris told me her husband was in the hospital in Ventura. He was having circulation problems related to his diabetes. I picked up some flowers and headed over to visit him.

When I arrived, Mr. Williams-Morris's face lit up. "You are the only visitor I've had this week!" he exclaimed. "My wife is not able to drive so she has to wait for the neighbor to bring her. And you know our kids are in England and don't talk to us anyway. We're 'estranged' as they say."

"Well, I am so glad I could come, then. How are you?"

"Gangrene, in my legs. It's not looking good. They want to amputate below the knee."

"I am so sorry."

"Yes, it is very unfortunate indeed. I will probably have the surgery tomorrow. I'm still debating. But let's talk about something else. How are you, my dear? It is so good of you to visit me. You really made my day walking through that door just now. What are you reading these days?"

"Well, actually I'm getting into the classics again. I'm reading Jane Austen and loving it. What are you reading?"

He held up a paperback copy of Tolstoy's *Anna Karenina,* "I never tire of him."

We talked for an hour about literature, politics, movies, and the weather. Mr. Williams-Morris was delightful and interesting as always.

"Well," I said, "I better get going—back to the grind, you know. I'll check in on you again later in the week."

"Thank you again, dear, for coming. It was so good of you. I was feeling very down and now I feel quite happy." I smiled and kissed him on the cheek. The next morning Mrs. Williams-Morris called to tell me her husband died five hours after my visit. The infection went to his blood. I was the last friend to see him and she was so grateful.

Claire, the executive director of Sunset Oaks, often spoke of the "gift of service." I never really understood the concept, that idea of getting more out of the interaction than we gave, until I worked in elder care. Visiting Mr. Williams-Morris that day, knowing I had made a positive difference right before he passed, gave me a feeling of purpose, heartbreak, and peace.

There were many times I felt that fulfillment of service, knowing I had a valuable effect on someone's life, like the time I visited Clyde Lewis at a nursing home. He was 75 and suffered from emphysema. I gave him my business card and brochure and answered his questions. He agreed to move to Eldersview when his stay at the nursing home was done. As I was leaving, something in his expression made me pause. Then I said something I didn't usually say, "Mr. Lewis, you're going to be here four more weeks. Is there anything I can do to make you more comfortable?"

"Do you know how to play Gin Rummy?"

"Yes, I used to play with my grandma when I was very young."

"Will you play with me when you have some spare time?"

"I'll pick up a deck of cards and see you tomorrow around this time. Sound good?"

I didn't have time to play cards with Clyde. I visited five to seven places a day trying to get referrals and find parking in San Francisco. I barely had time to go to the bathroom. But the look in his eyes when he asked just killed me. So, I went several times over the next month, turned off the ringer on my phone, and sat with Clyde while he lay in that hospital bed. He tried to teach me strategy to no avail. We talked about our lives, travels, and relationships. He asked about my career; I asked about his. He had been an engineer and was also a Korean War veteran.

"My dad is a Korean War vet, too," I told him, "Marine Corps."

"I'm a Marine!" he said.

"Semper Fi! I bet you celebrate that birthday every year."

"Yes ma'am, November 10th—I never miss it."

The next time I visited, Clyde asked, "So, what's your deal? Are you married, divorced, boyfriend?"

"I'm married. I love him dearly, but we have our challenges."

"Are you at least still sleeping together?"

"God, Clyde, I'm not going to talk about that with you! How about you? What's your deal?"

"I wasn't good at marriage. I've been divorced twice. I have a girlfriend. She's 20 years younger than me. I'm hoping for some conjugal visits when I get out of here."

I visited Clyde twice a week and he told me it meant a lot to him. The card games were a bright spot in my day, too. Clyde made me laugh and I actually relaxed for 30 minutes during the middle of my day. Every time I left the nursing home, I felt uplifted. I usually had at least 5 missed calls, 4 new voicemails, and 20 new emails on my phone, but I didn't care. I needed a break from the stress of trying to hit my numbers and Clyde gave me that gift.

Downtime was rare for me since the pressure to make sales was tremendous. I got my first taste of that stress at The Gables and it continued in every job after that one.

The first time I met Sofia Flores, co-owner of The Gables, we talked for about 20 minutes and when she left, Mary asked me what I thought of her. "She was pleasant enough," I replied, "but I have no doubt that woman would screw me over in a New York minute if it meant an extra buck for her."

The Gables was the Flores' only profitable property. They managed two low-income, nonprofit communities in Santa Barbara (which weren't supposed to make money) and three others in Texas and Arkansas that were complete money pits. Rather than focusing their energy on the money losers east of the Grand Canyon, they took another strategy: *squeeze as much revenue as we possibly can out of our only cash cow.* This meant raising rates for existing residents at the highest percentage possible, raising rates even higher and more frequently (every three months) for new people coming in, and cutting care staff, housekeeping, and food budgets relentlessly. When our chef, Carlos, asked for the first budget increase in three years, 25 cents per resident, per day, Sofia flatly refused. "We can't afford it," she said.

"These people are paying an average of $5,000 a month to live here," I said to Sharon, "and she can't give Carlos an extra quarter per day for their food?" Sofia also put exorbitant amounts of pressure on Sharon, Olivia, and especially me, to keep all of the rooms full. One time, Sofia wanted me to start calling the wait list when a lady went on hospice. Sharon relayed the message to me, "Just let people know the apartment will be available soon."

"If you want, you can call the wait list on that apartment, Sharon. Personally, I need to wait until the woman stops breathing and her heart stops beating."

I was so worried about empty rooms that I often found myself waking up in the middle of the night thinking: *how am I going to fill that parlor in independent living?*

One year we had an unexpected wave of losses in November and December. Fifteen residents died in less than two months. Sofia began calling Sharon every day asking how many deposits we had. Sharon, Olivia, and I put our marketing efforts into high gear, bending over backwards for every prospect.

"You want a tour at 5:30 p.m. on Christmas Eve? That sounds great! I would love to meet you there."

"Sunday at 6:30 a.m. is the only time you can come? No problem; I'll be there with donuts and coffee."

"Your mom wants to paint the apartment bubble-gum pink to match her favorite flowered bedspread? By all means, send me the paint chips and I'll have our maintenance department take care of that."

We gave tea parties, sent fliers, and made phone calls from our homes at night. We had marketing meetings twice a day. The only strategy we did not implement was to lower prices, because Sofia refused to approve that proposition.

After five months of sleepless nights and overwhelming stress, we finally reached 100 percent occupancy again. I was elated and incredibly proud of the three of us. There is an interconnectedness involved in successfully marketing an assisted living community, a team spirit. Even the best marketing director will not succeed without a strong team behind him or her.

My success at The Gables was because of Sharon, Olivia, the chef, activities director, gardener, and everyone else who worked there. About a week after reaching the 100 percent milestone, I ran into Sofia at a local fundraiser for the American Heart Association. The Gables had a booth there which I was supervising. She walked across the grass to say hello and I left the booth and walked towards her, unable to contain my excitement, "We're finally 100 percent full again, Sofia," I beamed. "We made it!"

She looked at me with pursed lips, towering over me at 5 feet, 11 inches tall, scanning the crowd, "Well, you're really the only game in town. There's no real competition for The Gables." I was dumbfounded. *No competition? We had plenty of competition.* "And, you've got a beautiful piece of property." There was a long pause while I scraped my jaw off the grass. "That's all I'm going to say," she continued in her condescending tone. "You have a beautiful piece of property. I'll just leave it at that." In that moment I decided that I would take the next decent job offer that came my way, and there had been plenty.

At every job, there was no getting away from thinking about the numbers. Someone died and we could not dwell on that fact for too long. Many times, I got the news that a resident had passed away, and my first thought was, *who do I have for that room?* I became wired that way; I had to be if I was going to keep my job. I had a colleague at a place in Ventura who got so mired in grief every time someone died that she could not move on to the next prospect, and eventually lost her job because of it.

Sometimes when a resident died at The Gables, my office mate, John, joked saying, "Cha-ching! More commission for Liz. Another bed to fill."

"It's not that way, John. A death means more pressure for me. Plus, I actually liked Mabel."

When I was in management, one of my marketers lamented, "I had three move-ins this week, Liz, and all three have fallen in the night. One died and the other two are in nursing homes now. Three in, three out. My census is dwindling. Is it legal to bubble-wrap people?" I conjured an image of the three new residents taped up in bubble wrap like crystal vases.

The nursing facilities also worried about their census. One day, I called the social worker at the skilled nursing facility (SNF) down the road and asked what time our new resident Lynette Kinsley would be transported over.

"What time is the least convenient for you?" the usually jovial guy asked. At first, I thought I had heard him wrong or that he was kidding. But his tone sounded malicious. I let out a nervous laugh and said nothing. "I'm not joking," he continued. "I am very unhappy with you guys right now. I had three more weeks of Medicare days on her." I sat there stunned. *Medicare days,* I thought, *oh yeah, red meat for nursing homes.*

"Our nurse assessed her and she's ready to move to assisted living," I said. When I had visited Lynette the previous week, she was in tears because she hated being at the SNF.

"Well, *our* nurse evaluated her and said she needs more time here and more physical therapy and isn't ready to go to your place."

Lynette needed more physical therapy but it could be done by home health at Casa Amanecer. She had lost her motivation at the SNF. When they told her she had to stay three more weeks, they might as well have told her she needed three more years. Lynette called me in tears. "I can't stay here three more weeks, Liz. It's so depressing. I just want to move to Casa Amanecer. I am going to stop my dialysis." If Lynette stopped dialysis, she would be dead in a week.

Lynette's daughter called me and begged to have our nurse re-assess her, which I arranged. Our nurse, Tamara, said Lynette was good to go. She even spoke privately with the SNF nurse, who agreed she was ready. The SNF nurse secretly told Tamara that she thought it was deplorable they were keeping her for financial reasons, those precious Medicare days.

Medicare pays for a skilled nursing facility, provided that the person has spent at least three days in the hospital. Medicare paid four times the rate that Medi-Cal paid and three times what private insurance paid. The day a person converted to Medi-Cal dollars, the SNF wanted them out of there, regardless of their condition. Medicare will pay for up to 100 days or until the resident plateaus. If they are making progress with their physical therapy or are still in need of skilled nursing care, Medicare will pay.

That is why so many SNFs do evaluations that claim the person still needs to be in skilled care, even when the person doesn't need it. Assisted livings, of course, want their residents back because they do not want to lose the rent money. This causes tension. Usually, the senior prefers to go back to assisted living. I understood the importance of the bottom line. I worked on commission. I loved money as much as the next guy. But I also understood the need for basic human decency.

The social worker continued his rant, "I thought we were supposed to work together on these things." *Not work together to lie to people*, I thought. He was angry about lost revenue for his building and for himself. His quarterly bonus was directly tied to Medicare days. My chest tightened, but I bit my tongue because I needed referrals from him. I ended the conversation as politely as I could, replaced the receiver on the phone, and left my office in search of the nearest exit. I needed a moment to breathe and regroup. In the stairwell, I ran into Tamara who noticed I was upset.

"What's the matter, Liz?"

"Sometimes I hate this job," I exclaimed. It was an unusual outburst for me. I usually kept my cool publicly and saved the outbursts until I got home.

Lynette Kinsley's daughter threw a fit with the SNF and they discharged her "against medical advice." Lynette moved into Casa Amanecer the next week. She was a "full assist" when she arrived, meaning she needed two people to transfer her from her wheelchair to the bed or toilet. She needed wheelchair escorts to meals, incontinence care, and someone to bathe and dress her.

Still, she was ecstatic to be at Casa Amanecer and so motivated to get better, that within two months she was getting dressed and walking to the dining room on her own. I ran into her one day and said, "Lynette, you amaze me. I am so proud of you!"

"I'm proud of me, too," she beamed.

I stopped doing marketing visits to that SNF, deciding I really did not want referrals from that social worker. I preferred to increase my efforts elsewhere to make up for the loss of business from him. I found out months later that the same SNF had a lady who had lived there a year and a half with no medical need. Her Medicare days had run out and she was paying their exorbitantly high private rate because they convinced her she needed to be there when she really did not.

I saw many examples of healthcare companies deceiving seniors in an effort to make a profit. One of the worst I saw was private health insurance companies convincing seniors to sign over their Medicare benefits. Medicare is the best insurance a person could have. It usually pays far more than private insurance for hospital stays, nursing home stays, home healthcare, outpatient physical therapy, and doctor visits.

Healthcare providers actually fight for Medicare patients, but many seniors don't know this. They fall for the scam, they sign over their benefits and then the private insurance company gets the majority of their Medicare dollars and the senior gets subpar medical care. Now that they have private insurance, the hospitals want them out sooner. Patients have to fight with the insurance company to get the surgery or medical equipment they need. Home health companies and doctors do not want them as a patient.

Similar to SNFs and insurance companies, assisted living facilities have their share of questionable practices, such as the "community fees" they charge. The charges usually range from $750 to $2,000. When people ask marketing directors what the fee covers, they say it is the fee to get the apartment ready, process the paperwork at the corporate office, etc. It's a false narrative. Years ago, nobody had community fees. Then someone got the idea as a way to drive more revenue and now everyone has them. At Casa Amanecer, senior management told me I could waive the community fee at my discretion as a negotiating tool to get a move-in.

"Why do we even have the fee in the first place, then?" I asked. "Either it is a legitimate charge or it isn't." One time I gave a tour to a guy named Mr. Clothier who asked, "What's this community fee?" He was already living in an assisted living and had paid their $2,000 community fee when he moved in there. He didn't like their food and was shopping around for a new place to live. I gave Mr. Clothier the usual line about how it covered the paperwork, getting the physician's report done, etc. "They have all that," he replied. "Just call them up. I've got to pay *you* $2,000 to make a goddamn phone call?" Mr. Clothier was right. That was exactly what I planned to do: call the marketing director, who was a friend of mine, and get the paperwork from her.

"I've got an idea," he continued. "How about I make the phone call and keep my $2,000?"

"Sounds good," I said. I liked his style.

While doing a market survey I once called a place that charged a $25,000 community fee! They were 100 percent full with a waiting list. I asked what that fee went towards. I was curious to hear the answer this marketer would come up with. "Well, we have a nurse seven days a week and we have a doctor who is our medical director and sees patients here."

"Do you pay the doctor for seeing your residents?"

"No, Medicare pays the doctor."

"So, the community fee doesn't pay for the doctor?"

"That's right."

"What does it cover, then?"

"Well, we use it to keep the grounds up, building maintenance, things like that."

"Okay, does it cover anything else?"

"The paperwork, getting the apartment ready for move-in."

It covered the same thing the community fee at every other place covered. The honest answer would be, "We are charging a $25,000 community fee because we can."

It was always about revenue. When I moved into management, I was the one pushing marketers to bring in the income. I had conversations with them about moving residents from assisted living to memory care when assisted living was full. I pressured the executive directors to have conversations with families of residents who were showing signs of early dementia. It was all part of the people shuffle to keep the building full.

I was laser-focused on filling beds, increasing profits, and keeping my job. I sometimes lost sight of the fact that these were people's lives we were dealing with, and that maybe moving mom from assisted living to memory care would be really hard on her and her family.

Under pressure from corporate, the nurse and executive director often had conversations like these with families:

"Your mom is a fall risk. You can either hire a 24-hour caregiver or move her to a skilled nursing facility."

"Your dad is not cooperating with taking his medications. If he does not comply, we'll have to give you a 30-day notice to move him out."

It all depended on census. If the building was full, residents who were a fall risk or wander risk or who had a wound that was borderline skilled-nursing level had to go. If you are unable to bear weight and need two people to transfer you, sorry, our license will not permit you to stay here. Oh, we cannot do hospice because we don't have a nurse to do the morphine injections. (Even though the morphine is administered orally and done by the hospice agency.) But if the census was low, well then, suddenly that wound didn't look so bad, it was fine to be in our building on hospice, fully bedridden. We'll just write a letter to the state and get an exception.

Executive directors told people all the time, "Your mother has to get physical therapy and be able to transfer from her bed to the toilet or she cannot come back to our place after her hospital stay," or, "We already have two residents on hospice and that is our limit according to the state regulations. It's not me, it's my license requirement." When a more honest statement would be, "Hospice is a lot of work and I just don't want to deal with it if I don't have to. I do not have the staff for it and I don't want to spend the money to hire the staff."

Assisted living is often more about profit than it is about doing the right thing. The rent increases and room shuffles were a far cry from the warm and fuzzies these families got when the facility was trying to get their deposit check. Once they had moved in, management sometimes did not care as much about them. Suddenly the people who were so compassionately trying to get dad's deposit are now trying to figure out how to give him the least amount of services possible for his $5,000 a month. I stress the word "sometimes" because there are fantastic companies out there who truly focus on giving great care, but they are the exception.

When I came across an assisted living community where compassion permeated the entire place, it was usually because the executive director was an extraordinary person. She found a way to balance the budget, keep her job, and still provide great care. She also had to deal with licensing requirements, such as residents who were fall risks or not taking their medications. She had a corporate office telling her how many caregivers she could have on each shift, what she could pay them, and how much she could spend on food. Executive directors were in a predicament. They had to toe the line, yet there was a point at which they could and should push back at corporate in order to advocate for their residents and staff. I worked with some who took the right stand and others who didn't.

Nancy was the executive director at Casa Amanecer when I moved in a resident named Harvey Kennedy. Harvey was an 85-year-old World War II veteran who had lived in San Francisco all his life and raised three responsible, kind children. I felt a fondness for Harvey the minute I met him on his first tour. There was something so sweet about the way he spoke of his children and the gentle way they spoke to him. The day Harvey moved in, I stopped by his apartment with a welcome gift and marveled at his Army medals, his Purple Heart, the pictures of his grandkids. Harvey had tears in his eyes when he showed me the picture of his wife, Edith, who had been gone 15 years.

Harvey rented a one-bedroom apartment in assisted living and paid top dollar for it. He was also paying for Level Four assistance, our highest and most expensive level of care. His daughter, Elaine, said to me, "I want my dad to have the best care possible. I don't mind what it costs. We will find a way to pay for it." The family was not wealthy.

Harvey had a strong, clear mind, but was physically frail and wheelchair-bound. He needed help getting to the bathroom. He could hold his urine for 15 to 20 minutes, but no longer. So, when he woke with the urge at 5:00 a.m., he rang his call button and waited for the caregivers to come. Forty-five minutes often went by and when the caregiver finally arrived, it was too late. Harvey would wet the bed. The morning shift was understaffed. Plain and simple.

Harvey was a proud man and felt embarrassed that they had to change his sheets almost every day. Finally, a few weeks after moving in, he reluctantly spoke with his daughter. Elaine complained to Nancy about the long wait time and thus, we found ourselves discussing this matter at the weekly Care Plan meeting. In attendance were myself (marketing director), Sister Louise (chaplain), Tamara (nurse), Valerie (assisted living director), and Nancy (executive director and our boss). We went down the list of residents, discussing medications, upcoming surgeries, and care needs. When we got to Harvey Kennedy, Nancy said, "His daughter complained. She said it's taking the caregivers too long to get there when he rings his call button."

"How long is it taking?" I asked.

"She says he waits 45 minutes, sometimes an hour. I think she's exaggerating," Nancy replied. She got up and walked to the copy room to get the printout of the computerized call log. It kept a record of what time someone rang their button and what time the caregiver arrived to re-set it. When she came back with the logs, we checked and sure enough it was taking an average of 45 to 50 minutes.

"Maybe we need to add more caregivers on that shift," Tamara said.

Nancy snapped, "We're *not* adding more staff on the morning shift. It is not in our budget."

"But we just had five new residents move in, all paying Level Two or higher of care in addition to their rent," I retorted. "Our revenue has gone up significantly, but we haven't added more staff."

"It is not enough to justify more caregivers. Mr. Kennedy just needs to wear Depends. It's nothing to be ashamed of. I had the conversation with my own father recently and it is no big deal. I explained to him that sometimes, older people have trouble holding their bladder and that's why we have these products."

"But, he's *not* incontinent," I said. "He can hold it. He just can't hold it for 45 minutes. I don't think I could hold it for 45 minutes and I'm 37 years old." I immediately felt the tension rise in the room. No one said a word. My workmates looked down and started re-arranging the papers in front of them as Nancy glared at me and said, "Mr. Kennedy will wear Depends. We are not adding more caregivers to the morning shift and I don't want to hear another word about it. Valerie, will you speak with Harvey's daughter, please, and explain to her?" *Typical Nancy. Didn't do a damn thing, especially dirty work. That's right, make Valerie have the conversation.*

I was fuming, but years of biting my tongue had gleaned me a great deal of professional success. I wasn't going to start blowing my top and walking off jobs now.

That night, I vented to Dave, "Nancy wants the guy to wear a diaper and he doesn't even need it. No respect for his dignity. No putting herself in his shoes. No asking herself how *she* would feel if someone told *her* to wear a diaper when she didn't need one."

"That's bullshit," Dave said.

"You're damn right it is. No one deserves this. This guy is a decorated veteran, a sweet man, a devoted father. And he's paying six fucking thousand dollars a month to live there! It's infuriating. It's neglect to make that guy wear Depends and I think I am going to call the ombudsman or Adult Protective Services or licensing on this one. I never thought I would be in a position to report abuse at my own community, especially by the executive director, but I am really tempted on this one."

"Won't they know it's you?" Dave asked.

"Probably. It would be pretty obvious given the heated conversation we had at the care conference this morning. But I don't know what else to do. This is just so unacceptable." I would probably get fired if I called licensing and Nancy found out about it. Then again, maybe this was worth getting fired over.

Dave agreed I should do something, then I slept on it. The next morning, I knew how I would handle the situation. I covertly called Harvey's daughter from my cell phone in my car. "Elaine," I said, "when Valerie comes to talk with you, don't stand for this." Elaine was no weakling and she pushed back. When she demanded to see the call logs and staffing ratios, Valerie backed down. We added another caregiver to the morning shift and Nancy never found out about my conversation with Elaine.

When I got to the corporate management level, I thought I would have more power to make a difference about these things. Instead, I just went to a lot of meetings. People were flown in from all over the country for these gatherings. Money was spent on food, audio-visual equipment, conference rooms, hotel rooms, rental cars, and entertainment. With every company, our agenda was always focused on this question:

How can we make MORE money?

We put our heads together to come up with answers. Led by people higher than myself in the organization, we sat around for hours saying things like: Let's look at our profit and loss statements. How can we fill these buildings? How can we cut our labor cost by five percent? (*No matter that the caregivers were already making less than a living wage.*) How can we increase our revenue per unit by 15 percent? Let's look at all the apartments with views or close to the dining room. Could we charge a premium for those? Maybe a dollar a day more? (*Old people have a hard time walking down that long hallway to the dining room. They will pay more to be closer.*)

If we increase our medication charge $25 per month and multiply that by 30 communities with an average of 65 residents, that brings an extra $48,750 to the bottom line. (*People have to take their medication, right? So, they'll pay the increase.*)

These were the conversations we had at corporate. It was a given that we would increase residents' rent seven or eight percent each year. Our costs did not always go up seven percent, but that's the line we told executive directors to deliver. They were the ones who had to sit across from family members and residents and deliver the news. Family members were usually angry at increases, but they were in a tough spot. They did not want the stress of moving their 90-year-old mom to a different place. So, they paid and paid and paid.

We also increased market rates (the price new people moving in paid) every year. These usually went up 10 to 15 percent. The marketers got the unenviable task of delivering this news, "Well, when you toured six months ago the price for the one bedroom was *this*, but now it's gone up to *this*."

Those revenue increases were a given. These meetings were focused on finding new revenue streams, increasing census, and doing a better job at sales. I did not go to a *single* meeting that asked:

How can we better care for our residents? or

How can we improve job satisfaction for our staff?

I live in a capitalist society. I get it. I am a marketing geek and I read sales books for fun in my spare time. I love making money. But *still*, I wondered, couldn't we spend 10 percent of the meeting discussing ways to improve quality of life for our residents? Was that too much to ask? Weren't we losing sight of the focus that made us love assisted living in the first place? Wasn't our field all about *caring* for people? Ironically, I think it would actually help sales if we focused more on resident care and less on money. More people would want to move to our community. Suddenly, this "feel good" business I had gotten into wasn't feeling very good anymore.

When I worked for the nonprofit, corporate did actually spend a significant chunk of time looking at their mission and values, asking themselves, how are we doing with that? At the for-profits, the mission and values were something on our wall or website, something for marketing, not something we actually implemented. At the nonprofit, Casa Amanecer, the priorities were discussed in this order:

1. Are we living our mission and values?
2. Are the residents and staff happy?
3. Are we making money?

Still, despite this commitment to the mission and values, Nancy got away with exploiting staff and residents. Still her bonus was tied to net revenue.

Almost every assisted living company had a mission statement. Here are a few I came across:

Our Family Is Committed to Yours

Helping Seniors and Their Families Live Happier and Healthier Lives

A Unique Family of Retirement Communities Offering Vibrant Senior Living

Providing Exceptional Senior Living for Over 30 Years

We're the People Who Make Life Better

The Art of Living Well. Price Is What You Pay. Value Is What We Deliver.

Our Mission is to Champion Quality of Life for All Seniors

When I worked for Hale Senior Living as a regional sales director, our company stock was traded on the New York Stock Exchange. Hale owned 450 assisted living properties across the country. "Must show growth," was the company mantra. Every quarter we had to show growth in rent per unit, average daily units, occupancy, and profit. No matter that it was 2009 and the housing market had tanked. Seniors either could not sell their homes or were moving in with their adult children so that the kids wouldn't lose their homes.

Corporate did not want to hear that. If 10 people died or moved out of a building one month, that building had better move in at least 11 people to show a positive net gain. Going negative in occupancy was not an option if we wanted to keep our jobs.

Along with the regional director of operations and the regional nurse, I managed a territory of 11 buildings in Northern California for Hale. We had 33 direct reports and many more indirect reports. I received an average of 20 phone calls and 100 emails every day.

When I started, ours was the lowest-performing region in the country. However, quarter after quarter, our region and the company showed an increase in occupancy and revenue. We turned our region around. Our stock price went up while our competitors' went down. We acquired properties while others went out of business. The CEO was downright giddy on conference calls.

The company's mission statement was: "Our Family Is Committed to Yours," but our regional team changed it privately to a more truthful motto, "Our Family Is Committed to Wall Street."

In all the positions I held during my assisted living career, my life revolved around the numbers. When I was a marketing director, it meant I had to stay at work until 9:00 p.m. if there was a move-in or a hot tour. No matter how late I stayed, I still had to be back at my desk at 8:30 the next morning. When I was a regional sales director and a vice president, my world revolved around month-end and quarter-end. At Hale, that meant getting every single move-in I could get up until 7:00 p.m. on the last day of the month. Seven p.m. was the time the corporate office closed and was the official end of the month.

I felt tremendous pressure to get those two or three more to push me over the hump and make my monthly quota and I transferred that pressure onto the people under me. I always spent that final day of the month frantically calling, emailing, and texting people above and below me.

One month, the last day fell on a Saturday. It was October 31st, Halloween, and as usual, I started early with the calls and emails back and forth between the corporate office and the marketers and executive directors at my 11 properties. I was driving sales, cutting deals, doing everything I could to make sure my region had a net gain in occupancy. Failure was not an option. Dave heard me on the phone and said, "It sounds like you're running a car dealership in there, Liz."

On this particular Saturday, there was one move-in from my Vacaville property where the person had paid the first month's rent, but the executive director, Ryan, forgot to fax the paperwork to corporate. So, it would not count for October. The paperwork was locked in Ryan's office and he was the only one with the key. It was 6:00 p.m. when I found out about this and Ryan had left at 5:30 to take his kids trick-or-treating. My boss, Lee Katsaros, the senior vice president of sales, called me excitedly for the eighth time that day, "How are your numbers looking, Liz?"

Lee was a tall, broad shouldered, handsome Greek man. He was only a couple of years older than me and had worked his way up in the organization over 14 years. He had a great sense of humor. Whenever Lee visited my region, I learned something new about marketing. When we did sales trainings, he usually ended the day by singing a Tony Bennett song, lounge-singer-style, walking from table to table and cracking us all up. I liked Lee.

"I'm at 56 right now, Lee. One short of my goal."

"Can you find one more, Liz? I know you can. You always pull through. You're our star."

"Well, Vacaville has one more but the paperwork is locked in the executive director's office and he's the only one with the key. It will have to count for November."

"Can you call him?"

"No, he's left for the day to take his kids trick-or-treating." *Long silence.* I wanted to make my goal. I wanted to make commission. I wanted to make my boss happy.

"So, can you call him?" Lee asked again. Another long silence.

I thought about it, then said, "No, Lee, I'm not going to call him. You can call him if you want to, but I'm not going to." Asking Ryan, who worked 60 hours a week, to come back from Halloween with his kids—I just wasn't going to do it.

I hung up the phone feeling defeated. It was 6:30 p.m. and there was no way I was going to make my goal. Then, it happened. A miracle. An email from my marketer in Sacramento popped up: 'I got one more for you, Liz!'

I dialed her number, "Oh my God, Brenda, this is great! Where did you find it?"

"I got the call this morning from the family. Dad is at a hospital in San Francisco. They want him to come here when he discharges tomorrow. I offered them a discount if they start paying rent today. I hope that's okay? I didn't call you because I didn't want to lose them."

"Yes, yes, of course. You did the right thing. This is awesome—it will count for October. Where is the family now?" I was talking at rapid-fire speed and so was Brenda.

"They're on their way here to sign the contract and bring me a check."

"Fantastic! Fax it to corporate as soon as you can. I'm calling them now to give them a heads-up. Bye."

I called the corporate office then emailed and texted Lee, who was thrilled. Adrenaline was pumping through my body and I could barely think. I had three other properties calling with final paperwork on move-ins that had been sealed earlier in the day.

Brenda and I frantically got the last sale processed. Number 57. I had made my goal for the month. I ran downstairs and hugged Dave. "Oh my God, I made it! Let's go out to dinner. I am so fried, I can barely breathe."

Dave and I went to our favorite restaurant and we were an hour into our meal before I finally decompressed.

We went to sleep and the next morning, Sunday, when I could finally sleep late, I sat straight up in bed at 5:00 a.m. and thought of the guy, move-in number 57. *Where* is he now? Did he make it from San Francisco to Sacramento? Is he okay? Is he even appropriate for assisted living? We didn't do an assessment. I turned to Dave, "Oh my God, Dave, I forgot that guy was a person."

"What guy?" Dave said groggily.

"My last move-in yesterday. Number 57."

"The dude at the hospital here?"

"Yes. I forgot I was dealing with *people,* Dave." We were silent for a few minutes while I let that reality sink in and then I jumped out of bed, "Shit, I need to get on the phone and fix this."

In my desperate desire to get the last move-in, I had cut corners. Nobody went and visited this man at the hospital (which I could have done, since he was in San Francisco, but I was too caught up in the phone and email frenzy). No one had evaluated his needs or physically laid eyes on him, all of which were requirements of our license, not to mention *the right thing to do.*

By 10:00 a.m., I had sorted out the situation by putting a Band-Aid on it. I called our nurse who came in and assessed him at the Sacramento property, a day late. I had crossed a line that day that I did not like. I felt awful about myself. I had succumbed to the pressure and compromised my integrity.

At Hale, I worked 80 hours a week. I was on an airplane every other week and the pressure never let up. My hair fell out in big clumps. I had just turned 40 and the hair I had left was rapidly turning gray. I wept regularly. My doctor did blood tests and an exam and told me, "You are physically healthy. This is 100 percent stress."

It had only been a year since I started the job and I felt chewed up and spit out. I went to a weeklong manager's conference at headquarters. The purpose was for us to bond with each other and get fired up about driving profits. On day three, the chief operating officer stood up in the front of the room and said, "If you are looking for work/life balance at this company, you're screwed. I want you to drink the Kool-Aid. I want you to live and breathe Hale."

When he asked the room of 150 people how many had taken a vacation in the past few years, only four hands went up. Mine and my friend, Bonnie, were two of those hands.

The economy sucked and we were all supposed to be grateful we still had our six-figure incomes. The people above me, below me, and at my level had so much work piled on them each day that the only way to keep our heads above water was to work 12- to 15-hour days.

On one of our weekly regional sales calls with Lee Katsaros, he announced, "We are going to start having you guys do conference calls with your properties at 9:00 every Saturday morning. That way the manager on duty can report any tours or marketing activities for the day. We need to keep people focused on driving sales on the weekends, too." No one said a word.

"Lee," I finally piped in, "are you kidding me?"

"Well, Liz, I knew this wouldn't be a popular idea, but we really need to move the needle at these properties."

"But, Lee," I continued. "I already work every weekend just trying to catch up on emails and paperwork. Now I have to do mandatory conference calls every Saturday?"

"Yes."

We were all angry about the calls, but of course, we did them because we wanted to keep our jobs. Most Saturdays, by the time I finished those calls and all my other catch-up work, it was 6:00 p.m.

Some little girls dream of being teachers, doctors, or movie stars. When I was young, I dreamt of being a businesswoman. When people asked "What do you want to be when you grow up?" I responded, "I want to carry a briefcase, wear suits, and go to business meetings. I want to be the boss, fly on airplanes, and stay in fancy hotels. I want to give speeches, make decisions, and make lots of money. I want to go to power lunches."

So here I was, living my "dream." Co-workers left and right of me were ending up in the hospital. One vice president of sales, a 40-year-old woman, went to the hospital for elevated adrenaline levels. A 38-year-old regional director of operations had a heart attack. A 42-year-old regional director of sales went to the hospital for exhaustion. These were just the examples I knew of in California. I am sure it was happening all over the country. Hale's response was always to give the person a week off and then expect them to get right back at it. They hired the best and the brightest people they could find, then churned and burned through them.

Meanwhile, the CEO of the company did a news segment about his running club at the corporate office, to demonstrate how his company was committed to "health." I watched the segment of him jogging on a city street and thought, *Huh?* Everyone in his organization was falling apart and this guy was on television talking about health, fitness, and a balanced life?

I tried pushing back and setting boundaries. I even said "No" once to a trip to Los Angeles. I got my hand slapped and was told I had to go on the trip. I had meltdowns that frightened Dave. He became collateral damage to my stress. He reacted with anger, not towards Hale, but towards me. "You wanted to be an executive," he said. "Well, this is what executives do. They work long hours. They deal with a lot of pressure. That's why they get paid so much."

"Well, I didn't realize that," I snapped back. "I don't want to be an executive anymore!"

"We're kind of screwed now," he said.

It was true; I was our only paycheck and Dave was working on a house we had bought as an investment. We had stuck our necks out in the hopes of retiring early. All I had to do was keep this job for three more years. One of my dear friends and spiritual advisors, an 85-year-old man named George said to me, "Get the fuck out of there, Liz. It is killing you." Meanwhile, my husband was saying to me, "Quit being a victim. Buck up. You're stronger than this. You can do this job."

I listened to George. I began looking around and when another large assisted living company came calling, I met with them. They had gotten my name from a recruiter. They had a regional sales position open. I interviewed with Kyla, the vice president of sales and marketing. We had breakfast at a cute hotel in San Francisco on a Saturday morning in April. I had just returned from a weeklong conference at the corporate office. I sat across from Kyla, who had pink cheeks and nails. She had good energy. She was warm and witty. I believed I would enjoy working with her. At the end of our two-hour breakfast, she asked, "So, are you interested in the position?"

"Well," I said, "the thing is, Kyla, I really like *you*, but Creekstone is a big publicly held company run by a bunch of white men. Why should I believe it would be any different than where I am now?" Senior living employees were predominantly women, but like most companies in the U.S., those at the very highest level were middle-aged white men.

She seemed taken aback by my directness. Then replied, "Well, it's a great company. We have people who have been with us for 15 years."

"Oh, we've got those, too. Plenty of them. Guys and gals who drank the Kool-Aid. I'm just afraid this job would be a case of going from the frying pan to the fire. I thought the opportunity was at least worth exploring, though. I do have some friends who say they like working for your company."

"What's important to you, Liz?"

"Work/life balance. I don't think it exists in corporate America." My mother-in-law, a vice president of a bank, was forever chastising me for bringing this up in job interviews.

"Okay," Kyla said, "I'll be in touch."

I was surprised when their recruiting department called me the following week for a second interview. "Kyla liked your candor," she said.

I had two more interviews with Creekstone, then the person who was going to vacate the regional sales position decided to stay put. I was not disappointed. I knew they wouldn't offer me any more balance than my current job. I might as well stay with Hale, the devil I knew, until an opportunity with less travel and less stress came up. My region was now among the top performers in the country and Lee, my boss, was happy with me.

I was with him one night in Rocklin, California, having dinner, when he got the call from Bridgette, my counterpart in Los Angeles. "Bridgette gave her notice," he said when he came back to the table. "I'm devastated. I don't know how I'm going to replace her."

"It's a big loss," I agreed. Bridgette had told me earlier that week she was going to quit. The job was taking a toll on her family and she rarely saw her kids. "I've learned a lot from her. She trained me my first month on the job," I continued.

"You know, Liz, I would hate to lose you. You're actually my strongest regional. I want to make sure you're happy."

"I enjoy the work and my team, Lee, but I have no life. I want to see my husband and my friends and family more. I want to go to the gym. Maybe take a cooking class."

"I know. The hours are long," he said nonchalantly.

"Yes, they ARE long," I said tersely. "Take today for instance. I have been physically with *you*, my boss, for 14 hours now."

"I know." Lee said he understood, but after that night, nothing changed. I don't think there was much Lee could do about the situation, even if he wanted to. Wall Street was not going to stop putting pressure on us. Still, I was honest with him. Why was he so surprised when I quit six months later? "I feel like someone cut my arm off, Liz," he lamented.

The hardest part of leaving Hale was saying goodbye to the people I had met at every level. They were knowledgeable and talented. We gelled quickly, bonding and supporting one another through the hardship and struggle. I just couldn't take the stress anymore.

At Elder Care Communities, where I worked as vice president of sales and marketing, I experienced a different sort of stress, the kind which comes from working for a dysfunctional organization. The company was falling apart almost from the day I arrived. A year into my job, we were behind on payroll taxes, mortgage payments, food supply bills, utilities, and many other debts at the company's 22 properties. The CEO was a charismatic guy. He believed in me and had given me opportunities that most companies would not give to a woman. I loved him for that but still, I wondered, where was all the money going? In the midst of putting out fires, I tried to keep sales going because we desperately needed the revenue.

One afternoon, I called Dennis, the executive director at our property in Pasadena, California. "How's it going?"

"I'm here," he responded flatly.

"So, how are sales going?"

"How are *sales* going? How are SALES going?! Our bills aren't getting paid. That's how sales are going. My lights got turned off today, my produce didn't get delivered, 10 employees had paychecks bounce, and the elevator company removed the motherboard from the third floor because we didn't pay their bill. That's how sales are going."

"I'm sorry, Dennis. I am working on it. I promise you. So, we are running this sales contest," I said meekly. I felt like a complete idiot trying to get these people to concentrate on sales but I had to do it.

"We won't be participating in that, Liz."

I didn't argue with him. It was hard to command respect when the corporate office wasn't holding up our end of the deal. I wondered did the CEO have a gambling problem? Or a drug problem? What the hell was going on? Where was the money going? I asked many times but never got a clear answer.

It was difficult to lead under those circumstances and I wanted to be a good leader. Throughout my career, I have had ineffective, narcissistic, stupid, and abusive bosses. I've had bosses that lied, cheated, and publicly demeaned people. I always swore that if I ever found myself in a position of power, I would not abuse it. When I became the boss, I would remember all the smart, kind, supportive, and inspiring bosses I'd had, and the one thing they all had in common was this: they led by example.

I imagined the type of boss I would want to have and then I tried to be that. I kept my word. I aimed to give people five pieces of positive reinforcement for every one bit of criticism, knowing that positive reinforcement is often a more powerful motivator. I acknowledged people publicly for their achievements. I recognized when someone was burned out and told them to take a vacation before they asked for it. Sometimes I had to insist they take time off, like the time I arrived at the Fairfield property and found my marketing director, Sandy, talking a mile a minute, telling me about all the tours, move-ins and phone calls she needed to handle in the next hour.

"Sandy, take a breath."

"All right, it's just I have this booth at the senior fair tomorrow and I have two move-ins today and four tours and—"

"That's great, I really appreciate the fantastic results you are getting here. I want you to leave at noon tomorrow after your senior fair. Go home and spend the afternoon with your daughter."

"But there's no way I can do that. Adam and Bill won't let me." Adam was the executive director and Bill was the other marketer.

"Well, I'm their boss, so I guarantee they will let you."

"I can't, I have too much to do. What if they tell me I have to stay and do it?"

"Then you tell them 'No.' Remember, Sandy, 'No' is a complete sentence."

Mostly, I tried to make work fun for the people who reported to me. I hosted bowling days and scavenger hunts with the whole team. I held contests like the "Wheel Spin," where anyone who got three move-ins in one week got to spin the wheel and win a prize. Everyone called into the conference call, I put them on speakerphone then spun the prize wheel I had in my office. They could hear it clicking as it was about to land on a prize. "You won theater tickets!" I would exclaim. Or a spa day, or a box of See's candy, or a Starbucks gift card. My team loved those calls.

Of course, I wasn't always fun. I expected a lot of myself and those who worked with and for me. Fire in the belly and a sense of urgency were things that salespeople either had or they did not. It could not be taught and I got frustrated when people didn't have it. Maintenance people rarely had it. When I worked at The Gables, the maintenance department became the bane of my existence. John was the director of the department and managed two employees, Mario and Pete. John was my office mate and friend and an intelligent and funny guy. Yet, when it came to getting his department to do their job, my frustration level mounted daily. It was beyond irritating trying to get them to prepare apartments for move-in. I regularly complained to Sharon, "Why are they allowed to just blatantly refuse to do their job? I can't refuse to do *my* job!" Sharon would shrug and say, "That's just maintenance guys, Liz. They're like that everywhere."

If I gave maintenance three days to complete the move-in punch list, they complained endlessly and got half the list done. Sometimes I even had to call new residents and postpone their move-in date because the apartment wasn't ready. It was the same outcome if I gave maintenance a month's notice. I had worked hard to get deposits on those apartments, to get all the paperwork and doctor reports for the new resident, spent endless hours on the phone with family members to seal the deal, and John's team couldn't just touch up the paint and replace a few switch plates?

I tried everything with them: begging and pleading, whining, even reverse psychology, pretending I didn't care if the apartment got done. I did the Buddhist "loving kindness" meditation every morning for two weeks holding each of them in mind and reciting their names: *may Mario be free of suffering. May John be happy. May Pete have wellness and wellbeing, may he be love and kindness.*

I practiced patience and positive reinforcement, praising them for any tiny thing they actually accomplished. I asked in two languages: Spanish and English. I baked them my famous chocolate Kahlua bundt cake. They appreciated the cake, but nothing changed.

It was apartment 11 that pushed me over the edge after a year of this plight. Apartment 11 was a spacious, well-lit, ground-floor, one-bedroom surrounded by magnolia and ginkgo trees. It was one of the best apartments we had in terms of size and location, but it needed repairs. Its occupants, Mr. and Mrs. Patterson, didn't like anyone coming in to fix things.

The Pattersons had lived in apartment 11 for eight years and were going to be moving out, but they did not know it yet. Mrs. Patterson had progressed considerably in her dementia, well beyond the point of being "pleasantly confused," and they needed to move from independent to assisted living. The Pattersons wanted to stay in apartment 11. However, Sharon and our nurse, Joan, had decided, along with the Patterson's children, that the move was going to happen. The question was, when to tell them?

The Gables was completely full and I was under tremendous pressure to keep it that way. This meant I needed to find a way to rent the apartment *before* the Pattersons moved out. So, at Sharon's direction, I did something risky. While Mr. and Mrs. Patterson were having lunch one day, I snuck in and showed their apartment to Bill and Martha, a couple on the waiting list. I nervously scurried the new couple through, pointing out the large windows and gorgeous views, all the while holding my breath and hoping the Pattersons would not return from lunch.

Bill and Martha loved the apartment and put down a deposit that same day. It was quite the sales coup: the room was rented and the Pattersons still had not even been told they were moving. "Zero lost revenue days" is what we call that in assisted living. Sharon was thrilled when I told her the news. Two weeks later, the Pattersons moved to the assisted living Cottages. Mrs. Patterson didn't fully understand what was happening. Her husband fought the move but ultimately succumbed since Sharon and Joan gave him no other choice. Their assisted living spot was much smaller and the communal dining room was missing their peers they had known for years. I felt relieved that I had rented apartment 11 and at the same time glum that the Patterson's had to leave the apartment they loved in independent living.

We now had six weeks until Martha and Bill's move-in date, plenty of time to do the renovations. I gave John the checklist of what needed to be done on the apartment and began working on my own list of action items: doctor reports from Bill and Martha, contract, tuberculosis tests. Martha and Bill were wonderful about everything. They even came by three days before the move-in date to pay their rent. Each week leading up to move-in day, I went over to the apartment to check on the progress. Every time, *nothing* had been done. I patiently and continually asked John, Mario, and Pete to get the apartment ready.

Now here we were, three days before move-in, I had four other pending move-ins and I was exhausted. I went by apartment 11 one last time, bracing myself in the hopes that something had been completed. The carpet, paint, light fixtures—I would be thrilled with anything. I walked in, stood in the living room, and did a 360-degree turn with my hands on my hips. Not a single thing had been done.

I stormed out of the apartment and stomped up to the assisted living Cottages where I knew the team was working that day. I pushed open the door of apartment 7 and there stood Mario, Pete, and a new guy. "Hey," Pete said to me, smiling and casually looking up.

"Hey," I responded, "who do I have to fuck to get apartment 11 done?" The new guy dropped his hammer, Mario jerked his head around, and all three stood there staring at me. Tentatively, Mario raised his hand. "Don't be a smart ass, Mario. Just get the damn apartment done!" I turned on my heels and walked out. Apartment 11 was finished three days later. "*Why*," I asked John, "why did I have to get mad in order to get you guys to act?"

"Because that is how maintenance guys are. You shocked us. We've only seen the sweet side of you. Those guys had never heard you say the 'F' word!"

"This is bullshit," I said.

"And the cursing continues. There's a new Liz in town."

I dealt with apathy and laziness from people in all different departments at every company where I worked. One August morning, at my Lodi, California property with Hale, we were in the morning stand-up meeting with all of the department heads. My boss, Lee, was visiting from corporate.

"So," I addressed the team, "we are at 70 percent occupancy. What are we going to do to get to 100 percent?"

Silence and blank stares followed. I waited a couple minutes.

"Very well," I continued, "I've got an idea if no one else does. How about we make phone calls and do home visits to our hot and warm leads? Let's go through the list right now." More blank stares. I glanced at Lee and raised my eyebrows.

I had been working with this property for eight months, driving two-and-a-half hours each way from San Francisco, staying in hotels, spending long hours trying to increase their census and the needle was not moving. Nothing I seemed to do inspired these people to fill their building. In fact, they appeared quite happy with 70-percent occupancy. I was successful at my other properties, but not Lodi.

"How many people can we connect with today if we divide up the list? I'm thinking 20 calls and 6 home visits," I said.

Kathleen, the marketing director, quietly interjected. "I think that's a little ambitious. Maybe we could do 10 calls and 3 home visits?"

"Really? What else do we have to do today, Kathleen? This building is 70-percent occupied! What else could possibly be more important than filling it? What is it going to take to get you people motivated?" Now I was raising my voice and increasing my hand gestures. I was so angry I actually forgot Lee was in the room.

"It's just that I'm not sure we can get that done," Kathleen continued, with a sheepish look, while the others stared at the carpet or the trees out the window.

"Well, maybe we're going to have to stay late, then." I turned to Tyler, the maintenance director, "Your hair is on fire, Tyler, and you don't seem to care!"

"My *hair* is on fire?" He didn't get the analogy.

"Yes!" I yelled. "This building is 70-percent occupied. YOUR HAIR IS ON FIRE!"

"All right, then," Lee interjected, "I think we've all got the message. So, why don't we conclude the meeting and get started on these calls?"

A few moments later I was sitting in the private dining room with Lee.

"It's not effective to scream at people and tell them their hair is on fire," Lee said in his nicest tone. "I know you're frustrated, Liz, and I appreciate your passion. It's just not good leadership."

"I know, Lee. I'm sorry."

Another approach I took when a property wasn't performing was to go out and pound the pavement myself. This usually motivated the rest of the team to get going. One day, I did this for our property in Sacramento. Their census was low, so I hit it hard with visits to hospitals, doctors' offices, and nursing homes. It was winter and pouring rain.

Meanwhile, 25 miles down the road, my executive director at the Fairfield property was supposed to be doing his own marketing blitz. His building was struggling as usual. I called him at the end of my day:

"Hi Adam, how did your marketing blitz go today?"

"Oh," he said. "It was raining so we didn't do it." I looked down at my drenched silk dress.

"What do you mean, you didn't do it? Your building is 60-percent occupied! I went out in Sacramento all day in the rain."

"Yeah, maybe we'll go out tomorrow."

The next week I visited Adam and handed him a nicely wrapped box with a gift. He removed the wrapping paper, took out the umbrella, and got the message.

I got angry, maybe a little too angry sometimes, but overall, I believe I was a good leader. Even some of the people I fired told me so. Like Sam, who still sends me a birthday message every year. Gabriela, the executive director at Elder Care's Fullerton property, called me after her summer luau and said, "Liz, in my 12 years with this company, you are the first person from corporate to attend one of my events and actually roll up your sleeves and help."

"All I did was set up some tables and go to the store to buy barbecue sauce," I said.

"You know, you work really hard and you don't give yourself enough credit. Have you thought of maybe keeping a record of the positive feedback you get from your employees? It might be a good thing to pull out on challenging days, just to remind you that you are a pretty great boss."

I took Gabriela's advice and started the journal that day. Here are some entries of feedback from my employees:

Marketer from my San Diego property at Elder Care: *You made going to work fun.*

The executive director from my Fremont property: *I love when you come, Liz. I always feel so safe and grounded when you're here.*

Business office manager from Hale Vacaville: *I wanted to say thank you!! It is always so nice and uplifting to get your emails. Thank you for always finding the silver lining in everything. It is truly refreshing.*

Business office director at Rancho Solano: *I'm usually so intimidated by regionals. But you're so open and welcoming, so approachable. I never felt afraid to go to you. You have such a good heart.*

Marketer at Hale Roseville: *I really enjoyed working for you, Liz. For once, I actually looked forward to a call from my boss.*

Marketer at property in Boise: *You're soft and kind and you inspire confidence in people.*

I was successful because I treated people like human beings, not machines that had been put on this earth to produce numbers for me. My first questions when I arrived for a site visit were usually:

"How is your husband doing since his surgery?"

"Did your daughter make the cheerleading team?"

"How was your weekend?"

"How was your parents' anniversary party?"

I did not start visits by asking, "How many move-ins do you have?" or "What's your census?" They knew that's why I was there. I didn't need to draw attention to it. I sent my marketers flowers. I bought them certificates for spa days and held down the fort at their building while they were off getting a massage. Here was the twist: when I treated people like human beings, they actually *became* machines that produced numbers for me.

With most people, I did not have to pressure them. I got respect by giving respect. I talked with them about what was important to *them* (new carpet in their model room, a raise, time off to see their mom in Minnesota), and they in turn cared about what was important to *me*: getting sales. This was what made people stay an extra 20 minutes at the end of the day to make one more phone call or give one more tour when no one was looking. It was Leadership 101: people want to be valued and appreciated.

Because of the staff and residents, there were days when my job was splendid, days when I did chair yoga or arts and crafts or played Bingo at the Senior Center. I loved the afternoons when I made Easter bonnets with residents or sat for eight hours on a golf course at a charity event, handing out water bottles while chatting with friends and colleagues. Much of the time, I got paid to socialize.

The job also came with a lot of laughter. While working as vice president of sales, I was visiting our property in Eagle, Idaho, a cute little mountain town where all the buildings are the same color of dark wood. I always felt like I was on vacation, breathing the crisp mountain air and seeing people in jeans and flannel on every corner.

As usual, I was staying in one of the model rooms at the property. At 8:00 in the morning, I was getting dressed when the door opened and in walked Daisy, our marketing director, along with a couple in their late 80s who were touring the building. Daisy screamed, "Oh my God!" when she saw me standing there in my bra and underwear, "I forgot you were staying here." I grabbed my blouse and covered my bare body as best I could, laughing so hard I couldn't respond. The husband asked, "Does she come with the room?"

Daisy had tears of laughter running down her face. "No!" she said, "she's my boss!"

The overall best day I had in my assisted living career was a day in December while working as regional sales director. My region's numbers were down and I got the idea to dress up in Christmas costumes and do a sales blitz to hospitals and nursing homes throughout our region, spreading holiday cheer.

At first my marketers and executive directors were not too keen on the idea. They found it silly. I cajoled on my weekly conference call, "Come on, you guys, it will be fun!" Eventually everyone started to get excited about the costumes. One guy wore a reindeer outfit, another gal was a gingerbread man, a few dressed as elves, some dressed as Santa, and two of us wore sexy Mrs. Claus outfits. There were 20 of us in all. We went out in teams of three, meeting halfway through the day to swap stories, have lunch, and switch up the teams. We sang carols and handed out red velvet cupcakes. The nurses and doctors loved it.

During one of the hospital stops, we got the idea to visit the pediatric ward. This was, of course, not related to assisted living sales in any way whatsoever, but we thought, *Hey, I bet the kids would love this.* And they did. One six-year-old cancer patient, with a little cap to cover his bald head, shrieked with joy when we walked in, "Rudolph!" he said, pointing at Tom who was wearing the reindeer costume. We spent a half hour with the little boy while his mom chatted with us and took pictures.

When I got home, I excitedly showed the pictures from our blitz day to Dave. When he saw my costume, he shrieked, "Oh my God, Liz, what are you wearing!" It was a short, low-cut velvet dress with red tights and black boots.

"A Mrs. Claus outfit," I said. "Okay, I realize it's a bit on the sassy side."

"A *bit*?! What exactly were you *selling*?"

"Come on, Dave, it was a really fun day."

"You're going to get fired if anyone at corporate sees those pictures."

I know it wasn't very professional of me to wear that outfit while representing the company, so I didn't show the pictures to Lee or anyone at corporate. But my region had a record-breaking December, ironically because we forgot about the numbers that day and focused instead on having some fun and lifting spirits. I suspect the people on my team have not forgotten that day either. It didn't seem like work. It felt more like holiday time with family. The way family is supposed to be.

Chapter Seven

We Are Family

*How sharper than a serpent's tooth,
it is to have a thankless child.*

— William Shakespeare, *King Lear*

My second year of college, I brought my boyfriend home to meet the family. His name was Patrick and he lived next door to me in my apartment building in Westwood, California. We arrived late Friday night and since everyone was asleep went straight to bed. The next morning, I headed downstairs in my pajamas. Patrick put on his dress pants, belt, a long-sleeved shirt, shoes, and socks. I asked him if he wanted to add a tie to the outfit. "It's Saturday morning and it's 80 degrees out! You don't need to get so dressed up," I said.

"I'm nervous about meeting your family."

I walked past my older sister, Amy, who was on the couch watching television, went to the kitchen, and got out some eggs and a frying pan. Patrick sat on the couch with Amy and picked up *Good Housekeeping* while she flipped through channels and glanced sideways at him a few times, not saying a word. *She's not quite awake yet*, I thought. *She'll warm up to him as the day progresses.* My mom had gone to get the newspaper and my stepdad, Bob, was still asleep.

"Do you want scrambled or fried eggs, Patrick?" I asked from the kitchen, which opened onto the living room.

"Either is fine." He picked up my sister's Danielle Steele novel, read the back cover, crossed his legs and uncrossed them a few times, then set the book back down.

I put some butter in the pan, then opened the bread box to see what was there. "Do you want sourdough toast?"

"Sure, that sounds good." He looked at the television, watching the show my sister had landed on.

"Do you want jam?"

"No thanks," he said.

"Coffee?" He nodded.

My sister then turned to Patrick and asked, "Why don't you make your own fucking breakfast?" These were her first words to my new boyfriend.

"Amy!" I exclaimed. "He's my guest!"

"Well, what the hell? You're waiting on him like you're some kind of servant."

My mother entered, introduced herself to Patrick, and began putting pastries and beverages on the table: Bloody Marys and Screwdrivers. When we sat down, Patrick asked me quietly, "Does your family always have vodka with breakfast?"

"Yeah, on weekends," I said, realizing for the first time that this might be odd.

We all have family dynamics. Working in assisted living gave me a front row view to other people's.

I sat in the plush dining room with Miriam Moreau and her mother, Hazel, who was 83, active, healthy, and went on cruises frequently. Hazel lived alone and was tired of cooking and keeping up her home of 57 years. On most nights, she got takeout and ate alone in her dining room. This was their second tour and I had suggested we all have lunch so she could try the food. We chatted about Hazel's career and what it was like raising her three daughters in San Francisco.

"I was a nurse," she said. "Miriam followed in my footsteps. She's a nurse practitioner, now. I'm so proud of her."

"Thanks, mom."

My cream of asparagus soup smelled delicious and I took the first taste of it as I leaned back and relaxed into an amiable conversation with Hazel and Miriam. *They're so fond of each other, that's nice to see.* Hazel spoke of her husband, how he had insisted that the girls stay local and go to a private, Catholic college. The only choice was University of San Francisco, so that is where they went.

"How long ago did your husband pass away?" I asked.

"Almost 20 years now." She looked across at Miriam, with a slight smile and said, "We couldn't reach you the day your father died. You were living in North Dakota or somewhere, I can't remember." She said it in a quizzical tone, as if it were the first time she had pondered this curious fact.

The tension at our table had spiked in a matter of seconds. I sat there thinking: *Where the hell did that come from? We were having such a pleasant time.* Miriam, on the other hand, was not blindsided. She had seen this coming a mile away and did not miss a beat.

"That's right, mother," she retorted with a broad smile on her face that did not match the tone of her voice nor the glare in her eyes. There was a long, uncomfortable pause. I wanted to say something to smooth it over, instead I just put a little more salt in my soup and waited for the other shoe to drop.

"Your phone was disconnected, I believe," Hazel continued in a chirpy voice.

"I know," Miriam said, with the phony smile still mortared on her face. "I remember, mom."

"We had no idea what had happened to you. It was months and months, maybe even a year that we couldn't reach you."

"You can reach me now, mom. Anytime."

They continued this exchange for the next 10 minutes, as I wondered, *Why did Miriam disappear? She told me she's gay. Maybe her parents weren't okay with it when she first came out?*

Our lunch continued and I eventually introduced a new topic to ease the stress in the air. I never found out what the deal was with that odd exchange between Hazel and Miriam. Sometimes I got a mysterious glimpse like that of people's relationships, sometimes I was thrust into the middle of those relationships for weeks, months, or years.

Donna Connolly came to our memory care after several failed attempts by her family to keep her at home with caregivers. Donna was 80 years old and had alcohol-related dementia. She had a broken ankle, a huge bump on her head, and an angry attitude the day she arrived at Casa Amanecer from the hospital. Her injuries were due to falls. The orders from the attending physician were that she was to be placed in a secure environment "with absolutely no access to alcohol." She owned a beautiful home in San Francisco's St. Francis Woods neighborhood and reminded us daily that *she*, not her kids, not her ex-husband, had paid for it. She had run a successful investment business for 30 years.

We gave Donna a private room overlooking the golf course and brought some of her furniture and pictures from home, hoping this would calm her down. It actually enraged her even more. I went to see Donna two days after she moved in. She told me to take the clothes off of the chair across from her and sit down. I did as I was told, as I imagine was the case with most people Donna had met throughout her life.

"I noticed my furniture is here and I'm starting to think this is permanent. When am I going home?" she asked.

"You're going to stay here for a while, Donna. It didn't work out at home." *Why am I having this conversation with her instead of her kids doing it?*

"What do you mean, 'It didn't work out?'"

"It's not safe there; you fell and hurt your ankle. Your house has lots of stairs."

"I didn't fall because of the stairs. I fell because I was drunk. What is this place, anyway? Is it some kind of rehab? Am I in a rehab because my kids think I'm an alcoholic?"

The activity director, David, popped his head in to invite Donna to Movie Night and immediately made a U-turn when he saw the looks on our faces and felt the vibe in the air. David had told me earlier that he thought her kids should take her home and let her drink. "She has lived her life, raised her kids, and run a successful business. Let her go out as she pleases," he said. He had a point.

"Is this a rehab?" she asked again, breaking my chain of thought. "And why is my furniture here? I'm starting to think this is permanent."

She asked me that five minutes ago. Her short-term memory is shot.

"Your furniture is here because you're staying a while," I said. Donna was stylish, statuesque, and clever.

"How did those clothes get on the floor? Did I put them there? I am in a prison cell," she continued. "Look at the size of this room."

"You don't have to stay in this room, Donna. You can go out into the living room and the activity room."

"Have you *been* out there?" she asked incredulously. "Have you *seen* what's out there?"

"What do you mean?"

"Those people are *nuts*. They stare into space with a blank look. What is this place, anyway? Is it some kind of rehab?"

"I'm sorry, Donna. I can imagine this feels very difficult."

"Don't say you can imagine how I feel. You have no idea how I feel. Has someone taken you from your home and locked you up in a place like this or are you free to come and go as you please?"

She was right. I didn't know how she felt. "I'm sorry. I know this is hard. I'll be back to check on you after lunch."

I went to my office and called her daughter, Erika. "I know a great geropsychiatrist. He does house calls. I think you should call him," I said. Donna's anger was valid. Perhaps a professional could help her work through it in a way in which we were not equipped.

Three weeks later, Donna had met with the psychiatrist and was doing much better. Her son, Russel, called me. "I think we are going to take my mom home and try it out there." I was perplexed. Donna was actually settling in. She was calm, cheerful, and taking far fewer medications than she had when she arrived. She was enjoying the art classes and made a friend named Jane who was also in the early stages of dementia. And because of her short-term memory loss, she barely spoke of her house anymore. She loved the view from her room.

"Do you think that's a good idea, Russel? I mean, it didn't really work at home. She ended up in the hospital with a huge lump on her head and a broken ankle."

"Well," he continued, "we're going to have 24-hour caregivers with her."

"Isn't that what you had before?" I wasn't trying to be mean to Russel. I just didn't think it helped the situation to participate in a family's denial. I understand denial can be a great coping mechanism at times. But there comes a time when reality breaks through our avoidance of it and for some reason, the universe had chosen me as the messenger to break through the denial of many families.

"Well, yes," Russel responded. "The thing is, we are going to have her sign a contract agreeing not to drink alcohol. She really wants to be in her own home."

"But she has dementia. She is going to forget she signed the contract."

"I know; we're just going to show it to her every time she asks for a drink." *Oh, that will go over real well.* I didn't say anything more. I decided to let Russel and his two siblings work it out. Russel's sister, Erika, came to talk with me the next day.

"Russel is a drunk himself, Liz. Who is going to get the call when mom falls down? I AM!"

"I figured that."

"I told him there's no way we're taking her home."

The family argued for weeks, sometimes in front of me in my office while I was trying to get work done. Donna ended up staying at Casa Amanecer. Russel visited once a week and took her out to her favorite restaurant where they got drunk together.

Like Donna, many people moved to assisted living unwillingly. The best scenarios happened when mom or dad was lucid and made the decision themselves to move before they really needed it. This was rare. One day a man named Jim Ainsworth came to see me. Jim was a local mortgage broker who wore Wrangler jeans and flannel shirts. He had weathered skin and a handsome face. His mom, Mabel, was 86 and had been working in the administrative offices of J.C. Penney for the previous 25 years. Mabel's boss called Jim and said that he hated to do this to her, but she could no longer work there.

Mabel had stopped bathing regularly and wasn't doing much real work anymore. She wasn't really doing anything except filing and half the time she put things in the wrong place. The boss didn't have the heart to tell her. The job was Mabel's life. Her routine was to drive the same route to work every day, do her eight-hour shift, then go home.

During our first meeting, Jim shifted in his chair and rung his hands frequently. He looked at the floor when I asked probing questions about his mom. Jim toured four times and called me nine times with questions over a two-month period before coming in one day with a deposit. Jim shared during our conversations that he was terrified of his mother. She had beaten him during his childhood. Sometimes, instead of hitting him, she yelled and broke plates. He grew up walking on eggshells, never knowing when her rage would flare up. Even though he was now 52-years old, the fear of Mabel's outbursts was the same as when he was 8.

I learned that Jim had a brother who was addicted to drugs and capitalizing on mom's failing mental capacity. "He is stealing money from her bank accounts faster than I can keep up with him. I need to get her away from him before he completely depletes her resources. She has worked all her life. She deserves to live in a nice place like this. I'll take the studio apartment you showed me, number 45."

"Great. You have 30 days before you need to start paying rent. This will give you time to make arrangements for the move. Have you talked with your mom yet?"

"No, but I'm going to."

During the next 30 days, while we were getting the paperwork together, I asked Jim a few more times if he had told his mom about the move. The answer was always no and each time I said, "Jim, you have to tell her. You can't just move her here."

"I know, I know," he responded.

On moving day, as the movers were setting down the couch and Mabel was in the bathroom freshening up, I tried to lighten the mood and asked Jim jokingly, "So, have you told your mom yet?"

"Actually," Jim replied, "I was thinking maybe I could just put her suitcase in the room and leave and then you could tell her she's staying."

I laughed hard, "That's funny." Jim wasn't smiling. "Oh my God," I said. "You're serious! Jim, you need to tell her. We cannot keep the people in independent living against their will."

"I'm afraid to tell her."

"It will be good. Don't worry. Just tell her."

When Jim finally told Mabel later that day, she wasn't happy about it, yet she didn't unleash the rage he expected. Within a month, Mabel got into a new routine. She ate breakfast with Millie every day, went to the local senior center for Bingo, then came home and watched her favorite TV shows. She found her way around just fine. Jim visited once a week for dinner and told me their relationship was better than ever and he didn't have to worry about her anymore.

Gina, the 50-year-old daughter of Manny, struggled with the same dilemma. She spent six months in therapy trying to figure out a way to tell her dad he needed to move out of her home and into a retirement community. She toured twice with me, then picked an apartment and geared up to tell him. When the day finally came, Gina did her meditation, prayer, chanting, phone calls, sage burning, and visualizing to prepare for the big moment. Then, at dinner, she dropped the bomb, "Dad, I think maybe we should look into a retirement community for you."

"Thank God!" he said, "I thought you would never suggest it. I am really tired of living with you, actually, and I didn't know how to tell you."

"You're kidding? I had no idea!"

"I'm so relieved," Manny said. "I've been trying to think of a way to talk with you about this and I didn't want to hurt your feelings." Manny moved into our community the next week.

When to have "the conversation" about assisted living was a question with which many adult children struggled. Most experts suggest having it sooner rather than later. Yet the majority of people wait until there is a crisis, which is a terrible time to shop for assisted living. The good places are full and the family has lost all negotiating power because they are in a hurry to find something. They have also lost all calm and sense of reasoning for their choice in a community. For the elder, they have lost decision-making power in the matter. They are usually laid up in a hospital or nursing home and other people are making decisions for them.

I read an article, "Parenting Your Parents," which included a guide, "What To Ask: A Checklist. Suggestions for having the conversation with parents who are still healthy and active." These are some of the questions included in the article:

Their Living Situation:

- *Do you want to live in your house for as long as possible? Are there things we need to do to your house so it's safe and comfortable for you as you age? Can we make some of those changes now?*
- *Would you be willing to hire someone to help you at home if you can't do it on your own anymore?*
- *Would you consider moving in with me or one of my siblings if we all agree that you need help with your personal care or aren't safe at home alone anymore? How do you feel about moving into an assisted living facility?*
- *Can I help you scout out quality assisted living facilities and nursing homes now, so we know what's available and what you would prefer in case you need one in the future?*

Their Health:

- *Can one of us accompany you to some doctor's appointments? We recognize your right to privacy, but maybe we can help keep track of everything your doctor says at your visit.*
- *Have you thought about what kind of medical treatment you want in the future and who would make those decisions if you can't make or communicate them on your own? Have you put these desires in writing?*
- *How do you feel about being kept alive with ventilators, feeding tubes, or other interventions? And under what circumstances would you want that?*

Their Finances:

- Have you written a will? Does someone you trust know where it is? Who should we contact about it?
- Have you consulted a reliable financial planner who can help anticipate your needs as you age?
- Will you give me or another trusted person power of attorney over your financial affairs in case there's a time you can't handle them yourself?

I loved that list and often gave it to families, telling them, "It pays to be proactive." Very few in the senior care world are going to take pity on someone who has failed to plan. I suggested sitting down and having a formal meeting with parents and going through this checklist. "Tell them you read a horror story about people not planning ahead and you don't want them to end up like that."

Even the thought of having this conversation invoked guilt, and most adult children had loads of it. Particularly fascinating were the kids who rarely visited. After a two-year lapse between visits, they showed up and were irate to discover that we were feeding mom bacon for breakfast. "How *could* you? Don't you know she has high blood pressure? And, why is the lightbulb out in the lamp next to her bed? And why is she taking all these medications?" Guilt often got projected outward as anger. It became so transparent after a while that we started bracing ourselves for it.

Family members who visited on a regular basis realized that the lightbulb next to the bed had been out for only a couple of hours because they were just here yesterday. They knew how much we loved their mother because they were at the community every week to witness the exchanges that took place between mom and our staff. They saw when a caregiver baked mom's favorite chocolate-chip-walnut cookies or when the executive director noticed she wasn't sleeping as well as usual and increased her exercise routine.

The ones who weren't involved showed up on a witch hunt. *If I stir the waters up enough and point the finger at you, maybe you won't have time to ask me why I haven't visited my mother in two years. More importantly, I will be so focused on what a horrible job* you're *doing, I won't have time to ask myself that question.*

There were adult children who had Power of Attorney over mom or dad's finances and healthcare even though they probably should not have. The years wore on with dad needing more care, clinging to life, yet having very little quality of life. It was at this point the adult children started making decisions based not on what was best for dad, but on what was best for their inheritance. They saw the money quickly dwindling before their eyes and decided that maybe dad would be fine in a smaller room, maybe he doesn't need a shower three times a week, perhaps twice a week would suffice.

Then there were the 50-year-old kids who strongly objected to mom moving to assisted living, asking, "Well, where will I live if my mom moves to assisted living?"

Eighty-nine-year-old Sylvia Walker said after her fourth tour, "I love the place, Liz, but my 60-year-old son, Bruno, lives with me and he'll have nowhere to go if I move in here."

"Sixty! Where will Bruno live when you die?" I asked her squarely over tea and cookies. "How will Bruno survive? You're not doing him any favors, Sylvia."

I called a fellow marketing director at a place in Camarillo and asked her advice for overcoming this obstacle. "Yeah, I had that happen again last month," she said. "This time it was a 52-year-old daughter. I dealt with it by finding the daughter a job. Then the daughter had enough money to afford her own place and mom was able to sell the house and move into our community. The rest of the time I do like you do and just try to break through their denial that this 'child' is never going to be okay and enabling is not helping."

We had one guy, the 55-year-old son of Rosalind Mirowitz, who actually moved into her apartment with her at The Gables. He was vegan and wore the same PETA (People for the Ethical Treatment of Animals) t-shirt every day. He had the nerve to actually complain about his baked potato even though we weren't charging him for food. He lived with Rosalind for six months and eventually, Sharon told Rosalind he needed to go because our license required people to be at least 65 years old to live at The Gables. Rosalind moved out with him. They got a one-bedroom apartment together in town.

Lynette Kinsley, the woman with diabetes who was reluctant to stay in the nursing home, had taken the tough love approach with her son. When she reached age 85, she decided to stop enabling him and take care of herself. He became homeless the day she sold her home and moved to a retirement community. "I think he's still homeless," she said, "living in some encampment in the desert. Every once in a while, the authorities tell him to move along. He packs up his tent and moves to another spot down the road. He calls me from time-to-time from a pay phone, just to say hi."

Lynette was 92 now, so I figured her son must be in his early 60s. "He's a sweet man," she said, "just has an addiction problem." She told me of the night he was still living with her and went to the hospital with a perforated ulcer due to drinking. "He bled all over the basement and the sheets on his bed and called the ambulance himself, because he didn't want to disturb me."

Adult children who were still dependent on their parents made up a fraction of the families. More often I met kids who were controlling every aspect of their parents' lives and getting burned out because of it. All of the books, articles, therapists, and support groups say the same thing: take care of yourself. But people still didn't. They took great care of the "patient," but not themselves. They gave and gave until there was nothing left to give.

One study said that the family caregivers' risk of death increases by 25 percent when a loved one needs more help. I often told people: at a certain point, if you keep pushing yourself, you're no longer effective. You get nothing done. When you're really stressed and tired, you can't think straight. You start spinning your wheels. Some people push themselves so hard, they never enjoy life and then, one day, they drop dead of a heart attack. "Do you want that? Is that going to be helpful to your mom?" I often asked.

One study said that 65.7 million caregivers in the U.S. adult population are providing care to someone who is ill, disabled, or aged. Many of these caregivers become martyrs in the true sense of the word, actually dying for the other person. They reach a point of physical, psychological, and emotional exhaustion and then they die. But as it is happening along the way, they don't want to hear about self-care. Taking care of themselves seems selfish, when in reality, *not* taking care of themselves is more selfish.

I often told people:

> *Let friends, family members, and neighbors jump in. Join a support group. Hire caregivers a few days a week. Look into adult daycare centers if your loved one has dementia. Look into respite stays at assisted living communities. Move your relative to an assisted living community sooner rather than later. You will still be their emotional caregiver even though you're not doing the day-to-day tasks for them.*

The adult children had careers, were keeping a marriage and house together, raising their own kids while also caring for their aging parents. They are known as "the sandwich generation." They often experienced a role reversal where they, the adult child, became the parent. Sometimes it happened so subtly that the kids did not even realize it until the roles had, in fact, been fully switched. Many times, the realization hit them at the moment when they found themselves sitting in my office, full of resentment.

This is not what they signed up for. Mom had become a job, an object, yet another task on their mile-long to-do list. As the years wore on and mom didn't die, the adult child became more condescending, micromanaging mom's every move, talking to her like she was a three-year-old. "Mom," I heard one adult daughter scream across the lunch table, "Say hi to Jim. You met him yesterday. Mom, don't eat that, it's bad for your diabetes. Mom, remember you're seeing your cardiologist tomorrow at 10:00."

Many parents get tired of fighting, finally relinquish, and lose all independence. General Braswell was not like most. His daughter, Kitty, signed him up for water aerobics and art classes, told the kitchen how to prepare his eggs (no oil or butter), and showed up with new shirts and pants about once every three months. She made all his medical and dental appointments, decorated his apartment, and came for lunch once a week so she could make sure he was keeping company with the right people. General Braswell continued wearing his old clothes, missed half the art classes, and slathered butter on his toast. "Your daughter wants to know if you have been doing your daily walks around the property," I overheard Mary, our office manager, asking him one day. "She called this morning."

"Tell her it's none of her business!"

Kitty's mom had died 15 years earlier and Kitty took it upon herself to become General Braswell's keeper. The thing was, he didn't need looking after. He was one of the healthiest 90-year-olds I had ever met. He walked without a cane or walker, lived in independent living, had friends and enjoyed hobbies like playing dominoes. Kitty was trying to fix something that wasn't broken.

Kitty was one of many loving daughters I met. It was almost always the daughters I dealt with, or the daughters-in-law. Even if the daughter lived 3,000 miles away and the son lived down the street, it was usually the daughter who called about mom's care and special diet needs, bought furniture for mom's apartment, sent flowers and photos of the grandkids, used her precious vacation time to fly out for a week to see mom. Sons were often clueless and self-absorbed, more than willing to let their sister handle everything.

I did meet a few sons who surprised me. Paul Alden was one of these exceptions. When his mom, Daniella, went on hospice, all of the family gathered around her. Paul, her middle son and primary caregiver, had been with her almost daily for the previous year. The other three siblings lived varying distances away and had limited contact with their mother. Paul put his life on hold to spend as much time as possible with Daniella. Paul adored his mom.

Paul was 38 years old, with blue-grey eyes, an athletic build, and a smile that radiated bliss. He was world traveled and fluent in Dutch, which he joked was completely useless living in Southern California. All of the female employees, myself included, drooled over him for his Adonis good looks and beautiful heart.

Daniella died on Christmas Eve. Everyone was bustling around, hurrying to tie things up and get to their families. It was cool outside and already dark at 5:00 p.m. I put my coat on to walk up to the Cottages to check on a new resident and on the way, I ran into Sharon. "I have to go to the hospital with Evelyn Bradford," she said a bit exasperated.

"What happened?"

"She had a fall. A minor one luckily, but we need to have her checked out. The thing is, Daniella Alden just passed away about 10 minutes ago."

"Oh, poor Paul," I responded.

"I know. I feel so bad for him," Sharon continued. "He's been with her constantly this past year as she declined and he left an hour ago to go home and shower. I left him a message to call in, but didn't tell him why. I hate to do this to you, but Joan is away and you are the next in line management-wise. I told Iris to send the call to you if Paul calls before I get back. Would you mind telling him?"

"Sure." I had never been the one to tell someone about a death. I usually dealt with people when they were moving in. Sure enough, Paul called while Sharon was gone.

"I'm sorry to tell you this, Paul, but your mom just passed away," I said. "I feel so bad this happened on Christmas Eve."

"It's fine. I'm not much into holidays anyway."

"Are you okay?" I asked. "I'm really sorry you weren't with her when she passed." There was a long silence.

"I'm good. I've been there with her all year. It's my siblings who struggled with her decline. They have a lot of guilt that they haven't been around. Even though they are here now, at the end, it's hard for them."

"Well, I am very sorry for your loss. I know how devoted you were to your mom."

"Thank you, Liz. Have a good Christmas."

I met other adult children like Paul who were incredibly kind and emotionally mature. The Spector family had four of them. All four of the Spector's adult children toured, called, asked questions, and took an active role in dad's choice of a retirement home. They were supportive and did everything they could to make it *his* decision. I watched the way they interacted with dad and one another ... it was so *respectful*. I thought to myself, *who are these people?* As the weeks and months went on, I looked for signs of dissonance and there were none. Everyone cooperated and did what they were supposed to do. They all flew in to take measurements of the apartment, buy furniture, fill out paperwork, take dad for his physician's report.

Then moving day came and I thought, *all right, here it comes, now the* drama begins. No one makes it through moving day without a fight. I waited and watched for the sister to get snippy with the brother, for a sarcastic or annoyed word to slip out, but it didn't happen. Then I thought, *oh, they're just the no-dirty-laundry-in-public types.* I stood outside dad's apartment door and eavesdropped. Still nothing happened. Their words and tone were just as nice behind closed doors as in front of me.

Finally, I asked the daughter, Linda, "How did you guys end up so healthy? Have you all been through a bunch of therapy or something?"

"We had great parents," she replied laughing. "It's that simple."

Over the years, I actually met quite a few families like the Spectors. The more I worked in assisted living, the more I saw that functional families actually do exist. They were the exception, though. Usually, I saw adult siblings retreat to the roles they had assumed as children. David is aloof, Susie steps in and takes control, Shawn makes it all about him.

Afton Jones, whom I met while working at Casa Amanecer, was one of the most memorable. Afton, whose mom had Alzheimer's, was in my office bouncing off the walls and using PhD-level words at rapid speed. I couldn't follow the conversation. It wasn't that my vocabulary was lacking. (Although I did look up the word *deleterious* when she left. It means *harmful*. Afton wondered if it would be "deleterious" to put her mom in a care home.)

She wasn't pretentious about the way she used big words, unlike my brother-in-law, who tried to sound smart by telling people they were "disingenuous" instead of just calling them liars. With Afton, it was just how she talked.

It wasn't so much her verbiage that threw me off, it was that Afton couldn't follow a coherent thought pattern. She was "wracked with guilt, in love with her mother, and angry at her abusive father." Twice during our tour, she asked if I had any wine available. She finally settled for chamomile tea. These are the notes to myself, from our tour, jotted onto my yellow pad:

Daughter is highly articulate and totally nuts

Mom is forgetful, lonely, physically healthy

Our relationship had begun when Afton called for a tour the week prior, which I scheduled for 4:00 p.m. the following day. The day of the tour, she called at 4:15 p.m., explaining that she was running late and that she could be there by 4:30 p.m. Then she said, "But, I don't want you cutting the tour short."

"I have another appointment at 4:45 so why don't we just re-schedule for tomorrow?"

"Oh, so you were going to give me a 15-minute tour?" she asked, indignantly.

"No, our appointment was for 4:00 p.m. I was going to give you a 45-minute tour."

We rescheduled for the next day and, on her way to our appointment, she got lost and called to yell at me because she felt the directions from our website were wrong. No one else had ever gotten lost coming to Casa Amanecer.

When Afton arrived, we sat in the dining room for a while and talked. "What do you do for a living?" I asked.

"Nothing for the past five years. I have been caretaking for my parents. Prior to that I worked for a software company."

Afton had Power of Attorney for mom, but her sister was making her life hell and calling Adult Protective Services to try and stop her from moving mom to a retirement community. "As if I don't feel guilty ENOUGH already! As if I WANT to do this!" she yelled.

After we looked around at the assisted living apartments and the memory care, we went to sit in the private dining room again. She began speaking with machine-gun rapidity.

"Okay, Liz, tell me why I should put my mother here. Sell me on this place. Tell me why I should choose you over the other places. Why I should put my mom here? Give me all you've got, Liz. Give me everything you got." I started to wonder if she was using cocaine.

"I've got one semi-private room available in our memory care. You are welcome to it," I said, hoping with all my heart that she *did not* want it. If Afton was any indication, this family was going to be a nightmare to deal with. Assisted living is not the kind of sales job where one seals the deal then never sees the client again. I saw them far more *after* they moved in.

Afton toured two more times and each time arrived 20 minutes late and found a way to blame me for her tardiness. She called me every day for two weeks. I went to the model room to take a nap after each conversation. I never met Afton's mom. Afton ended up moving in with her mom instead of choosing a retirement community and I was happy about that.

The Gables' Alec Hagstrom was another adult child who annoyed me. Alec was a big-shot lawyer from Los Angeles and he and his mom, Ines, decided after three tours that she would move to The Gables. Alec's clients included high-level politicians and CEOs, and he thought he was pretty important because of that. He was a multimillionaire and thought that made him pretty special, too. I backed down on many of his demands, but when his office called me a week before Ines's move-in date and said he wanted the bathtub cut done at no charge, I called him back on his cell phone. He seemed annoyed that I was calling *him* back instead of his secretary.

"You know, Alec, I was really clear during our first tour that we would be happy to split the cost of the tub cut with you, but we aren't going to pay 100 percent of it."

"You agreed to cover the cost."

"No, I didn't, actually. I have it right here in my notes."

"Well, your notes are incorrect, Ms. Breen, and I think you know that."

"No, Alec, my notes are perfectly clear and correct and I'd be happy to fax them to you if you would like to see them. We never cover the full cost of a bathtub cut. We rarely even cover half the cost. I had to get our investors' approval for this."

"You are legally obliged to cut out this tub for safety reasons. It presents a fall risk."

"You're right, a full-sided tub is a fall risk for frail seniors. That's why all of our assisted living apartments have either showers or cut tubs. But your mom is moving into independent living. If you think she is a fall risk or unsafe in independent living, I would be happy to put her on the wait list for an assisted living apartment."

Ines was 75 years young, healthy, and stable as a rhinoceros. She did not need or want to move to assisted living. As Alec pondered his next move, I sat silently on the phone wondering why a multimillionaire was quibbling over $350. I knew why I was quibbling over it. I was not allowed to ever promise that we would cover the full cost of a tub cut and I wasn't going to be bullied. Finally, when the silence became deafening, I broke in, "Alec, are you still there?"

"Yes."

"Listen, I have really enjoyed getting to know you and your sister, and your mom is lovely, but I have 20 people on my waiting list who would take that apartment, with or without the tub cut. So, I need you to make a decision on what you would like to do."

"I'll send you the check tomorrow," he said and hung up on me.

I smiled at my office mate, John, and said, "It is so nice to be full with a waiting list so I don't have to put up with that bullshit."

When dealing with bothersome family members, I tried to remind myself that prior to working at The Gables, the words *grab bars, incontinence, ambulatory, and congestive heart failure* were not even in my vocabulary. The first time I saw S.O.B. used in a medical context was on discharge papers from the hospital. The physician had written S.O.B. along with other abbreviations and notes in the history and physical section. I looked at it and thought: that's a little *harsh.* I went to Sharon, "I know Fred can be grumpy, but my God, how unprofessional of a doctor to call him a son of a bitch."

"It means 'shortness of breath,' Liz."

I tried to muster compassion for all that the adult children were dealing with. But sometimes, there were kids who were so difficult, I had to draw the line. When I worked for Hale, we once had to evict a 94-year-old woman because her daughter was so toxic. We liked the mom, but her daughter, Mary, screamed and belittled our caregivers and housekeepers on a weekly basis. We gave her repeated warnings then finally told her mom she had to either tell Mary to stop visiting or move out. She chose to move out. "I had kids so I wouldn't be alone in my old age," she said. "Mary is all I've got." *Yes, but wouldn't you rather be alone than deal with that?*

I met some women who had succumbed to the societal pressure to procreate yet could not handle motherhood. Penny was one such woman. She was the daughter of one of our residents at Eldersview. Penny walked around frazzled and confused, unable to accomplish anything, and frequently telling her two young children that she was going to call the police if they did not behave. She told me that she came home one day, looked at her one-year-old and said, "Aren't you 18 yet? Isn't it time for you to move out?"

Penny got pregnant with her second child at age 40, only to discover once he arrived that she really did not want him after all. Her baby, Adam, was so darn cute. It seemed Penny resented Adam's very existence. Adam was messing with her freedom.

I began observing the various choices women had made at all of the retirement communities where I worked. The whole spectrum was there to witness: ladies who had tried to have kids and couldn't conceive, those who had adopted, others who had eight kids, numerous grandchildren, and enjoyed an idyllic family life. There were people whose children had preceded them in death. I met ladies who had never married nor had children and ladies who had married and chosen not to have children.

I saw Katherine Conway, the talented 85-year-old artist whose two children were her biggest fans. I saw Jim Smith, the man with eight children, none of whom spoke to him, who died alone. I saw Mr. and Mrs. Pepper with their nine devoted children and beautiful home. I spoke with Eileen Fisher, whose biggest heartbreak was that she never had children. I began asking people how they felt about the choices they had made. I had women tell me, "I love my children, and God, please forgive me for saying this, but if I had it to do over again, I would not have had them. You have to give up your whole life."

Others said, "Having children was the most fulfilling, life-affirming, remarkable experience of my life." I knew that feeling. I had Jordan, who was living in San Diego with his dad. Biologically he was my nephew. Heart-wise, soul-wise, and all otherwise, he was my child, my heart walking around outside my body. I could not have loved him more if he had come from my womb. I held Jordan the moment he was born and that delivery room filled with a warm and radiant white light that I have never before or after seen. I remember thinking, *this is THE white light, the one people see when they die.* That light permeated every ounce of my being when he was born.

Gloria Armstrong, at the Gables, never had children but had 25 relatives at her 100th birthday celebration. One day, while sipping iced tea in her apartment, I asked, "Gloria, do you regret not having children?"

"Oh no, my dear. Children are a *huge* responsibility. Besides, when I was in my childbearing years, in the 1930s, I was on Broadway. There was no *way* I was going to give that up to have kids!"

"But do you regret it now? Now that you're a hundred?"

"No, I love being an aunt. You get to enjoy them and give to them and not have all the stressful parts."

Samantha Murray was another woman I met who had chosen an alternative path. She was 97, never married, and had no kids. She had traveled the world, was an avid reader, and had many dear friends of all ages. She started a Current Events group one week after she moved into Casa Amanecer. Samantha was also still highly active with an organization that aimed to get sex workers off the streets. Samantha had a joy about her that was infectious. I could barely keep up with all her visitors. Samantha had enjoyed a full life with authentic connections and she was still enjoying that life at her advanced age.

Samantha had many lives she had touched. No one was obliged to visit or spend time with her, so she became adept at making people *want* to spend time with her, by being a truly delightful, interesting person.

And then there was Genevieve, the self-described "spinster," who was one of the happiest octogenarians I met. Genevieve joked that whenever someone asked her why she never got married, she always responded, "Oh, I was so busy I forgot to get married!"

Chapter Eight

Happily Ever After?

Marriage is the ultimate form of assisted living.
— Pete (my neighbor for 14 years)

My maternal grandmother, Nanny, was born in 1921 and married seven times. Her first marriage was at age 19 and her last ended when she died of cancer at age 59. One of Nanny's husbands, Eldridge the judge, committed suicide when Nanny left him. Eldridge shot himself in the shower so he wouldn't make a mess. My mother told me this when I was 12 years old, as we drove past the large Victorian home in Michigan where it happened. Nanny's sister, my great-aunt Ruby, was married six times. Their other sisters were married one to five times each.

When I think about it, either my grandma or one of her sisters was always going through a divorce or burying a husband. Yet they never seemed depressed. I only remember laughter and dancing around Nanny's kitchen and I don't remember men being around much. The husbands were kept in the background, basically inconsequential, a mere backdrop for these bold women. When I was 10, I asked my mom, "How come Nanny and Aunt Ruby got married so many times?"

"I think they got bored easily," my mom replied without hesitating, "and most of their marriages lasted four to five years, because that's when you need new linens. Oh, and they also refused to put up with any crap from men." It was true. I could fit into the tip of my pinky finger the amount of bullshit my grandmother was willing to put up with from a man. Imagine that: leaving a man in 1940 simply because you did not want to be in that marriage anymore. My grandmother and her sisters were feminists before Betty Friedan, Gloria Steinem, *Ms.* magazine or birth control pills ever hit the scene.

In one of Nanny's wedding pictures, she is standing in a courtroom, with husband number four, and she has on a bright red suit. I always loved the audacity of that photo. A lot of women joke about wearing red to their wedding. My grandmother is the only woman I know who actually did it.

Nanny had a confidence about her that attracted men and drove them crazy. She was funny, too.

One day, when I was about seven, Nanny was in-between husbands and had a date coming over. I was watching her put on lipstick and get ready when Aunt Ruby arrived to pick me up. We watched Nanny place sheets of wax paper on the counter. She then took cookies out of a box from a local bakery and spread them on the paper. "What are you doing?" Aunt Ruby asked.

"What does it look like I'm doing? He'll think I baked these!" This was my grandmother.

When I entered the world of elder care, almost 30 years after Nanny's death, I began to meet couples who had been married 50, 60, even 70 years. My first thought was usually, *why would anyone want to do that?* We see the world not as it is but as *we* are. I saw the world from my family's perspective, believing that the institution of marriage was created for a time when life expectancy was 40. We were never expected to live to 90 nor to be married 60 years. It was counterintuitive. I learned in one of my college psychology classes that, from a purely biological perspective, human beings are supposed to be with one partner for a total of four years, because by that time, the child they have is walking, talking, and can somewhat fend for himself.

My mother was married three times, but never married to my father. My dad was an attorney and my mom was his secretary and they had an affair on and off that lasted over 20 years. On weekends, I went to my dad's house and rode horses with him or went shopping with Anne, my stepmother. I tried on clothes and Anne, who had impeccable fashion sense, helped me choose. My favorite part of these outings with Anne was lunch when we sat and conversed about current events, my classes at school, and life. I could tell, even from a young age, that Anne truly cared about me. She cared about my life turning out well. She treated me as one of her own children despite the fact that I was the product of her husband's affair.

One time, at lunch, I told her I wanted to be a fashion buyer and the next weekend, Anne had a gift for me. She had bought me a book called *How to be a Fashion Buyer*. She saved her copies of *Town and Country* magazine, *Vogue*, and the fashion section of the *Los Angeles Times* for me to read when I came to visit on weekends. She was always looking for that spark in me, whatever got me excited and enthusiastic. When I worked on my homework or a project for school at their house, she would say, "Remember, honey, God is in the details."

Years later, when I was in my 30s, Anne came to me with a box full of sparkling bugle bead evening bags. Knowing how much I loved attending the San Francisco ballet, she explained that she wanted me to have them since she no longer went to the theater. She wanted to think of her purses at the ballet and picture me enjoying them. The clutches were gold, black, silver, each carefully wrapped in tissue paper and displaying a quality of craftsmanship not seen in products today. I pictured Anne carrying the bags, 40 years earlier, wearing one of her satin or chiffon gowns, radiant and glowing back in the day. I hugged Anne and felt a flutter of excitement receiving this exquisite and unexpected gift. Anne was giving me a slice of the elegance I had admired in her for so many years.

My dad and Anne did right by me. My dad spent time with me, riding horses and picking macadamia nuts from his orchard in the backyard. I spent holidays and weekends with them and was welcomed into their family. My dad always told me, "You were not a mistake, my dear. You were a surprise." And, so it was, that I felt loved and felt like I had a right to be on this planet as much as any "legitimate" child. Anne, being the gem that she was, always separated me from the *fact* of me, which is remarkable to me and everyone else I have ever told about her.

When Anne was in her 70s and 80s, we talked regularly on the phone. We discussed my job, her job at a boutique, the weather, my sister and brother, the nieces and nephews. We chatted about politics, trips I had planned, her hip and knees that constantly bothered her. Our conversations flowed, as always, but I never asked the question I really wanted to ask, which was, "Why didn't you leave my dad when you found out he had an affair?" I was so curious, yet there never seemed to be an appropriate time to bring up that subject.

The first time my heart was really broken, when I was 27 years old, I went home for a visit and told Anne what had happened. When she saw the tears in my eyes, she said, "You're walking wounded," and then she started to cry with me. She felt my pain as if it were her own.

When I was 12, Anne was making dinner one night as I stood there talking and daydreaming about my future career. She told me:

> *Whatever career you pursue, make sure you keep up on it. If you leave it for a while to get married and have kids, stay current on what is happening in your field. Take classes, keep your resume up, stay connected with your contacts. Don't ever put yourself in the position of being financially dependent on a man. Always have the ability to earn an income and make sure you have the choice to leave a marriage if you want to.*

She said this all in a tone that was unusually serious for her, so I sensed it was a significant message she was giving me and I put her words into the "important" box in my mind. She went on to tell me about her own education and career, how she had studied to be a physical therapist but left her job to get married, have a home, and raise a family. "When I tried to get back into the field in the early 70s, I had been away for 15 years. Everything had changed so much that I couldn't get a job." I thought to myself, *I was born in 1969. Maybe the early 70s was when Anne found out about my dad's affair with my mom? Maybe she tried to leave and couldn't?*

Anne's generation of women had different views on husbands' fidelity. Many of the women I met from this generation had the attitude, "Men will be men." Many, like Anne and Marjorie Malore, whom I met while working at Casa Amanecer, stayed with their husbands despite infidelity.

Marjorie and her husband had been married for 55 years when they came to tour Casa Amanecer. The tour was going nicely and the Malores seemed happy and spoke sweetly to one another. After looking at the model rooms, we came back to my office. Mr. Malore excused himself to use the restroom and I asked Marjorie, "So how did you like the one-bedroom apartment?"

"Have you got a two-bedroom or better yet, separate apartments?"

"Well, yes, but may I ask why?"

"That man," she said, pointing towards the door, "cheated on me 30 years ago and I have hated him every day since."

"Oh!"

"I stayed with him for the kids."

"I'm so sorry that happened to you, Marjorie. But aren't your kids in their 50s now?"

"Yes, but I don't want to upset the apple cart, discombobulate the whole family, you know. Besides, I am not exactly going to get a divorce at age 80." She went on to pour out her heart, telling me about the affair and how it had crushed her soul.

The majority of women I met from Marjorie's generation accepted men's infidelity. But that didn't mean they liked it.

When Mr. Malore returned from the bathroom, I walked them out to the lobby, said goodbye, then went back to my office and remembered my own brush with being "the other woman."

I was a 20-year-old college student and Matt Richardson was my 33-year-old boss. I worked for him at a real estate investment company on weekday afternoons. He was vice president of the company and I reported directly to him. At 33, Matt seemed ancient, yet I liked him. I liked Matt because he paid attention to me; he was cute, funny, and married—forbidden fruit. His wife, Maggie, was devoted. He told me her main goal in life was to make him happy, which seemed a bit excessive to me. Matt was my unavailable boss, just like my dad had been to my mom.

On my 21st birthday, Matt took me to a fancy restaurant in Westwood for lunch and I had too many vodka martinis. That was when the flirting began in earnest. Six months later, we traveled together to San Diego for a meeting at one of the condominium complexes the investment company owned. We drove there in his black Porsche Carrera. The meeting ended at 11:00 p.m. and as we headed to the car to make the two-hour drive back to Los Angeles, Matt turned to me and asked, "Do you want to drive?" I couldn't believe it. Matt did not allow anyone to drive his car, not even his wife. I could feel my female parts tingling as he handed me the keys. "Yes!"

I was so glad my mother had taught me to drive a stick shift, insisting, "You just never know when you're going to find yourself in a situation where you'll really *need* to know how to drive one. Someone may need to go to the hospital and the only car around is a stick shift."

I eased into the driver's seat in my short skirt and put that car into first, second, then third gear. I drove and Matt told me to drive faster, "It's eleven o'clock," he said, "no one is on the road. Go for it!" I grabbed the stick shift, hit the clutch, and went into fourth and then fifth gear, driving faster and faster. "Push the peddle further. You're only going 90," Matt said. I did as he demanded and felt the adrenaline rushing through my body. I felt high.

Matt told me, "The Highway Patrol goes 80, so you'll come up behind them, not the other way around." I increased the speed even more. He told me going over 100 was considered reckless driving and I would go to jail. I went up to 100. "The Porsche is a race car," he said, "it's made to go over 100. It's a shame not to drive this car fast. It really hugs the road when you reach 100 per hour. Ironically, that is when you have the most control."

There was no one on the freeway. The road ahead and behind me was empty. I pushed my foot further down on the gas pedal, exhilaration coursing through me. I felt terrified and alive at the same time. That was when Matt reached over and began stroking my right knee and a little bit of my thigh as I drove his Porsche at 110 miles per hour up the Highway 5, past the nuclear power plants at San Onofre. I was 21 years old. What did I know? I knew the rush I felt from driving that car, at that speed, with that particular hand on my leg. I had wanted that hand to touch my body for the past year.

When we arrived at my apartment in Los Angeles at 1:30 a.m., I invited Matt in. More than a year of sexual tension had led to that moment in my kitchen. My bedroom was 10 feet from where we stood. I had Matt's jacket on. He leaned in to kiss me, I drew in a breath of anticipation and then, unexpectedly, he pulled back and did not kiss me. Instead, he said, "I need to go home." I gave him his jacket and he left.

The next day over lunch, I analyzed the night with my two best friends, Ben and Lisa, "He let me drive his Porsche, you guys! It was SUCH a turn on."

"That is so sexy," Lisa said.

"Dude, he's *married!*" Ben interjected and Lisa and I looked at him like, *yeah, so what?*

"When he put his hand on my leg, I thought I was going to lose it."

"That is so hot," Lisa said. "What happened next?"

"I kept driving. It was such a rush. All those months of flirting. I didn't know if he was really attracted to me. Now I know. Oh man and driving that car was so fun."

"He's *MARRIED*, you guys!" Ben interjected again.

"Dude, you're *fixated* on that," Lisa and I responded in unison.

I was caught up in the thrill of it all. Looking back, I see Ben had a valid point. After the Porsche driving night, Matt and I continued to work together and flirt, but we never again came that close to crossing the line and I was glad. I was especially relieved years later, whenever I met a woman like Marjorie Malore or when I thought of my stepmother, Anne, and the pain she must have suffered from my dad's betrayal, or when I thought of my own marriage. Dave was faithful to me and I to him and that was really important to both of us.

One time, when a friend's husband had been caught having an affair, I asked Dave if he had ever cheated on me. "Where would I be cheating?" he asked, "Home Depot? That's the only place I ever go." We both laughed because it was true.

Fidelity notwithstanding, I still believed there was no way two people could actually still love each other after 50 or 60 years of marriage. Most of the couples I met confirmed my belief. Most of them could not stand the sight of one another. I asked June Mittelman at The Gables, "How have you stayed married to John for 50 years?" She responded, "Every day, I say to myself: tomorrow I'm leaving him."

Sitting with the Mittelmans gave me flashbacks of my waitressing days. I remembered the couples who would sit through an entire meal without muttering a word to each other. The only conversation they enjoyed was with me. After I had taken their order and began to collect the laminated menus, the wife's eyes would say, "Oh, please don't go. Can't you stay just a minute longer?" She looked beaten down. Spent. *How many years had they been together? I always wondered. Ten? Fifteen? How did it get to this point of staring into space across a plate of enchiladas at Acapulco's? Do they still have sex? What was the point of continuing the charade? Why not just bring a book and eat alone?*

It felt tragic to see people so terrified of leaving that particular, unsatisfying, dead relationship that they would prefer to sit in silence with the person than to be alone. It wasn't the kind of silence that said, *"We're so comfortable with each other that we don't have to talk."* It was the *"I-hate-the-sight-of-you"* kind of silence, the *"you-repulse-me"* kind of silence. There was a look in their eyes, like they just did not have the energy anymore to be angry. Their apathy was palpable. That's what the Mittelmans' marriage was like. Whenever I saw them, it was the same emptiness. One day while having lunch, John, who was 85, said, "I went to the doctor this week and got a great report! He said I could easily live another 10 years."

"Oh God!" June blurted out, dropping her fork, "I don't think I can wait that long!"

The Mittelmans, like many of the long-married couples I met, were absolutely miserable together. Every once in a while, though, I met a couple who was deliriously in love after 50 or 60 years of marriage. They had seen every layer of the other person's onion, not just the sociable, professional, matronly, or sexy layer. *Every* layer. Even layers they really, *really* did not want the other person to see. And yet, even after seeing all those layers, they were still sitting across from each other at the dinner table, smiling and cooing like teenagers.

Henry and Tatiana Cartwright were one of these couples. They were married 54 years when I met them. They had been college professors together at UC Santa Cruz; he taught history and she taught sociology. Henry had advanced dementia and Tatiana was mentally sharp though physically frail. Every morning, Henry walked downstairs to kiss Tatiana's hand, say, "I love you," and sharpen her pencils so she could do her crossword puzzles. He could not communicate beyond this anymore. Tatiana would smile, take the pencils and say, "I love you more," and the tenderness between them was something lovely to witness.

Malcolm and Lana Chester were a similar pair. She was 88 and he was 89. It was the second marriage for Lana and the first for Malcolm. They both enjoyed politics and spirited discussions. They both loved poetry and walks in nature. They told me on their tour of Eldersview that it was love at first sight for both of them when they met. Malcolm was speaking at a Chamber of Commerce luncheon and Lana went up to him afterwards to shake his hand and compliment him. "The sparks exploded and it was game over," Malcolm said. They had been married 52 years when I met them, and she hung on his every word, gently taking his hand and saying things like, "Sugar, look at this beautiful vase."

This couple had flow. I could feel it. The look in her eyes when he spoke—there was just no way that could be contrived. I wanted a marriage like *that*. I thought of my own marriage. Dave and I loved each other, but we also fought a lot. We got so angry and yelled so loudly the neighbors could hear us. I could not imagine Malcolm and Lana screaming at each other the way we did.

One day when I was having an issue with Dave, I spoke with Phyllis, an 80-year-old resident at Casa Amanecer. I complained for 10 minutes about the recent argument we'd had. When I finished, Phyllis looked at me squarely and asked, "Does he have a job?"

"Yes."

"Does he beat you?"

"No."

"Then, shut up."

I think Phyllis' attitude reflected that of many women from her generation, and that is why their marriages lasted. The bar was pretty damn low.

Women did not have many choices in the 1940s, 50s, and 60s. I was talking one day with Bernadette Jenkins, telling her about my upcoming trip to Ireland with Kayleigh. "I'd give my eye teeth to go to Ireland," she said. "Where else have you been? Tell me."

"Well, I've been to Kenya, Paris, Rome, Athens, Peru, Rio de Janeiro."

"How?" she asked. "How have you been able to do all this?"

"Well, for the trip to Ireland next week, I had enough frequent flyer miles to get a free ticket. I flew a lot in my last job with the advertising agency. And I'm staying with Kayleigh's family there, so it won't cost much."

"That's lovely. What about your other travels? How did those happen? Doesn't your husband object?"

"Well, I traveled a lot before I got married. And Dave and I have traveled quite a bit together. I also take separate trips with friends. I have my own money, my own job, my own friends. Dave is a *part* of my life but he's not my whole world."

The scenario I described was not an option for most women in Bernadette's day. These were women who washed all the dishes and thought nothing of it. They traveled if they were lucky enough to land a husband who wanted to travel and had the means to do so. Or a husband who *gave* them that freedom.

I saw many perspectives on marriage as I got to know these women. Most of my views, though, were developed from my own union with Dave, which can be described the way Charles Dickens described the French Revolution: "It was the best of times, it was the worst of times."

It was February 13th and Dave and I were living in our home in San Francisco. I went out to dinner with a girlfriend, came home, and went to sleep. When I woke the next morning, I opened the curtains of our bedroom window, as I did every morning, but on this day saw something very different. I discovered our garden full of purple and pink tulips, my favorite flower. *Oh*, I thought, *it's Valentine's Day!* Dave had gone out in the dark night before. Wearing a head lamp, he planted tulips all over the garden while I was out to dinner. *Who does this after eight years of marriage?* I asked myself. I went downstairs to find him. He was reading the newspaper and I kissed him then we went for a walk on the beach and had a romantic dinner at home. It was one of the best days of my life.

Six months later, Dave and I were at a house auction in Ventura,

California. I did not want to buy another house. I didn't want the financial pressure, yet Dave had insisted we go to this. We already owned three houses and I didn't want the stress of a fourth, but Dave wanted another house. As we walked towards the huge building at the fairgrounds, Dave was nervous about the auction. "Liz, you need to get a sandwich," he said.

"Why? I'm not hungry."

"Because, you know how you get when your blood sugar drops and I don't want that happening during the auction."

We went to the deli and got a turkey sandwich. The auction started and Dave was sweating and fidgety. The houses were selling for more than we expected. There was one house in particular that Dave wanted. It was eighth in line to be auctioned. As the house approached, he got more and more nervous which made *me* feel more and more nervous. I began stressing out about the sandwich under my chair. *Should I eat it now? I don't want to be eating it when our house comes up, I need to pay attention. I don't want Dave to get mad at me.* I went back and forth in my mind and finally decided to get the sandwich out and take a bite, even though I was not hungry. I was worried I would get hungry at the exact moment I was supposed to be paying attention to the house. I reached under the chair, pulled the plastic box up to my lap, and looked at Dave who was glaring at me like he wanted to kill me. "Put the fucking sandwich away, Liz."

"Why?" I whispered. "I thought you wanted me to get it? I thought you wanted me to eat it before our house came up."

"Put it away now." I put the sandwich away. Our house came up for sale. We bid on it and someone else outbid us. Dave walked out of the warehouse and I followed him. He was 10 steps ahead of me.

"Dave, wait!" He was walking so fast I could barely catch him. Finally, he stopped, turned toward me and unleashed across the parking lot, "You are a fucking child! A selfish, idiot fucking child. I am so goddamn sick of being married to you. I don't even want to look at you. Right at the moment, right at *the* moment we are about to spend half a million dollars on a house, you decide to eat your fucking sandwich. You're clueless, Liz. You are a clueless fucking space cadet!"

He continued berating me in the car ride to the hotel and throughout the night until he finally got so tired of yelling, he fell asleep. He woke at 3:00 a.m. and started verbally abusing me again. In the morning, he got up, got dressed, walked to his truck without saying goodbye, and drove the six hours back to San Francisco, leaving me stranded in the hotel room. I called a friend who took me to get a rental car.

Who does this? I asked myself. *Who leaves their wife in a hotel room six hours from home because she ate a sandwich at the wrong time? A monster, that's who. The man I love, the man I am married to, has a horrible, awful, abusive side to him.* When I got home, Dave apologized profusely for his wrath, but his apology could not undo the damage.

Still, I stayed.

I had spent my 20s single, breaking hearts or having mine broken, fearing I would never get married. Spinsterhood was actually my biggest fear. It makes me think of a line in Barbara Kingsolver's book, *The Lacuna*,

> *People contort themselves around the terror of being alone, making any compromise against that. It's a great freedom to give up on love and get on with everything else.*

Throughout my 20s, I badly wanted a soul mate, someone with whom to share my life. I dated, did my positive affirmations and visualizations, went to therapy, and even saw a Chinese herbalist who concocted a potion for me to attract The One. Still, no man appeared in my life.

The night before my dear friend, Elena's wedding, my mom said to me, "I thought your plan was to get married by age 25?"

"It was."

"Well, you're 26." *Did she think I didn't know my birthday?*

"I know mom. I'm doing the best I can."

Elena's mom, Camila, was also worried about my marital status. Elena and I grew up together and Camila was my second mom. In Camila's world, 22 was the cutoff age when one's chances for finding a husband became seriously diminished. After Elena's wedding, Camila looked at me and shook her head, saying over and over, "Ay, mi hija, ay mi hija." That's all she said for a while, then she told me she would have to ramp up her efforts on my behalf. Her daily prayers were not doing it, nor were the candles she was lighting at the church for me. We went back to her house and she showed me the shrine she had built to Saint Anthony, the Patron Saint of Miracles. (I took a little offense to the "miracle" part.) There was a candle turned upside down.

"This one," she explained, "I will light as a sign of thanks when you find your husband, but not before." I didn't quite understand the concept of blackmailing a saint with candles, but whatever Camila did, it worked. A year later, I found Dave, the veritable needle in the haystack: a heterosexual guy in San Francisco who was also educated, financially stable, and wanted a monogamous relationship.

I met Dave at a birthday party for Kayleigh's daughter, Chloe, who had just turned one year old. Dave had recently ended a 14-year relationship. He walked in wearing jeans and a button-down shirt. His hair was in a pony tail that went to his waist. I remember his pine-colored eyes and tanned skin. He had a doll in one hand and a bouquet of calla lilies in the other. *Who does that?* I thought. *Who thinks to bring flowers for the mother?*

Two months and several dates later, Dave came to pick me up at my apartment. We were going to see Howard Stern's movie *Private Parts*. When I opened the door, he kissed me passionately right there in the doorway. My stepmom, Anne, always asked about any man I was dating, "Does he make your ovaries tingle?" The answer with Dave was unequivocally, "Yes." After our kiss, Dave walked into the hallway of my apartment and said, "I'm falling in love with you, Liz." I had heard *that* before and had been disappointed by what followed a month or so later, when the guy discovered that he had been mistaken and really did not want a committed relationship.

"You are not in love with me," I told him matter-of-factly. "You just had a Toyota for 14 years and now you have a Honda and it seems like the best thing in the world simply because it's *different*."

"You are a Porsche, Liz. And I am falling in love with you." We were married a year and a half later.

I told Edith Wetzler at Casa Amanecer the story of my meeting and courtship with Dave. Edith and I were having tea and cookies in the living room. "How about you, Edith? How did you meet Joe?" Edith began her story, taking me back to 1939. I could feel myself sitting in that San Francisco jazz club, watching Joe in his naval uniform, Edith in her pink polka-dotted dress. I could hear the big band music, feel the softness of her silk dress, smell her friend's red rose corsage, and see the way the men slowly and confidently approached them.

"Joe asked me to dance, then he asked me for my address, and the next week, we went on a dinner date. We dated for six months, going to movies and out for ice cream and then Joe sent a telegram to my parents asking for my hand in marriage. He got a telegram back saying, 'Permission granted.'" Edith and Joe were happily married for 62 years. "A part of me went with him when he died," she said. "A big part. I never cheated on him and I still haven't."

Adette and Caleb Lewis were another couple who were adorably in love. They met at Adette's first husband's funeral. "Caleb said I winked at him under my veil," Adette told me. "Now would I do that, Liz? At a *funeral?*"

"She did," Caleb insisted. They had been married 42 years and they traveled the world together doing volunteer work and enjoyed each other's company immensely. This was obvious as I sat in their San Francisco apartment drinking coffee. Adette and Caleb were both 86 years old and got up at 5:00 a.m., 6 days a week to go to the gym together. On Sundays, they went to church instead of the gym.

Monica and Bud had been married 65 years when I met them. I asked how they got together and Bud said, "We were living in the same apartment building in San Francisco's Mission District. Monica was 18 at the time and I was 19. My laundry was hanging on the line outside and it began to rain. Monica gathered my clothes and knocked on my door to give them to me. I was grateful but could not invite her in because I was home alone. You didn't do that back then. It wasn't proper." The next week Bud asked Monica on a date and she obliged. He courted her for two years before they were married. "There was no hanky-panky before the wedding," Bud proclaimed emphatically. "You didn't do that back then."

"So I've heard."

"We were married at Mission Dolores Catholic church and had our reception at a friend's Victorian home down the street. The reception was cake, champagne, and punch. In my day, we didn't have elaborate wedding receptions like they do now. Marriage was a simple, private matter and we saved our money instead for buying a home."

Dave and I had a modest wedding too, though not as low-key as Bud and Monica's. Ours was a lovely garden wedding at our home in San Francisco. It was one of those rare San Francisco August days when the weather was perfectly clear, sunny, and 80 degrees outside. I wore a spaghetti-strapped gown and danced until 11:00 p.m. It was one of the happiest days of my life. The man I loved actually loved me back.

Three weeks after our wedding, Dave told me he wanted a divorce. It was the first of many times he would ask for a divorce. We had gotten into an argument about a toilet Dave was repairing in our upstairs bathroom. He was fixing everything in the house to prepare it for the renters who would stay there while we traveled. There was a crack at the base of this toilet, I suggested he put some caulk in it, and he screamed at me that I had no clue of how stressful life was for him. The argument took a rapid downward spiral and within an hour he was telling me to get a lawyer. Our neighbor, Lisa, and my friend, Kayleigh, calmed him down and convinced him to stay married to me. The next day, we left for a year of traveling throughout Latin America. I woke up every day of that year next to a man who seemingly could not stand the sight of me. We fought and fought. He was such a jerk that first year of our marriage, that even *his* mother sat me down and told me to leave him. Yet I stayed. Things improved somewhat when we got home from our travels and we actually enjoyed some fun days together watching football, playing Scrabble, decorating our Christmas tree, and hosting dinner parties.

Mary Parsielli, a resident at Eldersview, said of her husband, "Sometimes I think: I am so lucky to have this man. And other times I think, I have to love him. God wants me to stay with him. I just *have* to love him because he is so damned difficult that *no one* else is going to do it. Then he will be all alone and somehow, I just don't think God wants that, because despite his stubbornness, he has a really good heart."

"That is exactly how I feel about Dave! There are days when I feel like I managed to fall in love with the most difficult person on the planet."

I, too, was difficult at times, doing things like buying piles of new clothes right when our property taxes were due. My anger came out in passive aggressive ways, like sabotaging tasks that Dave asked me to do for him. It was not a productive way to communicate.

The ladies from the Greatest Generation stayed despite feeling frustrated, despite infidelity, despite a lot of things. Divorce was rare for the women I met in assisted living. Most of their marriages had ended when their spouse died.

I ran into Dorothy one day and complimented the gold Police Chief star she wore on her necklace. "Were you a police officer?" I asked, and her eyes started to glisten with tears.

"My husband was, for 35 years. It was hard work, but fortunately he also had some good retirement years before he died."

"When did he pass away?"

"Three years ago. I miss him terribly."

"How long were you married?"

"56 years. We're still married."

"That must have been unbelievably hard to lose him after so much time together."

"You can't even imagine, Liz. It is indescribable. Going to bed alone that first night after sleeping next to someone for 56 years. The pain is truly unbearable."

Edith Wetzler's husband died when he was 55. Edith was 52 at the time. After Joe's death, she went back to school and got her nursing degree. "I was a stay-at-home mom for 16 years," she told me. "I did not know the first thing about being in the career world." She got her degree, worked, and raised their son, put him through college, all the while continuing her relationship with her husband, consulting him on every move.

"At night, I talked to him. While I was raising our son, I would ask, 'Am I doin' okay, Joe?'" Edith had received offers for dates, but she turned them all down. She said it just wouldn't be fair to the new guy. "Joe is the love of my life. They would be competing with a dead man, doomed to failure from the get go."

Lynette Kinsley was married 61 years. Her husband, Albert, died 5 years before she came to Casa Amanecer at the age of 91. "He was a gem," she told me.

"Losing someone after that long must feel like losing a limb."

"Pretty much. It is so hard. I went into a deep depression. My kids took me to see a psychiatrist. I met with her twice and then I sat myself down, alone, at home and I said to myself: 'Listen, you're on your own now, Lynette. You are alone. That is just the way it is. You're going to have to deal with it. Albert is gone and there's nothing you can do about it.' And with that I dusted myself off and got on with my life. I had to."

I almost said, "Oh, but you're so lucky. You had 61 great years with Albert. Some people never fall in love. Some people get divorced. Some people have 50 horrible years of marriage. Some people, like my grandma, have seven difficult marriages." But I stopped myself. Lynette did not feel lucky that she had 61 good years with Albert. Lynette wanted one more year, one more day with him.

One day I noticed Irene Dematei wasn't playing the piano like usual. "What's wrong?" I asked her. "You play the piano every day. Why aren't you playing today? Is your arthritis acting up?"

"Today is the anniversary of my husband's death."

"Oh, I'm so sorry, Irene. When did he pass away?"

She stared into space then whispered in a cracked voice, "Eighteen years ago. It's not the same, you know. My kids are great, don't get me wrong. I love them dearly, but it's not the same."

Irene was old-school San Francisco Italian and she had six kids. She was a tough lady. Watching her choke back tears, I wondered if she ever showed this side of herself to her daughters. I doubted that she did.

"My husband showed his love in concrete ways," she said, "like attending every Giants game because I was such a fan. Bill brought a book to entertain himself because he could care less about baseball."

"My husband does things like that, too," I said. "He is a staunch atheist, but he once flew home from working in Mexico to see me get baptized. It had always bothered me that my parents never baptized me. I have a strong faith, so at age 36, I went to the pastor at my church and asked to be baptized."

If Dave had to think of the last thing on Earth he would like to be doing, it would probably be standing in a church watching a preacher pour water over his wife's head. Yet, that is exactly what he did, probably thinking the whole time, *I can't believe I flew home from Mexico to watch this disturbing sight.*

It freaked him out, but he was there, sitting in the front row of the church, dressed in a nice suit, sweat pouring down his forehead, even though it was November and very cold outside. When I touched his hand, before walking to the front of the church, his palms were soaked. As the pastor poured water on my head, I watched Dave, looking like a terrified animal, yet smiling at me the whole time. My love for him grew tenfold that day.

One January night, a year or so later, I came home from work and it was freezing both outside and inside the house, even with the heater on. My hands, face, and entire body were as frigid as the water in the Pacific Ocean outside our window.

I put some fish in the oven and set the timer for 30 minutes. I whisked past Dave, who was lying on the couch. I had it in my mind that, while the fish cooked, I would take a hot bath to thaw out.

Dave took my hand and held it as I continued my motion towards the stairs. The inertia of his grasp stopped me, "You're ice cold, Liz."

"I know."

He lifted his blanket and opened his arms, "Come here. Let me warm you." I crawled under the blanket and nestled myself in his arms.

"You're so warm," I said. He felt like three hot baths and a heated blanket all in one. We had been married nine years and I lay there thinking, *what would I do without him?* I embraced and savored that moment. I realized this was what I had always wanted. *My whole life, this is what I've wanted: to be held exactly like this by someone I love.*

I thought of how much I would miss Dave if he were gone and again, I thought of all the ladies in assisted living who had lost their husbands. At one of the funerals, the wife was crying and throwing dirt at her husband's grave, yelling at him, "Why did you leave me? Why did you *leave* me?" They had been married 65 years and he died after a long, drawn-out illness. Somehow, I thought it would be easier to lose a husband at age 80, after all those years of marriage. Somehow, I thought she would have prepared herself mentally and emotionally enough to where it would not be quite so hard. I think, now, it is actually more difficult to lose someone after so much time together. After so many years, there was no separation between her and him, no way for her to have an identity apart from him.

I met many women in assisted living who lost their husbands and were deeply saddened by it, women who would give absolutely anything for one more hour with that man. So, I tried in arguments to see things from Dave's point of view, to create harmony instead of discord. I learned to spend as many moments as I could enjoying his company, because those moments could be gone in an instant.

The Blumenthals had been married 44 years when I met them. Ralph Blumenthal could not tell me about meeting his beloved Margaret without bursting into tears. He had three bad marriages, lost his job, went to work for his brother at the car lot, was ready to cash it all in and take his own life. Then he went to a "Parents without Partners" meeting. "And there I met Margaret." He always cried at that part of the story. "I had given up on finding love. Then, there she was." Ralph sat in the lounge and read the paper while Margaret played bridge because he could not stand to be away from her. They were always together. I often saw them walking around The Gables, holding hands, smiling and laughing, just thrilled to be together.

I figured the Blumenthals would be one of those couples where one spouse died and the other followed a few days or weeks later. It happened with Stanley and Rachel Price. She fell and broke her leg one day after Bingo. It wasn't a big deal. We took her to the hospital and she had surgery. The next day, she formed a blood clot which released and caused a massive stroke which killed her. Stanley died a month later from a broken heart. He just went to sleep one night and didn't wake up the next day.

There was nothing wrong with him before Rachel died. He was 82 and thriving. He and Rachel had gotten married at age 30. They raised five kids, all of whom were among the most devoted I had seen. Stanley and Rachel were proud when they told me they had only spent a total of 6 nights apart in their entire 52 years of marriage.

It was nice to see couples who were in love, especially since it was rare to actually see couples at all. Most retirement communities are about 80-percent single women, 10-percent single men and 10-percent couples. Women live longer than men and this is true, throughout history, in every country of the world. There are many theories as to why this is the case, such as the fact that women have two X chromosomes, which provides us a spare copy of every gene. Others cite lifestyle choices and the fact that women tend to drink and smoke less, exercise more, eat better, and go to the doctor more often. Some say it is the fact that we have less testosterone and testosterone contributes to cancer and heart problems later in life. No one knows exactly why women live longer, but the fact remains that even female chimpanzees, gorillas, orangutans, and gibbons consistently outlive the males of the group.

So, I met a lot of widows, some miserably married couples, and a few happily married ones. Some of the couples were still having sex, even after 50-plus years of marriage. One day Mrs. Patterson, who was 86, had to be sent out with a broken rib. Her husband had fallen on top of her while they were having sex. They were a happy couple, and I imagine their sex life contributed greatly to that joy and the longevity of their marriage.

I knew two couples, around my own age, who divorced over their sex life. They got along well in all other respects but there were big problems in the bedroom. One wife told me she wanted to vomit every time her husband touched her. She was tired of imagining movie stars every time they had sex. She really enjoyed her husband's company and truly loved him. They shared common interests like hiking and movies. They never fought. Friends and family were shocked to hear of their separation. Another woman I knew was a total knockout whose husband had not touched her in over a year. She literally begged him for sex. She told me that one day, while doing the laundry, she sat on the washing machine and gave herself an orgasm from the vibration of the spin cycle. *So, it's come to this*, she thought. A week later she asked him for a divorce. Seeing her situation made me grateful that, although there were many big issues in my marriage with Dave, sex was not one of them.

It always perplexed me when people oooed and aahhed over a 50- or 60-year marriage. *Why?* I wondered. *Why do they admire something simply because it has lasted a long time?* I admired *good* marriages, people who were clearly in love, unlike the mother of Joan Vidal. Joan sent me a letter before her mom moved into Eldersview, and part of it read:

> My mother is 95. She was 77 when my father died. I think the years since his death have been the best of her life. It is as though her life really began when he died. She was able to do as she pleased: no societal pressure to marry, no stigma of spinsterhood or divorce, no husband to deal with.

I told Kayleigh about the letter and she said, "Ah yes, we call that the Irish Widow's Syndrome." She explained that since divorce was illegal for so many years in Ireland, women who were miserable in their marriages would finally be freed when the husband died. "Then they went through a renaissance, looked 10 years younger, traveled the world, dressed sexier, got a lover, had lunch and shopped with girlfriends, enjoyed the best years of their life doing whatever they pleased."

I met another woman at a hole-in-the-wall nursing home in Santa Barbara. Her abusive, oppressive husband of 61 years had died a couple years before I met her. She lived at this skilled nursing facility from age 82 to 85 and told me they were the best years of her life. "I am free from him. I have friends. I do fun activities here like art classes and playing cards." I looked around at the scuffed beige walls, the ugly tile floor, the wrinkled people drooling and slumped in wheelchairs and thought, *wow, that must have been a Really bad marriage.*

It was not just women I came upon who had lost their spouses. There were also a few men I encountered along the way. Cyrus Teves, a resident at The Gables, often lamented to me about the loss of his wife, Ellen. Cyrus was 68, much younger than the other residents at The Gables, and an offensive guy to most people there. He sat in the dining room unshaven with his shirt unbuttoned, chest hair sticking out, reeking of cigarette smoke and whiskey. He said inappropriate things at the worst possible times. Cyrus was not cut out for community living, especially in an elegant place like The Gables. I felt sorry for Cyrus because no one liked him, except Mary, the office manager, and me. We liked Cyrus because he was real.

Cyrus and I were sitting out by the rose bushes one day and he was smoking a cigarette, looking like something Las Vegas had chewed up and spit out onto that red brick patio, when he told me how his beloved wife had died:

> *Ellen was a sweet woman who lived a clean and wholesome life. She stood by my side through all the years of boozing, gambling, and womanizing. I loved her. You wouldn't know it from my awful behavior, but I really did love her.*
>
> *Then, one day about 15 years ago, we were on this vacation. We had taken a train trip across the United States and we were in the dining car with some other folks and Ellen said her stomach hurt. The next day it hurt even worse, to the point where she could barely walk. So, we cut our travels short and came home. Two months later she was dead from pancreatic cancer. Imagine that. I abuse my body all these years, beat it to hell, and this woman who never touched a cigarette*

or a drop of alcohol, dies at age 50. It's not right. It should have been me.

It was obvious Cyrus's life had gone downhill without Ellen. The last 15 years had clearly been terrible for him. And now, here he was, in this old folks' home where no one liked him, wishing he had died instead of Ellen. *Maybe,* I thought, *despite her cheerful demeanor, Ellen was actually very unhappy in her marriage, and cancer was her way out. Maybe Cyrus's selfish ways took a subversive toll on her psyche and body.* It happens that way sometimes. Women want out of a marriage and illness subconsciously becomes their way out.

Arthur and Alice Russo were married 60 years and Arthur had been verbally abusive to her the majority of those years. One day, Alice had a massive stroke. We all talked about it, the nurse, the caregivers, and me. We came to the conclusion that Alice's stroke was a result of 60 years of being screamed at and put down by Arthur. She was so entrenched in that marriage, the stroke was her only way out, a subconscious choice to escape.

Watching Alice, who was practically comatose after her stroke, made me think of the verbal abuse I took in my marriage. Dave never hit me, but he did rage and throw tantrums. He also put me down, like repeatedly telling me I didn't really contribute to our financial well-being, despite the fact that I made a six-figure income and many times was our only paycheck.

I went by Juliette Wright's apartment at The Gables as she was getting ready to take her family on their annual trip to Nebraska to visit her husband's grave. "Are you ready for your trip?" I asked.

"Yes, I'm all packed and ready. Just need to call my cab."

"How many years ago did Joe die?"

"It's been six years now. I take the kids every year to visit his grave."

"How long were you married?"

"Sixty-five years."

"How did he die?"

"Cancer," she said.

"I'm sorry. That's very sad."

"Not really," she replied. *Not really?* That was all she said and we stood there in silence, awkwardly looking at one another.

"You see this statue, Liz?"

"Yes, it's beautiful." It was a bronze statue of a woman with her arms folded in front of her.

"The artist is from New Mexico and for many years her statues had no arms. All of the statues she did of women had no arms. Then she got divorced and started putting arms on her statues."

Juliette then told me about how she had left Joe one time when she was 25. After three years of marriage, she was fed up with his tyrannical ways. She mustered all her courage, packed a bag, and moved to Oregon. Joe followed her, cried and pleaded with her to come home. "He actually got on his knees and begged," she said. So, Juliette succumbed and never looked back. She figured that flight to Oregon was her one shot to get out. She resigned herself to stay after that, but nothing changed. None of the issues that bothered her changed. "We just weren't compatible," she said. "It was 65 years of hard work just trying to get along." *Imagine that. Regretting 65 years of your life. God, please don't let that happen to me.*

I thought back to a conversation I had with Violet York at The Gables. We were sitting in her apartment, looking out the windows at the redwood trees, and she asked me about my marriage, "Are you happy, Liz?"

"Yes. This week I'm feeling happy. Dave and I are settling into our home in Ojai. We got a rooster and a couple of hens to go along with our new rural life."

"That's nice."

"The first couple years of our marriage were hell. But things are better now."

"If you have a good one, hang onto him. I was married twice and both of them were complete shits. My first husband, when I was 19, was physically abusive and the second was emotionally abusive. He was particularly nasty when we were in a foreign country because I was stranded and dependent on him."

"Dave was a total jerk to me throughout most of our Latin America trip, but I spoke Spanish much better than he did, so I felt somewhat empowered by that. I had also traveled alone to Peru, Mexico, and Argentina before our marriage. So, I had no problem with the idea of taking off on my own and leaving him stranded if it came to that."

Violet admitted she was bitter about her marriages. Mostly, she was mad at herself. "I was just lousy at picking husbands," she said. "Luckily, I was really good at picking friends."

"I'm good at picking friends, too."

My marriage got better, then worse, then better again. During a particularly rough patch, I went to see Nadine White, a resident who had been married 50 years. I asked her, "Nadine, do you ever just feel like saying 'screw it' and leaving Tom?"

"The first 10 years of our marriage, I packed my bags at least once a month," she said.

"Then what happened?"

"I don't know. Somehow, we just worked through things. I got over it."

The Cohens were a couple where the husband was a gem and the wife was detestable. Mrs. Cohen had borne 11 children and still ruled her roost with an iron fist. All 11 kids obeyed their mom, despite the fact that they were now in their 50s and 60s. I sensed that even though they acquiesced, they did not like her very much. We certainly didn't. The activity director, the maintenance director who was forced to cater to her every whim, the dining supervisor, all of us could not stand Ellen. The kids sent her flowers for every occasion, had dinner once a week with her, even forced their own children to visit the miserable woman.

I stopped by one day and found Ellen's grandchildren running around on the grass outside her apartment, laughing and playing hide-and-seek as Ellen sat there with a scowl. "Keep your voices down," she yelled, then turned to her husband and demanded, "When are they leaving? Go get my book and glasses for me." Her husband dutifully got up and went to get her glasses.

I could never understand that relationship. The Cohens had been married 55 years. He was one of the gentlest, kindest men I had ever met, and brilliant, too. He had been a successful accountant for 40 years, had supported the family well, and all she did was bitch at him and order him around. I often watched them interact, looking for an inkling that he resented her, but I never saw one. What did Mr. Cohen owe this woman? Why did he love her? *Could* he actually love her? Or did he stay for the kids and then time just got away from him?

Dottie and Jack Wilson had been married 60 years when I met them. Whenever Dottie tried to interject a comment into the conversation, Jack always interrupted, bringing the focus back to himself. "You know, when I was in World War II, we had a saying...." Dottie did not seem the least bit affected by it. Each time he interrupted her, she would smile serenely. Sixty years of unchecked narcissism.

Jack flirted openly with other women in front of Dottie and told her repeatedly what a bad cook she was. He walked five feet in front of her, oblivious to her aching knees and hips. In private, Dottie told me how she dreamed of traveling, but it never happened. She wanted a social life, but instead spent the majority of her days living in isolation with Jack. I looked for any hint of rage seeping through Dottie, but detected none.

"I know marriage is about compromise, Dottie, but when do we cross a line where we have compromised too much of ourselves to make it work?"

"I don't really know the answer to that, my dear."

I thought of my dad and Anne's 50th wedding anniversary dinner. I sat across from Anne and asked, "So what is the secret to a long marriage?"

"I'm a saint," she replied. "That's the secret."

I knew I had already compromised too much of myself, my values, my soul, to make my marriage to Dave work. Yet, I stayed and stayed. Three years after that conversation with Dottie, I was still with Dave and working at Eldersview assisted living when Samuel Price's son, Louie, came to my office. Louie was a 26-year-old who had been a linebacker in college. He was six-foot-four, 250 pounds. He had done tours of combat duty in

Iraq and Afghanistan, seen friends die next to him, but nothing prepared him for watching his father sink into depression.

"What happened to your dad?" I asked.

"My mom left him after 45 years of marriage. He was a together guy, taught college English, coached football. She leaves him and he falls apart."

"Tell me more about that, how did he fall apart?"

"Within a few weeks of my mom leaving, he went from being totally functional to lying on the floor in a fetal position. Not eating or talking."

"Did he suffer from depression before?"

"No. He had some anxiety, but nothing like this. Forty-five years of marriage. Who DOES that, Liz?! WHO leaves in the fourth quarter?!" Louie was yelling at me now.

"I guess your mom does. I bet she feels pretty guilty about all this."

"No, no she doesn't. She's got ICE in her veins. How long have you been married?" Louie asked, pointing to a picture on my desk of Dave and me on the beach in Mexico.

"Thirteen years."

"Listen to me," he said, leaning in. "If you're even THINKING of leaving him, do it now. Don't do to that guy what my mom did to my dad. Leave him now when he still has a chance to get on with his life."

I *was* thinking of leaving Dave. What Louie said made sense. I felt guilty about the thought of leaving, but staying longer would only hurt Dave more. I read a magazine article that night and a line jumped off the page at me: *Are you breathing just a little bit and calling it a life?* "Yes," I said out loud to the magazine, "Yes, I am." My spirit was dying.

I believe most human beings both intensely crave and, at the same time, greatly fear intimacy. Dave and I were no exception. We got close and then, almost as if on cue, we created distance, usually in the form of a knock-down, drag-out fight which culminated in a lot of door-slamming.

Not all romantic relationships require this level of drama to achieve the needed break from intimacy. Some people just take a week's vacation and go visit their sister in Idaho. The level of drama Dave and I had was exhausting. After 13 years of it, I was sick and tired of being sick and tired.

All those years of volatility and intensity . . . and the end was so quiet. I packed a bag to take to Kayleigh's house, walked downstairs to Dave who was lying on the couch watching television, and said, "I'm leaving you." He just cried, shook his head, and said nothing.

The day after I moved to Kayleigh's, he called me and asked, "Did you really leave me? You're not just on a business trip right now?"

"Dave, I've been telling you for years what is wrong, telling you I am unhappy, but you did not hear me."

"I hear you now," he said. But it was too late. I had no hope left for our marriage. He had won every battle and lost the war.

I have known or heard of so many men who echoed Dave's sentiment, *I had no idea she was so unhappy.* Or, they knew she was miserable but never thought she would actually *leave.* They stand there shocked because their wife has divorced them. My therapist shared an interesting Darwinian view on this phenomenon. He said men have been genetically programmed, through natural selection, generation after generation, to hear what they want to hear. Men, particularly white men, have had all the economic and political power and therefore could tune out anything they did not want to hear because frankly, they did not have to listen to it.

Their wife could complain until the cows came home, she could threaten to leave every day, but they both knew she wasn't going anywhere. She had no way to support herself and the children if she left. My grandmother and her sisters left. They were willing to endure whatever financial hardship they had to rather than put up with bullshit from a man. I am very proud of these women, my beautiful, amazing, powerful ancestors.

The last two years of our marriage, I woke up every day wishing Dave would leave me. I wanted out, but I did not want to be the one to have to do it. Sometimes, if I woke before Dave and he wasn't stirring or didn't look like he was even breathing, the thought would cross my mind that maybe he'd had a heart attack and died in his sleep. I would think, *yes, please let this be it, let me be free to go on with my life.* Other days, when he woke before me and I heard him mulling about the kitchen, I would lie in bed and pray, "God, please give me cancer. Please just take me. I can't do this anymore."

That's how badly I wanted out of my marriage, and that's how badly I did not want to have to be the one to leave. Nora, a resident who lived at Eldersview, told me she had wished for cancer, too. "Death is a socially acceptable way out of a marriage," she said. "Divorce is not."

In one of the sessions with our marriage counselor, I turned to Dave and said, "I love you; I just can't live with you anymore."

And he replied, "If you leave me, I will destroy you." *Oh, now I really want to stay.*

During our separation and divorce, I called Dave regularly to check on him and ask how he was doing. "How am I doing?" he responded. "My soul has been destroyed by a soulless woman. *That's* how I'm doing!" I felt sad that he was in pain, but I couldn't go back.

I went to the county hospital during this time to meet a patient. He was 68-years old and had ended up in the intensive care unit with total organ failure. He was an alcoholic and not eating prior to his hospitalization. The doctors pumped him full of liquids and medications, stabilized him, and now he was ready to move to an assisted living. I met with his son and his doctor.

"My mom cooked him healthy meals and served them to him on the couch," his son said. "She laid out his medications. She controlled his drinking. Then he got alcohol-related dementia. When he got physically violent, she had to leave. That was three years ago. They were married 36 years."

I thought, *where would Dave be if I left after 36 years instead of 13?* I looked at this man and saw where 20, 30, 40 years of enabling could lead. It was not pretty.

I fell in love with Dave partly because of his refreshing honesty, then sat in court, watching in disbelief as his attorney lied under oath, telling the judge I had cut Dave off my health insurance. Dave sat there and nodded in agreement and my heart broke. Dave was awarded a huge amount of monthly alimony mainly because of this health insurance lie. The lying and fraud continued and I began to melt down. I spoke with my father almost daily for support and guidance, both emotional and legal, since my dad had been a successful attorney for 50 years. At age 86, he was as on the ball as any 35-year-old.

One day, as I cried on the phone, my dad said, "Honey, you are a Marine's daughter. You need to suck it up and kick ass." So, I dug deep and fought back with all the strength I could muster. Yet still, I watched everything Dave and I had built financially slip through my hands.

After 11 months, Dave and I finally came to an "agreement" on our assets. He got the San Francisco house, the Mexico house, the more expensive car, one of the IRAs, and the lion's share of proceeds from the sale of the Ojai house. I got to stop paying alimony. I had already spent $30,000 in attorney's fees and was looking at many thousands of dollars more if the divorce dragged on. I was also facing many more days of lost work and the potential of a nervous breakdown. My attorney told me I could surrender or face losing even more if we went to trial. "The judge clearly favors Dave," he said. "You might even end up paying his attorney's fees." It was true. The judge openly flirted with Dave in court, even going so far as to wink at him.

After signing the final divorce settlement, I went to see Kayleigh, who had stood by my side every step of the way through that horrible year. "Well," she said, "you've gone from Prada to *Nada*." She knows exactly what to say in the best or worst moments. I had lost everything yet found myself laughing out loud with my dear friend.

Months later, when the reality hit me that I had lost my life savings and moved from my ocean-front home in San Francisco to a boarding house in Daly City, I complained to an 85-year-old woman at a nursing home. I was devastated. She said, "That's the price of equality, my dear. Forty years ago, you couldn't have left him. You probably would have been financially dependent on him." She told me she envied the choices my generation had and reminded me to be grateful to the brave women who had paved the way. After that conversation, I felt a little better about the exorbitant price I had paid for my freedom from that marriage.

In the wake of my divorce, I could not help but think of my mother's marriages and divorces. My mother's first husband physically beat her and, somehow, she mustered the courage to leave him despite his threats to kill her if she did. For that, I will always admire her. My mom left her second awful marriage, too. I do not understand why people stay together and torture each other for the sake of the kids. As a child, I was very grateful when my mother got divorced. It took tremendous strength for my mom to leave her marriages, and thank goodness she did. If she had not left, she never would have married Bob, her third husband, who was a treasure and my only direct experience with caring for an ailing loved one. My mother finally found true love with Bob and then, 10 years later, he died.

Chapter Nine

Last Man Standing

The end is in the beginning, and yet you go on.
— Samuel Beckett, *Endgame*

My stepfather, Bob, was one of the great lights of my life. Bob was 60 years old when his health started to decline and 62 when he passed away. Slowly, over the course of two years, I watched him die. I was 21 when he passed and too young to grasp the enormity of what was happening and how the loss of him would impact me for the rest of my life. Bob was one of the people I loved most on the planet, and he was my introduction to walkers, dialysis, surgery, home-health nurses, and funeral arrangements.

I was away at college when Bob's late-stage diabetes escalated. He had to have four fingers and toes amputated. He had open-heart surgery. His one functioning kidney finally failed and he had to have his blood cleaned through dialysis three times a week. Every time I came home for a visit, Bob looked older and thinner. Still, I clung to the hope that he would bounce back and get strong again. A few months before he died, on a month-long visit home, I spoon-fed him and gave him his insulin injections because he no longer had the strength to hold a fork, let alone plunge a syringe into his leg. Bob was an athletic outdoorsman, a hiker, and a runner. He was a municipal court judge, active in community service, a supportive husband, father, and stepfather. To watch this man who had epitomized strength, lose his dignity, was excruciatingly painful for all of us, most of all for him.

During that trip home, my mom and I took Bob into town for a piece of his favorite blackberry crumb pie. He was so frail that we had to help him down the street, even with his walker. He smiled like a little boy as he bit into that pie and I started to cry because it was the first time I had seen him look happy in months. Bob asked me to play backgammon with him late at night. "Will you put on a strong pot of coffee, honey?" he asked. He told my mom he was afraid to go to sleep, fearing he would not wake up, so he stayed awake the entire night, drinking coffee. When he did leave his body, it was at 6:30 in the morning and he had just laid down on the couch after being awake all night.

Losing Bob was so devastating that I was unable to cry at his funeral. The pain was too recent and raw and so deep that it took several months to emerge from inside me. I remember the moment it hit me that Bob had actually died. I was in a grocery store in Los Angeles, eight months after his funeral, shopping with my boyfriend, Patrick, and his roommate. I walked down the coffee and tea aisle and while looking at the tea, I noticed a metal ball used for loose tea. I thought to myself, *that metal tea ball would make a great stocking stuffer for my mom. Christmas is three months away. Bob will not be here for Christmas . . . my first Christmas without Bob . . . Oh my God, Bob is dead.*

I began bawling uncontrollably in the aisle of Safeway, hyperventilating and wailing. I thought I might collapse. When Patrick found me, I was unable to speak. He drove me home and I stared out the window of his apartment, continuing to cry cathartically for another 45 minutes before I was able to tell him what was happening. His face was pale as he watched me, so frightened that he later told me he almost took me to the emergency room.

When I went to work in assisted living, 10 years after Bob's death, I was 31 years old. I had experienced the passing of two people I loved dearly: my grandma when I was 10 and Bob when I was 21. Death was a relatively unusual occurrence in my life up to that point.

One day at Casa Amanecer, I walked by a group of women playing bridge in the lounge and thought to myself, *they're just passing the time, waiting to die.* Then I thought, *wait a minute—am I not doing the same thing?* We just think when we are 32 or 24, or 44, the things we are doing are so much more important than what a 90-year-old is doing. But, why?

As I left the lounge and walked upstairs to the clinic, I remembered a play I had read in college, Samuel Beckett's *Endgame,* which ponders life as though it were a game. If life is a game, Beckett surmises, then the object of the game is to die, because that is what happens at the end of the game, every single time. Beckett asks, then, why don't we just get it over with in the beginning? He writes, "It will be the end and there I'll be, wondering what can have brought it on and wondering what can have ... (*he hesitates*) ... why it was so long coming." Now, Beckett was a bit of a depressing guy, but he had a point.

Why *don't* we just get it over with if death is what is going to happen eventually anyway? Maybe it's because we are afraid. None of us knows what happens in the afterworld. Shakespeare described death in *Hamlet* as "the undiscovered country from whose bourn no traveler returns...." And, there you have it. No one has come back to tell us what is on the other side of that door, so it is a bit intimidating, even for the most courageous, to walk through it. I have a strong faith and I feel deep peace when I go to church or connect with God through prayer or meditation. Still, I have some trepidation about what happens when we leave this earth.

After I had been working at The Gables for a short time, I walked into the office one morning and Sharon said, "Mr. Jones died last night."

"Oh my GOD!" I screamed and threw my arms up in the air, causing my cup of coffee to go flying over my shoulder. Sharon laughed loudly.

"Liz," she said, perplexed and still laughing, "he was 95."

"Still, it's so sudden. I just saw him in the dining room yesterday. He was fine. He was enjoying his clam chowder."

"Well, his heart stopped last night while he was sleeping."

"So, he's gone?" I said, stunned.

"Yes."

"My God . . . it's just so final."

The following week, Sharon found me standing in the lobby drinking coffee. She took the cup from my hand and said, "Liz, Mr. Blanchard died last night."

Again, I threw my hands up and yelled, "Oh my GOD! You're joking!"

Sharon laughed and said, "You're going to have to get used to people dying."

My education on death, my opportunity to look back at life from the end, even though I was young, began at The Gables. I went to work, I saw my friends and family, I cooked dinner, I watched my chickens in the back yard, scratching and pecking away, with an incredible sense of purpose, as if the work they were doing was of the utmost importance. I watched them and wondered, why *AM* I here?

When I was married to Dave, he had this annoying habit where he would ask me, "What are you doing today, Liz?"

And I would say, "I'm going to the grocery store." Then he would ask, "And then?"

"Then I'm going to do the laundry."

"And then?"

"Then I'm going to cook dinner."

"And then?"

This went on and on until I finally got irritated and yelled, "You're driving me *crazy* with your 'and then.'" This line of questioning could go on and on indefinitely with what I planned to do for the rest of my life, and the last answer would be, "And then I'm going to die, okay?"

We get caught up in the minutiae of life and forget what is important. We lose perspective. Then one day, someone we care about dies. For a brief period, we see things from a higher plane, until we get tangled in the nitty gritty again. My wakeup call was Mary. I finally got to a place of acceptance that the residents at The Gables were going to pass away. But I did not expect my co-workers to drop dead.

Mary was our office manager whom I loved. I popped my head into her office on a Friday, "Hey," I said, "do you want to go to the Ojai Garden Tour? I'm on the committee and I've got a couple of free tickets."

"No thanks, Liz. I'm not feeling well. My back is really bothering me. Actually, my stomach, too. All week they've been hurting."

"Oh, I'm so sorry to hear that. Have you gone to the doctor?"

"I have an appointment on Monday."

Two days later, on Sunday morning, Betty, one of our caregivers and a close friend of Mary's, found her on the floor of her apartment. Mary had advanced ovarian cancer and did not know it. The cancer caused a blood clot to be released which led to a massive stroke that killed Mary instantly.

She was 68 years old and as active as any 30-year-old I knew. She died on Mother's Day, which was ironic since our residents had nicknamed her "mom." She was a mother hen to them and to many of us staff as well.

That Friday, when I had offered Mary the Garden Tour tickets, I also told her I would be leaving The Gables. I had accepted another position and given my two-weeks' notice. So, by a fluke, I actually got to say goodbye to Mary right before she died. I told Mary about the new job and we expressed what we had meant to one another. "You were nice to me," I said. "From the very first day I started here, you were kind to me. I was afraid I would fail at this job and you took me under your wing."

"You are a good person, Liz. It was easy to be nice to you. And you are the best marketing director we have had." We cried a little and hugged. I had no idea she would be gone two days later.

All of us were stunned and saddened by Mary's passing. John, my office mate, saved his last voicemail message from her for months, just to hear her voice.

When I worked at Casa Amanecer, our chaplain, Sister Louise, would ask residents to describe their own "good death." People would say they wanted to be comfortable, no pain, at peace. No one wanted to die alone.

In every assisted living where I worked, there was an unspoken understanding among caregivers when a resident was in their final days. Rather than becoming hardened or desensitized to death because of the frequency of its occurrence, they became even kinder. They would not leave dying residents alone, even for a minute. They would always find a family member or another staff member to sit with the person. They made sure the resident did not die without another human there, holding their hand.

Sister Louise would next ask the elders to get more specific, describe the music and scents they would like, and the individual people they would want surrounding them. Then she asked them to plan their own funeral. At our staff meeting one week, Sister Louise asked the management team to describe our own "good death." I was 37 years old, still married to Dave, and here is what I wrote:

> *I am at my home in San Francisco. I am comfortable with no physical pain. I have time to tie up all my loose ends and say goodbye to the people I love. But not too much time, maybe a few months. I don't want to drag this out. I look good. I have makeup on and my hair is styled and I am wearing nice pajamas. Silk and colorful. I am at peace. I have no anger left for anyone, only love. I have made all my amends. I listen to music (disco, country, mellow rock, and classical). I go to the ballet one last time. I laugh a lot the last month of my life. People visit me and I communicate to those most important, just how much they have meant to me. I hug them close. Then, one night, I go to sleep with Dave next to me and I die.*

Sister Louise then asked us what kind of funeral we wanted. I knew I definitely wanted to be cremated. I wanted my ashes scattered in a few places that were sacred to me: Machu Picchu, the San Francisco Bay, and the redwoods. During the signing of our living trust, Dave and I had to express our burial wishes. My smartass husband said he wanted to be shot from a cannon. I looked at the lawyer and asked, "Do I have to do this?"

"Yes," she said, "it's a legal document. If he wants to be shot from a cannon, you have to respect his wishes and shoot him from a cannon."

"Where am I supposed to get a cannon? Do I need a special permit? Dave," I said turning to him, "quit being ridiculous. Think of your mother and me, standing there watching your body fly through the air." Our attorney laughed as we sat and argued.

"Is it even legal?" I asked her. "Do I shoot him into a lake or the ocean or what?"

"I'm not sure actually. We would have to research that."

"It's my funeral," Dave said, "I should have what I want." He finally relented, agreeing that we could shoot his *ashes* out of a cannon into a lake.

My sister, Leslie, wants a Viking funeral, her body put on a pyre, sent out into a lake where people shoot flaming arrows at her. Leslie's friend, Bailey, wants to be chopped into pieces and fed to the fish in the ocean. I also heard about "natural funerals" where the person is not embalmed nor cremated; they are just wrapped in cloth and lowered into the ground in a pine forest. There's no tombstone. Instead loved ones are given GPS coordinates to find where the body is buried and there is a tree planted next to it. That sounds like a beautiful way to be laid to rest.

I spent a lot of my assisted living days thinking about death and talking about death with residents and prospective residents. Part of the standard move-in paperwork involved asking the new resident if he or she had a Do Not Resuscitate (DNR) order in place. If they had one in place, we needed a copy in our Emergency Binder. If they did not have one, I was supposed to make sure they understood what would happen in an emergency without one. I never knew the appropriate time to bring this up. It seemed too harsh at the beginning of the paperwork signing and I did not want to end the meeting on that note. So, I usually put the DNR form in the middle of the stack of papers.

Some residents had been through the conversation already with their doctor and it was easy, "Oh yes, here you go, here is a copy of my DNR." Or, "Yes, I am fully aware of it, but I am just not quite ready to go yet, so I want to be resuscitated." For others, it was the first time they or their kids had heard of such a thing, so I had to explain, "A DNR means that if your heart stops, they will not re-start it. If you stop breathing, they will not bring you back to life. If you do not have one of these in place, emergency responders are legally required to do absolutely everything humanly possible to prolong your life."

I would then explain that for younger people, it is generally considered a good idea to be brought back to life. For older people, it could be quite traumatic for both the senior and the paramedics. They would look at me quizzically or ask, "What do you mean?" and I would continue.

> *They will use resuscitative measures including chest compressions, assisted ventilation, sometimes endotracheal intubation, defibrillation, and cardiotonic drugs shot straight into your heart with a hypodermic needle.*
>
> *Elders sometimes have brittle bones and their ribs get broken during this process. Their life is saved, but they may end up in a coma or brain dead because they stopped breathing for a few minutes and the oxygen supply was cut off.*

Paramedics have told me they hated to put seniors through resuscitation. It was often brutal to watch and I imagined even more brutal to have to be the one doing it.

I gave people the facts and asked them what they wanted to do. Dave thought I could have gotten my point across without mentioning broken ribs or hypodermic needles shot into the heart. But most people truly did not understand how intense resuscitation could be. It seemed worth it to go through the trauma at 30—but at 90?

I did not enjoy the paperwork-signing stage of move-ins. It was a tedious process. If it had been a particularly long and emotionally draining week, I sometimes did not even ask about the DNR. I never knew which way that conversation would go, and sometimes I just was not in the mood to find out. So, I took my chances, prayed the person wouldn't go into cardiac arrest that night, and left that page for the next day.

Mary White's move-in was a typical example of the conversation which could sometimes last 30 minutes or more. I explained the DNR. Mary looked at me and then her daughter with a questioning expression on her face. I explained in detail what it meant. Then her daughter repeated what I said. Then everyone started to cry, silent tears, two to three at a time, running down the faces of the daughter, son-in-law, and granddaughter. We all sat in silence for a while. It was as though they were all facing for the first time the fact that Mary would one day die. Then I said, "You don't have to decide right this minute. Just let me know sometime this week. It's just, if an emergency happens and you *do* want a DNR, we have to have a copy to give to the paramedics."

"No, no," Mary's daughter said and sniffled, "now is as good a time as any." *Is it? Is it really? Wouldn't later, alone as a family, without me here, be better?* "We have to talk about this. Mom, what do you think?" Mary, like most seniors, decided not to re-start her heart. She said to her daughter, "Look, honey, I'm 87. I have had a good life. If it is my time, then it's my time." They went on to have a conversation they had clearly never had before. They all talked about their feelings towards Mary and her inevitable death. She signed the DNR form, then I moved on to the next paper in the pile.

"So, are you planning to have your hair done in our salon or go out? It's a separate company that runs the salon and we have this billing agreement that needs a credit card number if you want to get it done here." Just like that, *Do you want us to re-start your heart? And how about a shampoo and set once a week?*

Mom or dad were usually the least emotional when the topic of the DNR came up. Seniors were often ready to die, but their adult children were rarely ready to lose them. Dr. Baker's daughter, for example, pressured him to go through radiation treatment for prostate cancer at age 92. He was miserable. It was unkind of his daughter to put him through this, but she could not let go. Regardless of their age or the relationship they had, when the day of a parent's death came, the adult child felt like an orphan. Because of this, they often kept their parents alive because they did not want to say goodbye or face their own mortality.

My mother got nervous about her own mortality on birthdays when she reached the same age as the death of one of her parents. Her dad died at age 54, and as my mom's 54th birthday approached, her anxiety mounted. I couldn't help but interject, "Mom, your dad fell into a MANHOLE! This is in no way connected to genetics unless you are a strict follower of natural selection. I mean, I suppose clumsiness could be genetic."

When my mom was 65, she was diagnosed with stage III colon cancer.

I was in no way ready to lose her. She had surgery to remove the tumor then received chemotherapy treatments. I sat with my mother and held her hand while the chemotherapy drugs slowly dripped into her body through a port in her neck. Four hours went by like five minutes. I looked at my mom and remembered her telling me about the first four months of my life, spent in an oxygen tank because I had infant's asthma.

I thought of how she slept next to me every night at the hospital, holding my tiny hand through the plastic. I remember how hers was the first face I saw when I woke up at age six after having my tonsils removed. There she was with chocolate Fudgsicles and stuffed animals for my sister and me. Again, at age 17 after having my wisdom teeth out, my eyes opened after a deep, long slumber, and there she was, holding my hand, smiling, just as I was doing now with her.

Compassionate friends softly said to me, "You know, your mom could die." They wanted me to prepare myself if it did, in fact, happen soon. I told them "No, no, she's going to be fine. She's going to be fine." I would not even let the thought of her dying enter my mind. I did not realize, though, just how entrenched that fear was in my subconscious mind until the day my mom called and told me she had received the results of her first CT scan. She was cancer-free. I let out a huge sigh and said, "Oh, thank God! Thank God!" I hung up the phone and cried tears of relief for half an hour. At age 37, I was not ready to be orphaned.

Like me, Zelda Derrickson's daughter was not ready to be an orphan either. Zelda was a special lady and we who worked at The Gables were also not ready to lose her. Sharon called Dr. Lazer, a local gerontologist, one day about Zelda, who was 92. "Dr. Lazer," she said, "I'm worried about Zelda. She looks kind of yellow." Zelda had ovarian cancer and was responding well to chemotherapy, so her change in color had surprised Sharon.

"Sharon," Dr. Lazer replied flatly, "people get *old* and they *die*."

Zelda's daughter took her to see Dr. Lazer and after the visit, the doctor and Zelda's daughter decided it was time for hospice. Everyone wanted

Zelda to be comfortable and free from suffering. But they didn't tell Zelda, who continued doing water aerobics, meeting with her book club weekly, and re-decorating her apartment. Finally, with Sharon present, Zelda's daughter told her, "Mom, we've decided to enroll you in hospice care. The nurse who visited you yesterday was from a hospice agency."

"What does that mean?" Zelda asked.

"Well, generally it means you have six months or less to live and the doctors won't treat your cancer anymore. No more chemotherapy." Zelda nodded that she understood, but said nothing. The next morning, a caregiver found her dead in her apartment.

"Oh my God!" I said to Sharon. "Can you believe it? How bizarre. You tell Zelda she's on hospice and the next day she's gone. What are the chances of *that*?!"

Sharon looked at me in her knowing way. "Well . . . maybe it's not so bizarre."

"What do you mean?"

"I mean maybe Zelda took matters into her own hands when she found out she was on hospice. Perhaps she had something stashed away for just such an occasion."

"You think she killed herself?!"

"Let's put it this way, her daughter did not seem surprised at all when I called to tell her we found Zelda dead this morning."

Coroners will do an autopsy if there is some question of how the person died. Sometimes families want one, even if there is no doubt it was natural causes, because Alzheimer's and some other diseases are best diagnosed postmortem. The kids want to know if mom or dad had it because they want to know if they might get it. There is a hotline people can call to get a private autopsy done for about $3,500. Zelda's daughter did not want an autopsy.

Zelda's time on hospice was clearly very short. Some people spend a week on hospice care, others spend years. Hospice is a beautiful service. It is a philosophy of care which treats the person rather than the disease and focuses on enhancing quality rather than quantity of life. The needs of the patient and family drive the activities of a team who not only address physical distress, but also emotional and spiritual issues. There is a physician, nurse, social worker, chaplain, home health aide, and team of volunteers who do everything possible to give the person pain-free, fulfilling days for whatever time they have left. They provide things like art, aromatherapy, and music, and they help people fulfill dying wishes such as trips to Hawaii or Disneyland.

They are available over the phone and in person 24 hours a day, 7 days a week to manage symptoms at home and prevent traumatic trips to the emergency room. Fighting to stay alive is an understandable and oftentimes admirable thing. But this journey called life that we are on *will* eventually end for all of us. Accepting that one's end is near and having people facilitate a peaceful, dignified death is a lovely thing. I am stunned at how many people in the United States have no idea what hospice is or resist it at all costs.

Hospice can also sometimes become a form of euthanasia. The morphine given to the patient for pain management starts to slow everything down. The hospice nurse gives morphine at her discretion and has great leeway in just how much morphine she is allowed to administer. Some nurses give large, regular doses. The line between keeping someone comfortable and easing them over the hump into death can get blurry. Doctors know it. Hospice nurses know it. Assisted living workers know it. Dr. Jack Kevorkian went to jail for this, but if we call it "hospice" or "palliative care," it is legal. It is what some people want and I respect that.

Hospice is also life-affirming. It is about giving people the best possible quality of life. Yet, some people find it inhumane. Liquids and nutrition are sometimes withheld from the dying person unless they specifically ask to have them. It would seem that withholding food and water from a dying person is cruel, but actually, I learned the opposite is true. When the body is shutting down and declining, it cannot absorb as much, so the food and liquids cause swelling that can be painful. Also, as the body starts to shut down, it releases endorphins. Putting nutrition and liquid into the body actually *blocks* the release of the endorphins, thereby making the person's death *more* painful.

When I left my last assisted living job at Eldersview and went to work in home health, we had a 95-year-old patient named Howard who shot and killed himself. His son, daughter, and our home-health nurse who had known him for years were all devastated. Howard had never been depressed. He left a note saying he was tired of all the tests and procedures, tired of going back and forth to the emergency room, tired of being in and out of the hospital, done with being poked and prodded and taking an ever-growing list of medications.

I talked with his distraught family. I went to see Dr. Braxton, his primary care physician of 25 years who was heartbroken by the news. "I had no idea he was done and wanted to die. I wish he would have told me." Howard could have had a beautiful, peaceful death if he had gone on hospice. But his family and doctor were in denial. They did not listen to him. They did not want to broach the subject of death with him. Howard shot himself because he thought there was no other option. He died a violent, awful death because his doctor did not want to talk about end-of-life. Like most physicians, Howard's doctor was hard-wired to keep patients alive, no matter what, which is admirable to a point. At some point, though, it becomes negligent.

"I wish he would have told me he wanted hospice," Dr. Braxton continued. "He didn't have to have such a horrible death."

"Did you ever talk with him about hospice? Did he even know what it was?" There was a long, uncomfortable silence, and I left the doctor's office soon after. It was Dr. Braxton's responsibility to bring up the subject of hospice with Howard, but doctors often pursue the most aggressive treatments, even with the elderly, and even at the expense of the patient's quality of life.

One resident's son, Joseph Wagner, came to speak with me after his dad's death. His mom was an absolute mess following the loss of her husband of 60 years. She wailed and cried for hours on end. She needed constant hand-holding. She was incontinent of bowel and bladder and had lost all dignity and decorum. She was 94. Joseph told me he wished she would die, for her own sake and his. "Can we put her on hospice?" he asked.

"The problem with that plan, Joseph, is that your mom does not have a terminal diagnosis. Medicare requires a prognosis of six months or less to live. Some of the approved diagnoses for hospice are congestive heart failure, cancer, end-stage liver disease, end-stage dementia—she doesn't have any of these. I don't think a doctor will put her on hospice just for being old and difficult and falling apart emotionally."

"I see."

"Although, I do understand why you want her to go and maybe even she wants that, too."

I went to a luncheon where the speaker was from a hospice agency. He told a funny story (at least it was humorous to all of us who worked in elder care) about the wife of a man who was on hospice. The man was 88, had lung cancer, and had been given six months to live. "That was three years ago," the speaker said. "Several times, it seemed he was close and might expire." When the man miraculously pulled through a close call for the third time, the hospice guy said to the wife, "Wow, what a miracle, I think he might live quite a bit longer."

"I think he might grow a new lung!" she said disdainfully.

Many families were ready to say goodbye to their loved one, but they did not want to admit it because this stirred up guilt. "I love you. Now, could you please die?"

It was not because they did not love the person, but rather because they had been preparing themselves emotionally for the event for 15 to 20 years. The parent had chronic illnesses and the family called everyone in from the East Coast for a bedside vigil when dad was at death's door. Then dad would miraculously bounce back. After three or four times of this happening, it got a little tiresome for everyone, including dad. The general consensus was, *could you please just go ahead and die already?*

Tracy Balinski actually said the words out loud to her mom. When her mom was on hospice and rang the bell at her bedside to ask for a glass of water, Tracy said in a joking tone, "Mom, would you stop ringing that thing? You shouldn't be drinking water, anyway. You're supposed to be dying."

It was unusual to hear an adult child speaking so candidly with her parent about death. Tracy adored her mother but knew it was not good for anyone if she hung on too long. Julia was another adult child I met who did not tiptoe around the subject. Her parents were pack rats and she called them on a regular basis to say, "Will you guys please start going through your stuff? We don't want to have to do it when you die." Both Tracy and Julia had great relationships with their parents.

Our society has an aversion to death, talking about it, thinking about it, or facing it in any way. At a seminar on long-term care insurance, I heard that, thanks to scientific advances, kids born in 2004 could live to be 140. In fact, it will probably be common to live to be 140.

An article in the *San Francisco Chronicle* talked about a scientist who is working on a way to prolong life indefinitely. I'm not sure I would want that. The scientist, Aubrey de Grey, claims he will develop a way for people to live 1,000 to 5,000 years, or possibly never die. He says that there are people alive today who will live for 1,000 or 5,000 years. Reading his article, I recalled Gertrude Wilson's 100th birthday party at The Gables, where half of the people at my table, all in their 80s and 90s, exclaimed, "God, I hope I don't live to be a hundred!" The birthday girl was doing remarkably well, both physically and mentally.

"Well," I chimed in, "I wouldn't mind it, if I could be like Gertrude." One of the ladies at my table shot me a scowl and turned off her hearing aid.

Reading de Grey's article, I wondered, what would it be like to be at someone's 900th birthday? Or their 2,010th birthday? My God, a life without death actually sounded like torture.

De Grey's goal was to find ways to alleviate and eventually reverse the debilities caused by aging. He planned to "radically postpone aging, giving indefinite life spans." He identified seven causes of aging, all related to cell mutation and loss, and argued that if we reengineer the body to eliminate these seven causes, we'll live forever. Most people in the scientific community think de Grey is a complete whacko. But there are people who believe in what he's doing and give him large sums of money to find the fountain of youth. My thought on that is, *what's wrong with dying? What if things are actually better on the other side?*

If everyone lives for hundreds or thousands of years, we are going to need a lot of assisted living facilities and nursing homes. When asked about overcrowding, de Grey suggested we have fewer children.

I saw many people who lived too long. They *were* a burden to their families, both emotionally and financially. Their kids weren't free to enjoy their own lives because they were spending so much time, energy, and money caring for their parents. I had a few adult children confide in me about their resentment over this. One woman told me, "This is why I didn't have children. I did not want this responsibility. Now I'm being forced into parenthood because my mother has become my child."

We live in a society obsessed with youth, yet doctors and scientists do everything to preserve people into old, old age, far beyond anything resembling quality of life. We work so hard to keep seniors alive yet we don't want to see them with their walkers and hearing aids, don't want to be around the smell of old age.

When I was at Casa Amanecer, we had a resident named Victoria Connolly. She broke her hip, went to the hospital and then to a rehabilitation facility for physical therapy. When she came back to Casa Amanecer, she was never the same. A team continued physical therapy with her, the doctor prescribed anti-depressants, we encouraged her to get back to the novel she was writing. Nothing worked. Victoria wouldn't even go into the dining room or participate in activities that she once loved. Eventually, she refused to even get out of bed. Victoria died soon after her return to Casa Amanecer.

That is when I discovered that "Failure to Thrive" can be listed as the cause of death on a death certificate. It basically means a person is miserable and has given up on life and their body responds and shuts down. It is different than depression because it has actual anatomical symptoms. The person's muscles and organs atrophy and then they die. They don't have a disease. They just have no will to live.

I saw it happen to Paulette Hayes, who was 85. She was so sad about leaving her house and moving to The Gables. She kept her home, which was only five blocks away, and often went over there during the day, just to sit in her living room. Four months after moving to The Gables, Paulette died and the coroner wrote "Patient Expired due to Failure to Thrive," on her death certificate.

In U.S. culture, when someone dies, we usually say, "He passed away." Somehow, it just sounds gentler than saying, "He died." In healthcare circles, the term often used is, "He expired." Whenever I saw this on paperwork or in emails, I wondered who came up with the notion that this sounded good. *Expired? Like a carton of milk?*

I went to a lot of funerals. There were days when the ambulance literally followed me to work. When, in my rearview mirror, I saw that there were no lights on the ambulance and I heard no sirens, I knew someone had died. During one particularly rough patch at The Gables, we had 15 people die in a span of two months, an unusually high number in such a short span. Our custom for the memorial service was to plant a rose bush in the person's honor. We were having funerals so often we couldn't keep up with buying the rose bushes. So, at one memorial, Sharon asked our gardener to go and dig up a bush from the other side of the property and bring it over to the service. Afterwards, we had a bit of a dark humor chuckle over that.

I often sat at these services wondering why people waited for the funeral to express their feelings about the person. Why not tell them directly, while they were still alive? When Mary Russo's daughter spoke and said what her mom had meant to her, how she had been an amazing support and role model, I remembered many conversations with Mary when she told me she felt she had failed as a mother. Somewhere around my 10th assisted living funeral, I started telling people on a regular basis what they meant to me. Instead of just writing "Happy Birthday" in someone's card, I started telling them, "Happy Birthday. You have a great sense of humor. I love your loyalty. Your commitment to your kids is inspiring."

John Wagner's funeral was the one where things sort of gelled for me. The sons, three of them, were all there. One son had not spoken with his dad in 10 years because of an argument. He stood awkwardly at the podium with nothing to say. I wondered why he even went up there. Maybe he thought the words would come to him in the moment? I felt sad for him. I sat there thinking, *how is my relationship with my mom today? With Jordan? With my dad? What have I done to make a positive difference in the world? What if this was my funeral or one of theirs? When was the last time I called my mom?*

My friend, Nadia, who worked at a retirement community, had a mother who drove her crazy on a weekly basis. To cope, Nadia would often stop and imagine herself saying the eulogy at her mom's funeral. "I'd have to think of something nice to say," she told me one afternoon at lunch. "I cannot stand up there and talk about what an incredibly hateful, tequila-drinking bitch she was."

So, Nadia would think about things like the fact that her mom had done the best she could providing financially for her children as a single mom. She had created a lucrative bookkeeping business. She was an avid gardener who gave her heart and soul to planting and pruning. She had a lot of dear friends who adored her. Nadia would think about how, despite being a terrible mom, she was actually a good grandma. "This job, seeing people die so often, really helps me with my relationships in the here and now," Nadia said.

It helped me too. Assisted living taught me how to better love the living and how to grieve those who had passed. With my stepfather, Bob's death, after that day in Safeway, I shoved the pain away and moved on with my life. Then, one day, many years later, a rabbi walked into Casa Amanecer and made me realize I had never fully grieved the loss of Bob. The rabbi was giving a presentation on grief and loss, speaking about losing loved ones and how the grieving can go on for years. He taught us about the value of creating grief rituals to help us remember our family members in healing ways and with a sense of peace.

"Too often, bereaved people feel they must hold onto pain, seemingly forever, in order to remember those they love," he said. He gave us various tools for grieving, such as lying face down on the earth and letting the grief drain out. He said it was important to tailor our rituals so that they would have meaning and healing significance. I thought of Bob. It had been 16 years since his death and tears streamed down my face. The wound was opened and fresh again. The rabbi handed out a list of ways we could honor our loved one, even continue our relationship with them. One of the suggestions was to light a memorial candle which represented that person's spirit. Another was to do volunteer work in a loved one's memory, perhaps doing something they enjoyed or felt passionate about. Another was to read spiritual or other books that were meaningful to the person as a way to remember and connect. Another was to write a letter to them.

One man raised his hand and said he had lost his wife 10 years earlier. He said he lit a memorial candle the day she died and he never let it go out, and wouldn't until the day he died. The elders I met had suffered many such losses. Arriving at age 80 or 90 meant many, if not all, of the people they loved were now on the other side. How very lonely it must feel to be the last man standing in one's life. Some had even outlived their kids. This was the most unnatural and excruciating pain, a true hell on earth.

That night I went home and lit a candle for Bob's spirit, which I knew lived on somewhere in this big universe. Someone that special could not just disappear. I went on the internet and ordered writings by John Muir and books about President Lincoln, Bob's heroes. I went to the Purisima Creek Redwood Preserve, just south of San Francisco, and lay face down on the soil with my arms stretched out, and allowed the grief that had been locked in my heart for so many years to flow into mother earth.

Then I wrote Bob a letter:

Dear Bob,

I wish you were still here and I could call you up just to say "hello" or ask your advice on life matters. I wish I could give you a hug and look into your smiling Irish eyes. I wish I could give gifts, trips, and other things, to you and my mom to say "thank you" for all you did for me.

I wish we could talk about your love of Yosemite, politics, current events, and so many other things.

Thank you for all the love and support you gave me during my childhood and teen years. You contributed so much at a crucial time in my life. Much of the self-esteem, values, and other good qualities I have are because of you.

I graduated from college shortly after you passed away and I am so sorry you couldn't be there for the ceremony. I know how much you wanted to. I strive to be there for the kids in my life the way you were there for me. I volunteer and do community service like you did. I haven't reached your level of commitment in that area, but I'm working on it. You touched a lot of lives.

I have many wonderful memories with you: the camping trips, the family weekends in Palm Springs and Mammoth, the museums and your love of history. I always stop and read the roadside plaques explaining monuments, just like you taught us to do. I will never forget that backpacking trip we took to the Sierras, with Tammy and the switchbacks, drinking from the streams, seeing deer and even bears up close. What an adventure that was! Thank you, Bob. I could write a book about all the gifts you gave me. I love you, I miss you, and I hope that wherever you are, you are happy and at peace and you know that your life here on earth mattered.

Love,
Beth

I put the letter in a drawer. I donated money to the Sierra Club. I read the books about Lincoln. The rabbi was right. I did feel some peace. I did reconnect with Bob through all this. It is a law of physics that energy can neither be created nor destroyed. So, somewhere out there, in some form or another, Bob still existed and I felt his presence.

Two years after my friend Eve lost her beloved mother, she was struggling with grief. I shared some of the suggestions the rabbi had given us. So, on her mother's birthday, Eve bought a bouquet of long-stemmed, red roses for her mom and kept them in the living room. She had breakfast with one of her mom's friends. She lit a candle for her mom's spirit. She called her brother in Los Angeles, the one she rarely spoke to, and they shared memories about their mom. Throughout the day, Eve told me, she felt *light*. And I thought, *how beautiful to feel light on what could be such a difficult day*. She thanked me and said she felt connected to her mama.

After the rabbi spoke, I had lunch in the dining room with Tim Daniels, a resident who had lived at Casa Amanecer for three years. "What did you think of that talk about grieving?" I asked him.

"It was good. Made me wish I had told my mom more of what she meant to me when she was alive. It made me wonder if I've had an impact on anyone's life."

"Of course, you have! Your daughter and son have shared with me many examples of the positive influence you had, how you made them the people they are today. Haven't they told you?"

"No, not really."

Tim had coached his son's Little League team which meant the world to his son. He had helped his daughter with her math homework almost every weeknight of her high school years because she struggled so much with the subject, never once complaining or saying he was too tired after working all day. It struck me as odd that they told me these things, but hadn't thanked Tim. Older people want to know their life meant something, that they are leaving some kind of positive legacy. These are the things people think about in their later years. They think about dying, too, and for many that thought is surprisingly not a scary one.

When Virginia Cotter brought her friend Millie to tour, the three of us had lunch, looked at independent living apartments, and walked around The Gables' gardens. When Millie left, she thanked me and told me she would mail a deposit check later that week. I sent her a thank you note then called two days later to follow-up. No response. I called again two days after that. Still no response or call back and no check arrived in the mail. I waited, then called again the next week. Nothing.

"This is so strange," I said to my office mate, John, after hanging up from leaving my final message. "She loved our place and the tour went well. She even connected with Fred Snelson—they had a lot in common. You would think she would at least tell me *why* she changed her mind?"

"Maybe she was just being nice because she felt sorry for you," John said dryly.

"Oh, shut up," I laughed.

An hour later, I ran into Virginia. "You know, Virginia, your friend Millie hasn't returned any of my calls. It's odd because she seemed really interested in the parlor apartment."

"Oh, she died," Virginia said plainly. "Sorry, I meant to tell you."

"What do you mean she *died?!* She was only 78 and perfectly healthy."

"She got hit by a car on the way to church the Sunday after she toured. It's very sad. She was really looking forward to moving here." With that, Virginia shrugged her shoulders and walked on.

Like Virginia, most of the elders I met were pretty matter-of-fact about death. They would talk with Glenn, our activity director, after memorials and say, "That song you sang was beautiful. Will you sing it at my funeral?" Or they would tell Sharon the kind of rose bush they wanted planted in their honor.

I arrived for work one morning and saw Lilian sitting in the tea room reading the obituaries. "Good morning, Lillian, how are you?"

"Well, my name isn't in here, so I guess I'm pretty good."

Lillian was a healthy, active 85-year-old. *Imagine if I started my day just feeling lucky for the fact that I woke up?*

On election day, Martha Wallace, from The Gables, got her picture in the newspaper. A local reporter had snapped a photo of her coming out of the polling place in her pink visor and matching sweatsuit. It was a great shot, capturing Martha in just the right light, showing her bubbly personality and the joy in her eyes. When I ran into her, I said, "Martha, that was a really nice picture of you in the paper. You look beautiful!"

"I know," she said. "It *was* a great picture, wasn't it? I told my daughter to keep it for my obit."

Another day I saw Greta Lombardi, a 93-year-old resident at Casa Amanecer all dressed up, and I asked her where she was going. "To the mortuary, for a viewing. My friend, Bill, died."

"Oh, I'm so sorry," I said.

"It's okay. I think I'll get measured for a coffin while I'm there, you know, kill two birds with one stone," Greta said with a chuckle. She continued, "Father Mahoney is doing Bill's service. One thing is for sure, I don't want that jackass doing my funeral!"

With people dying all around, I figured the time would come when I would see a dead body up close. I was both nervous and curious to see one. I remembered seeing one from a distance at an open-casket funeral when I was eight years old. I didn't walk up to the casket; I just saw the guy's nose sticking out and got a slight glimpse of his profile. I was fascinated, of course. The dead guy was Esther Barbieri's husband. Esther was Nanny's best friend and her husband had dropped dead of a heart attack at age 54.

One morning at The Gables, Thelma Addington didn't show up for breakfast, and had not shown up for dinner the night before. Mary asked me to go check her apartment to make sure she was okay. I walked into the living room and it felt very still. I called out Thelma's name and there was no answer. I came around the corner of the bathroom and saw the shower curtain was completely closed. I wondered if she had slipped and fallen or maybe had a heart attack and died in the bathtub? I began to have dreadful visions of her dead body behind that curtain. I reached my shaking hand out to pull the curtain open but couldn't do it.

I stood there, breathing quickly and prayed, "God, please help me open the curtain." I walked back to the living room and said to myself silently, "For fuck's sake, Liz, get a hold of yourself. It's just a dead body. Just open the damn curtain." I went back to the bathroom, my heart pounding, and again I could not do it. I walked back to the living room, paced around and talked to myself some more. Mary was probably wondering what was taking me so long. Finally, I charged back to the bathroom and flung the curtain open with one hand while shielding my eyes with the other. I separated my fingers and peeked through at the empty bathtub. *Oh, thank God!*

It turned out Thelma had skipped dinner the night before, gone to bed early, then gone to breakfast with her family and forgot to tell us. When I told Sharon about my morning, she said, "Liz, you have to take someone with you when you check on a resident who hasn't shown up for a meal. Don't ever go alone."

"Have you ever found a dead person?"

"Oh, yes, of course. Many times."

I never saw an actual corpse up close during my assisted living career. I saw one from afar, on a stretcher, in a body bag, and I saw a lot of ambulances and coroner vans drive away with dead bodies in them and the thing is, not one of them ever pulled a U-Haul behind it. Not one casket had property deeds or stock certificates stuffed in there with the body. It seems obvious that material things do not matter at the end of the day, that no matter how much we have, we still cannot take any of it with us, but I didn't really grasp that until I started spending time surrounded by death.

I remembered a trip I took to Peru when I was 26. I visited the ruins of the Chimú indigenous people who had lived in Trujillo in the north of Peru around 900 AD. Their rulers' tombs were filled with treasures, furniture, gold, and the remains of their wives and servants. They tried to take everything to the next world with them, yet there it all sat, in a pile of dirt.

In the final analysis, character is what matters. I learned that from watching Dorothy Stansfield and other socialites like her, at the end of their lives. Mrs. Stansfield was not a nice lady, even on a good day. Now that she was dying, she was constipated daily, worn down, and having frequent bad days. Our nurse gave her enemas when prunes and laxatives didn't work and after one of these, a caregiver named Peggy handed her the toilet paper to wipe her bottom. "You wipe it," Mrs. Stansfield said. "It's your job."

"No," Peggy replied sweetly. "You're able to do it, so you should do it on your own."

"It's your job," Mrs. Stansfield replied again with bitterness. I imagine Dorothy Stansfield had had people wipe (or kiss) her ass in the figurative sense for many years and now she wanted it done literally. Whereas most people would be mortified to need this done by someone else, Dorothy wanted the services she was paying for. All of them.

To Peggy's credit, she did not wipe Mrs. Stansfield's butt that day, nor the next day, nor any day after that. It was not because Peggy was not a good caregiver. The caregivers are there to provide care that is needed. They are not there to be demeaned. Dorothy Stansfield was a miserable, mean woman, who had not one ounce of elegance, despite her mansions, restaurants, and millions of dollars donated to charities. Money buys many things. It doesn't buy class.

So, if the point of life is not the accumulation of wealth, what is it? Is anything I do today going to matter a hundred years from now? If not, then does it really matter today? I would sit at funerals and think about life, about how 50 years from now, everything I was doing would be meaningless. The exception, of course, is someone like Abraham Lincoln or Mahatma Gandhi who changed the course of history. But what about the rest of us?

I contemplated the meaning of life pretty regularly before working in assisted living. Being around death increased that contemplation tenfold. Socrates said, "The unexamined life is not worth living." What about the overexamined life? I was definitely at risk for that.

One article I read claimed that work is the central meaning of life. It said that leisure is a response to work and not essential to a good life. This explains why some people retire and are dead within a year; they have lost their sense of purpose.

Another researcher named Joffre Dumazedier said that leisure is more important for human life than work. He considered leisure purposeful in satisfying human needs for relaxation, entertainment, and self-development. He predicted that a time will come when personal growth, not working for a living, will be life's primary motivator and that leisure will become the primary goal in life.

When I worked as vice president of sales for Elder Care, we had an office in Mongolia. They handled all of our technology, websites, and search engine optimization. I spoke with a guy from our office there, a Buddhist named Bartan, on one of his visits to California. I told him about my theories of reincarnation, of learning different lessons in each life and then having those areas go smoothly in the next lifetime. He said, "In Buddhism, people who live a really good life come back as birds or humans with a wonderful life full of blessings."

"What about people who live a bad life? People who murder or do mean things?" I asked him.

"They come back as cockroaches."

"Really?"

"Yes."

When I started working at Casa Amanecer and met Sister Louise, our 62-year-old chaplain, I was excited about meeting a nun for the first time. I had a lot of questions.

"Did you always know you wanted to be a nun?" I had only met Sister Louise two weeks earlier and she seemed taken aback by my nosiness.

"Well, yes, since I was 17," she said, and then went on to tell me about the spiritual services she provided to our residents.

"Do you think life is destiny or free will?" I continued. Somehow, I thought being a nun for 45 years gave her insights into the meaning of life, knowledge not readily available to the rest of us.

"I don't know," she said.

I told Sister Louise about a dementia care community I had toured the previous week where I met a woman who was only 53 years old. She had been an accomplished attorney. Then her husband and two kids were murdered in front of her during a home invasion and she had a break with reality and was now living at the assisted living, staring blankly into space, saying nothing.

After telling Sister Louise the story about this woman, I asked, "Why do people say, 'God never gives us more than we can handle'? What exactly does that mean?"

"I hate when people say that," she replied bluntly.

"That's it? That's all you have to say on this subject?" I asked.

"I think God gives people more than they can handle all the time."

"THANK You! I've always thought that, too!"

I went to yoga that night after work and as I lay there during *shavasana,* also known as "corpse pose," in silent meditation, focusing on my breath, I thought, *one day I will take my last breath; it could be tomorrow, it could be 60 years from now. What am I going to do between now and that breath?*

I began thinking about how I wanted to help other people more, even if no one would remember my efforts generations from now. I called the American Cancer Society, donated some money, and signed up to drive radiation patients to their appointments. Then I signed up to sponsor a woman in the Congo. I started writing her letters of encouragement and sending her money. It wasn't enough, but it was a start in the right direction.

I watched a *60 Minutes* interview with LaDainian Tomlinson, a running back for the San Diego Chargers. This guy was an NFL superstar and the episode showed how he was such a humble, quiet spirit. His community service efforts were almost limitless. Florence Nightengale would be hard-pressed to catch up with this guy. He had a work ethic that would not quit. He had grown up black, poor, with an absent father, and he had made something of himself. Now he was giving back.

Just seeing this guy talk made me want to be a better person. Maybe *that* was the whole point of life: face our demons or obstacles, whatever they may be, work through them, then get on with the business of being someone who makes other people want to be better people. As much as possible, be part of the solution, not the problem. Be like my friend, Betty, who will drop everything and drive someone to the airport. Or my friend,

Chandler, who is one of the kindest people I know. He spent 15 years of his life in Cambodia, sleeping on a dirt floor, cooking his food on a chicken-poop fire, and dedicating his life to building schools, hospitals, and infrastructure so that Cambodians would have options for financial survival other than poaching tigers.

At The Gables, I attended Jean Katz's funeral, where her daughter read this quote by Mother Teresa about the purpose of life:

> *People are illogical, unreasonable, and self-centered.*
> *Love them anyway.*
> *If you do good, people will accuse you of selfish ulterior motives.*
> *Do good anyway.*
> *If you are successful, you will win false friends and true enemies.*
> *Succeed anyway.*
> *The good you do today will be forgotten tomorrow.*
> *Do good anyway.*
> *Honesty and frankness make you vulnerable.*
> *Be honest and frank anyway.*
> *What you spend years building may be destroyed overnight.*
> *Build anyway.*
> *In the end, it is between you and God.*
> *It was never about you and them anyway.*

This quote has stayed with me since that funeral.

When I worked at Eldersview, the CEO, encouraged us to look at our lives from the perspective of our residents, from the end of our lives. He told us to go home and do an exercise where we imagined our 90-year-old self, sitting in a chair across from us. He told us to have a conversation with this person. I was 41 at the time. I sat in the dining room of my San Francisco home overlooking the Pacific Ocean and it became very clear that if I did not leave my marriage to Dave, I was going to have a whole lot of regret when I reached age 90. My 90-year-old self begged me to leave that marriage before I completely lost myself and my connection to so many of the people I held dear. This wise and strong old lady also thanked me for all of the traveling, living, and loving I had done up to that point.

One morning in meditation class, I had my eyes closed for an hour as the teacher guided us. When I opened my eyes, the dull blue blanket beneath me had turned a vibrant, intense turquoise. The color popped. The only time in my life I had seen colors change like that was when I took psychedelic mushrooms. I realized that through meditation, I had gone to another level of consciousness. I just kept staring at the blanket until the teacher said something that jolted me out of my trance. I went on to have the most productive, wonderful day, completely in the moment and full of bliss at every little act. Stapling two pieces of paper together was a joy that day. Talking on the phone, photocopying, eating—it was all a spiritual experience.

The quiet sweetness that comes over me in these moments makes me feel lighter than air and at the same time, completely grounded and safe. I feel an absolute joy and rightness with the universe. I feel like I deserve to be here. I am where I'm supposed to be, doing what I am supposed to be doing. I know there are spiritual masters who live in this state of grace all the time, but I have only experienced fleeting moments of it. The Hindu yogis call this state *turiya*, the fourth level of human consciousness.

I went to a violin recital one Saturday afternoon at a church in San Francisco. It was a rare warm day and Kayleigh's daughter, Chloe, was playing. The back door of the church was open, allowing a calm breeze to blow through, and the sun shone through red, pink, and yellow stained-glass windows. I was surrounded by people I had known and loved for years. Chloe, this precious 10-year-old girl whom I had held minutes after she was born, was playing Mozart. I was present and feeling every moment of it. A wave of pure joy washed over me. *Maybe*, I thought, *maybe the whole point of life is to raise my consciousness enough that I always live in this state.*

I thought of that violin recital one day when I was out driving around with Don Antonelli. Don was a retired journalist who lived in the independent living section of The Gables and we sometimes cooked together. Back in the day, Don had been very successful in his career in Los Angeles. He enjoyed friendships with the likes of Frank Sinatra, Dean Martin, and Marilyn Monroe and showed me pictures of himself with all of them. He was working on writing his memoirs. Don and I were on our way to Trader Joe's, talking about the cooking ingredients we were going to buy, when, out of the blue, he said to me, "You've had a full life, Liz." It was an odd thing for ta 78-year-old man to say to a 34-year-old woman.

"Yes," I replied. "I have lived a full life." I had loved and been loved, both platonically and romantically. I had numerous close, authentic relationships. I had been on safari in Africa, swum naked in the Indian Ocean, been to the Running of the Bulls in Pamplona. I had hiked the Inca trail to Machu Picchu. I had seen the Sistine Chapel and the *Mona Lisa* up close.

I had overcome obstacles, both physical and spiritual. I had made a positive difference in some people's lives. While there was still more I wanted to do, I felt pretty complete. The odd thing was that Don did not know half of the things I had done in my short life. "You know, Don, it is so funny you say that. Honestly, I'm only 34 but I have actually done everything on my bucket list. I was thinking of starting a new one. How did you know that about me? I haven't even told you much about my life."

"I'm a journalist. I have a knack for reading people."

Don often spent hours in the clubhouse kitchen on Saturdays making an Italian feast that he and I would devour when it was completed. I always brought dessert. Sometimes we invited guests, like staff members, other residents, or Don's grandson, Finn. But a lot of times, it was just Don and me. During one of these lunches with just the two of us, we ate linguini with sausage and peppers as I lamented about my recent woes.

"I need to lose weight, Don. None of my clothes fit anymore!"

"You look great to me, sweetie."

"And my sales are down. It is totally stressing me out. I'm so worried about getting move-ins that I'm not sleeping at night."

"The tide will turn. You'll get move-ins. Didn't you once tell me this is a slow time of year?"

"Yeah. But on top of everything else, my sister and I are in an argument."

Don listened attentively. "I'm sorry, sweetie. Family can be tough."

"Thank you. How about you, Don? What's going on with your daughter? Is she still dating that guy you don't like?"

"Yeah. He doesn't have a job and he doesn't treat her very well. But there's not much I can do about it."

We sat in silence for a bit and then Don said, "Hey, kid, you and I both know I am probably going to leave this world before you do."

I nodded and stared at him. "Remember something when I'm gone, okay?"

"Sure, what?"

"Don't sweat the small stuff."

"All right . . . but what's the small stuff?"

"Everything."

Chapter Ten

Life

> *There is a fountain of youth:*
> *it is your mind, your talents, the creativity you bring*
> *to your life and the lives of people you love.*
> *When you learn to tap this source,*
> *you will truly have defeated age.*
>
> — Sophia Loren

Kristi, my assistant at Casa Amanecer, walked into my office and said, "My cheeks hurt from smiling so much. This happens to me almost every day here."

"I know," I said, "me too."

I stayed in assisted living for eight years because despite the illness and death, despite the pressure for numbers and the long hours, there was so much inspiration and life to be found in every community where I worked. One day while driving around doing outside marketing, I heard a report on the radio. It said a recent survey had revealed that 85 percent of people hated their job. *Wow*, I thought, *that is so sad. I love my job. I actually cannot believe I get paid to do this job.*

Contrary to what many believe, assisted living communities are not depressing places. Nursing homes, for the most part, are depressing places. They are cold, institutional, medical environments. I have seen a few that were joyful, positive atmospheres with plants, animals, young people and activity, but they were the exception. These places were modeled after the Eden Alternative, a revolutionary approach started by Dr. Bill Thomas. But they are rare, probably because it is just too much work, costs more money, and provides a quality of life not necessary to simply keep people safe and alive. Skilled nursing facilities serve a purpose, but God help me if I ever end up in one.

Assisted living, on the other hand, is a social, rather than a medical model. The communities tend to be vibrant, life-affirming environments. People do not move into them to die. On the contrary, when I began working at The Gables, I met residents who had lived there many years. Gertrude Wilson was 99 when I met her during my first tour of The Gables. She had moved there 19 years prior at age 80. Estelle Collins was 97 when I met her and had lived there 16 years. The residents who moved in when they were still active and healthy tended to thrive longer and stay healthy into their later years. There was something about getting support before they *really* needed it that helped them to flourish.

Yet even many of those who arrived unhealthy and beaten down seemed to bounce back after moving in. There were days like the day Judy Cofod said to me, "My mom is very happy here," and my heart melted, because Judy's mom did not arrive at our community happy. She arrived in a deep depression. Then there was the day Sean O'Leary said to me, "It is nothing short of amazing what has happened to my dad here." Sean's dad had been incontinent and helpless when he moved to Casa Amanecer. After a few months, he was more independent, managing most of his own activities of daily living, and reduced the care he was receiving from our staff from level three to level two.

I think the reason for this is that retirement communities provide some of the main coping tools for addressing the challenges of aging. Many provide pets, faith, family, friends, community, hobbies, and giving back to the next generation. Elders in assisted living are surrounded by their peers, people who listen to the same music they do, remember the wars and other historical events they lived through, and often share similar values like ladies who believe you should dress up when you go shopping. Most of their friends and family who lived through these eras with them have passed away. Then they move to a community where there is a whole new group of friends who also lived through that era, people who remember when airplanes and television sets were invented, and it is like coming home. One resident, Pam, said to me a month after she moved in, "I have more of a social life now than I had in my 20s!"

I asked Dr. Lazer, the Ojai gerontologist, "What is the secret to aging well?"

He responded, "It is very simple. Stay engaged physically, intellectually, socially, and spiritually. That's it. Have a reason to get out of bed in the morning."

For many seniors, their pets provided this sense of purpose. There was a woman named Emily who used to come to The Gables and help our residents find pets and take care of them. Emily had an amazing effect on giving people a will to live. Gertrude Wilson, for example, with Emily's help, adopted a cat from a woman who was dying. That cat changed Gertrude's life. Gertrude was 102 years old at the time and the cat was 18, and they fell in love. Gertrude derived so much joy from feeding and taking care of that cat. One afternoon, she asked me to take a photo of her with her cat, whom she named Sophie. She put it on her Christmas card and sent it to everyone she knew. Gertrude had not sent out Christmas cards in 20 years. I had never seen Gertrude smile as much as she did after she adopted Sophie.

Since embarking on my career with elders, I have read a lot of books on the topic of aging well. *The Blue Zones: Lessons for Living Longer from the People Who've Lived the Longest,* says: "Eat less. Make family a priority. Banish stress." Having fun and relaxing will prolong life.

Giving to the next generation is another way to age well. It is called "generativity" and it means "a concern for people besides self and family that usually develops during middle age; especially: a need to nurture and guide younger people and contribute to the next generation." Generativity includes activities such as teaching, mentoring, social activism, and grandparenting. Elders who thrive have usually found an activity, any activity, that fulfills the desire to feel needed and connected to society and family. I learned it is dangerous to our health, at any age, to spend too much time alone.

I saw residents in assisted living giving back to the next generation by forming a "Peace and Social Justice Group." One of their causes was the eradication of human sex trafficking. They wrote letters to Congress. They called the manufacturers of feminine products and sent letters asking them to put a toll-free number on tampon and maxi-pad boxes. The Peace and Social Justice Group figured women who had been brought to the United States as sex slaves could call the number and get help. They also figured the women's captors would not take time to read a tampon box, so they would not notice the message. They convinced the tampon manufacturers not only to put the number on the box, but to put the message in a couple of different languages. They knew the women would have trouble getting access to a phone, but this message at least told them someone cared and it gave them the number to call if they did get access. This group of residents showed me how people in their 80s and 90s could still do work that made an impact on society.

Lifelong learning is another way to stay engaged. I taught a Spanish class at Casa Amanecer to a group of 80- and 90-year-olds who showed up every week with their completed homework in hand. During class, they focused intently, devoting themselves to getting the pronunciation just right, even though they knew they might not even wake up the next day. What an inspiration it was to see people tackling new goals and interests at age 90.

I read about another place in Ann Arbor, Michigan where the assisted living residents took classes with university students. "While a growing number of retirement communities are affiliated with universities, this is one of the few assisted living centers that have established ties with one. Each year university students are paired with residents for research projects, and they take classes with them at the facility." The place has a fitness program, classes, and discussion groups on things like the novels of John Updike, the music of Louis Armstrong, and Medicare. The residents hang out with the students, get to know one another and go to lunch together.

"If you give people a reason to get out of bed, activities that engage them and allow them to feel successful, they will be at the top of their game, whatever it is," said Cameron Camp, the psychologist who directed research at a facility called Menorah Park Center for Senior Living.

This was what I saw as our main responsibility working in elder care: challenge the myths of aging. Embrace wellness. Embrace the spirit of the heart. Jumpstart people's hope. We did this through art classes, like the one Glenn from The Gables and I taught at a local senior center. We called it "Cutting Edge Crafts." Our class was full every week and Glenn would always start by saying, "Remember, people, when it comes to glitter, less is more."

Zoe, the activity director at Eldersview, was truly cutting edge. She did not believe in an activity program based on the three B's: Bingo, Bibles, and Birthdays, which was the "go to" plan for many of her counterparts at competitor places. Instead, Zoe did things such as an art class in which residents would study Jackson Pollock, look at his artwork, take a field trip to the museum, read his biography, watch a documentary film about him, and then paint a painting in the same style as Pollock's. Zoe believed in activity programs which treated elders like adults, not children.

One of the most delightful ways I got to see people stay engaged in life was when they fell in love. It happened more often than one would think. I saw people fall in love at 80, 90, 95. Valorie Branson was one such lady. She arrived for her first tour of The Gables wearing three-inch heels, her white hair swept into a sophisticated updo. Valorie was 93 and exceptionally beautiful. "Valorie," I said, "this place is on eight acres. Are you sure you're going to be okay in those heels?"

Valorie's skin, jewelry, and clothes were gorgeous. She was just as pretty on the inside too, a truly sweet person. A month after she moved in, at the weekly happy hour gathering, Valorie met Floyd Broder, who was 95. She came into my office a few months later and exclaimed, "Liz, I thought I was going to come here and play Bingo, watch movies, take up arts and crafts. Instead, I met a man! I am in LOVE!"

"That's wonderful, Valorie! I saw you and Floyd in the lounge before dinner last night and you both looked very happy."

Valorie and Floyd were inseparable. They went on field trips together, ate every meal together, and walked around the property holding hands (with Valorie still in her high heels). One day I went to Valorie's apartment to give her a package that had been delivered to the office. As I walked onto the porch, the curtain to the front window was open and there they were, on Valorie's sofa, making out like teenagers. I didn't want to interrupt the steamy scene, so I turned around and headed back to my office smiling.

When Dave's grandma moved to The Gables at age 90, the first few months she enjoyed the meals in the dining room and playing piano by herself in her apartment. About a year later, Dave and I stopped by for one of our regular visits and noticed she was wearing lipstick and a new blouse. "Goma," Dave asked her, "are you wearing lipstick?"

"Yes, I am. I have a gentleman on his way over to watch my Andrea Bocelli DVD with me so you two better not stay too long." Ten minutes later there was a knock at the door and I opened it to Harry Minassian, wearing a suit and holding a bouquet of flowers. I looked back at Goma, who was beaming.

One of the communities I oversaw in Auburn, California had a population that was 50-percent male. It was highly unusual to have so many men in a retirement home. *This is our selling point,* I thought. *This will get women from the area to come tour and move in here.* I suggested to the marketing director that we do a monthly activity of "The Dating Game" and invite women from the town to come.

The men were often looking for a mate, too. When Sharon and I signed paperwork with Bob, a 96-year-old who was moving into independent living, Sharon explained that the cost of the apartment was $4,000 a month but that was for one person. A second person would cost another $700. "What do you mean?" he asked.

"I mean $4,000 is the price for just you. If you want a girlfriend to move in, it will cost an additional $700."

"All right," he said, "I'll take it. That sounds like a great deal." Sharon looked at me quizzically and then back at Bob.

"You'll take what?" she asked.

"I'll take the girlfriend for $700 per month."

Sharon bellowed, "Oh, we're not going to *provide* the woman! You have to get her yourself."

"Oh!" he said. "That sounded like a bargain to me!"

Another time, a woman called me inquiring about memory care for her dad. "He has Alzheimer's and is being kicked out of his current assisted living community because of inappropriate sexual behavior."

"We can handle that," I told her.

"He loves gardening and dominoes."

"Great," I said, "let's schedule a time for you to tour."

"Okay. There's one other thing," she continued. "There is a woman he sees once a week for two hours . . . a lady friend. I would need you to provide transportation to her house."

"Oh, that's fine. We can do that."

"I will be honest: it is a professional relationship. Sex has always been very important to my dad. I don't think he should miss out on it now just because he has dementia. So, I pay this woman. She calls herself a sex therapist but she is basically a prostitute. Do you have any issues with that?"

I wanted to say, "*Lady, sex is up there with eating and sleeping in my book. I think it is great that you have made this arrangement for your dad.*"

"I have no issues with that," I replied. "We will just make those visits part of his care plan along with his doctor appointments."

"Great, thank you."

Many seniors still want sex and romance. Why do we think they wouldn't? One article I read said that the National Council on Aging's website informed the author that "48 percent of seniors are sexually active once a month and nearly 75 percent of those randy oldsters find their sex lives as emotionally satisfying as they did in their forties – or more so." We had a 22-year-old receptionist at The Gables whom I had to remind about this a few times. Her name was Stephanie and she often came to work in mini-skirts and crop-tops which broadcast her pierced belly button to the world. She was like a walking bottle of Viagra for the male residents. "These men may be old," I told her, "but they're not dead."

One day I ran into Rose Paganini, a 96-year-old resident who had lived at Casa Amanecer for 5 years. She had on turquoise-colored raw silk pants with a white cotton top that had turquoise and green flowers on it. Her jewelry was also turquoise. To see a woman dressed so perfectly at age 96 was just splendid. "What are you up to, Rose?"

"Well, over the past few months I have discovered a new passion: water aerobics! On Tuesdays and Thursdays, I take a cab to the public pool near Ocean Beach and I work out for an hour. I feel so *invigorated* on the days I do my water aerobics," she said with a big smile.

Two days later I ran into Rose wearing a peach-colored sweater, a shell-pink blouse, rose-colored pants, and a gold necklace with matching earrings. She said to me, "I took a trip to North Beach and bought chicken apple sausages, and do you know what the chef here said when I asked him to cook these up for me?"

"No, what did he say?"

"He said: *I would be HAPPY to!*" Glee sprung from her voice. Rose was in love with her life. It seeped from her pores and I wanted to hug her whenever I saw her. I left each interaction with Rose wanting more of her.

One day I overheard Rose saying to the receptionist, "I need the number for Chevron Oil."

"Sure, Rose, let me get that for you."

"The stock has gone up to sixty-two dollars per share and I own 8,000 shares."

"That's great," the receptionist said, as she pulled up Chevron's telephone number on the internet.

"My husband worked at the refinery for 30 years and they gave him the option of getting a percentage of his pension in stock. "I figure if I sell 1,000 shares, I'll have $62,000 to play with. I'm planning to take this cruise next year to Ireland," she said, showing the receptionist a brochure. Sitting in my office, listening to Rose through the open door, I thought, *I want to be taking cruises to Ireland when I'm 96! You go, girl!*

Contrary to popular belief, elders are not just waiting around for young people to call or write. A lot of them are actually very busy with full lives. Filomena Meyer was an 87-year-old writer and political activist. She was not adept at computers and one day asked me if I could help her out. "Do you know how to block emails from coming in?" she asked.

"I can help you with that, sure, Filomena. Are you having a spam problem?"

"What's that?"

"Marketing and sales-type emails."

"No, it's not that. It's that I have all these relatives on the East Coast who email me incessantly. Grandkids, nieces, grandnephews, sending me jokes and articles. They think I'm a little old lady with nothing better to do." At 87, Filomena had more friends than most people I knew. She was also on the City Council and was writing her third book. "Why can't they just send a Christmas card once a year like everyone else?" she asked.

Like Filomena, many seniors I met were busy and thriving. They were also resilient. When Evelyn Bradford didn't show up for breakfast one day, a caregiver went to her apartment to check on her. She found Evelyn splayed out on the living room floor in her pajamas, unconscious. She had been there since the night before. It turned out Evelyn, who was 94, had a brain tumor the size of a hen's egg that had been growing in her head for six months. That was exactly how her doctor described it, "A brain tumor the size of a hen's egg." *This is it*, we all thought, *Evelyn is on her way out.*

Two days later, she underwent four hours of brain surgery. I felt miffed with Evelyn's family and thought, *brain surgery? Really?! At 94? My God, people, let the lady go in peace.* But, I was wrong. It was not Evelyn's time.

When Evelyn was discharged from the hospital, she moved to the skilled nursing facility across the street, to rehabilitate before coming back to her apartment in our independent living. I decided to take her flowers. I went to the rose garden and started snipping yellow, orange, and red roses, carefully matching them to the ribbon I had bought at the craft store. Then I thought to myself, *what the hell am I doing? I have a million phone calls to make and this lady just had brain surgery two days ago; she's not going to know either way if these roses match the ribbon.*

I walked across the street and found Evelyn in her room. She had staples across her forehead and a little pink beanie on, which was supposed to cover them, but didn't. The staples were large and grotesque. She looked like the creature from Frankenstein. It was hard not to stare at her forehead. Evelyn was happy, animated, and lucid. She loved the roses and told me she could not wait to get back home to her bridge and bingo buddies and her gardening. Sitting there talking with her, it was hard to keep a straight face. I thought, *this is so unbelievable that it's comical. The woman is 94, just had brain surgery, and she's having a conversation with me like one of my peers would.*

Evelyn was still at The Gables when I left a year later, and still there when I visited two years after that. At 97, she was walking gracefully without a cane or walker, smart as a whip, enjoying life in her same independent living apartment, and playing bridge three days a week. Evelyn was very much alive.

Thinking of her reminds me of a poem, written by a woman in San Francisco, submitted for a poetry contest we held at Eldersview:

Happy

You may say, I am a Senior,
Does it mean that I am old?

You may see my pretty hair
Saying: "She is going bald."

You may take me by the hands,
Feel the lacking of the warmth.

I am sure they look bland
With the diamond rings on them.

You may say: "Oh, she is stout
And she shouldn't wear a dress."

But of my figure I am proud
And enjoy my own self.

I get compliments from people
Whatever their sex may be.

I am proud to be eighty,
Have a better look at me.

— Genya Ehrlich

On a trip years ago to visit my nieces, Chelsea who was 10 and Kara, who was 6, I sat at Kara's soccer game and watched 20 little girls run around, chasing a ball, giggling, and jumping in the air. Later that day, I took the two girls to a pumpkin patch and as we walked from the car to the entrance, I noticed their hair shining brightly in the sun. I kept staring at it, wondering, *what is it about their hair? Why is it so shiny?* Then it hit me: youth. That's what was in their hair: a shine that could never come from a bottle, a shimmer that could only come from being 10 years old.

When we got inside the converted farm, we discovered there was much more going on than just a pumpkin patch. There was a scarecrow contest, a corn maze, a petting zoo, hay rides, and more. We were excited by all the choices and couldn't decide which activity to do first. This prompted Kara to jump into the air and yell, "Oh my God, we just barely got here and we're ALREADY having fun!" Youth. Only youth could make someone squeal with joy like that.

The gift of youth is possibility. The possibility of adventure, travel, greatness, love. The possibility is often far more extraordinary, wonderful, and enjoyable than the actual attainment of these things. My friend George Birimisa was one of the few people I knew who achieved this sparkle of youth and enjoyed the gift of childlike wonder into old age. George was the one elder whom I did not meet through work. We met before my assisted living career, when I was 28 years old and George was 72. For the next 16 years he supported, loved, and encouraged me to be the very best person I could be. He was my writing teacher, spiritual guide, and dear friend. He was my Yoda and whenever I spent time with him, I felt like a Jedi.

Every day, George found something to look forward to. He was blogging at age 88 and wrote this post about our visit one day:

> OLD-OLD AGE BULLETIN: Very tired today – my right foot is weak, weak, weak. I'm wondering if I'm overdoing it with the 18-minute walks in the hall. But I had a great day. Liz, one of my students that I've known for 15 years, dropped by with her friend, Kelly, from Oregon. We had lunch at a restaurant with beautiful orange flowers.

Then they took me to Ocean Beach. Huge crowds but we found a spot with my handicap placard. They went for a walk while I sat on my walker seat and watched the people. I noticed that no one was wearing a swimming suit. In the distance, I could see the ugly box-like Cliff House. An elderly lady lifted her dog on my lap so I could give him a hug and a kiss. I watched the waves and the tears started – no longer catching a wave or even wading. On the way back to my house Kelly checked her iPhone and found out that 15,000 people had attended an Occupy SF rally. When I got home, I had enough energy to compose this blog. I have a new friend in Kelly – a lovely young lady. And, of course, I adore Liz.

I adored George, too. I always felt energized after spending time with him. Everything was an adventure for George, even walking up and down the hallway outside his apartment, which was almost impossible for him that last year of his life. I would go to visit with him in the evenings and he would tell me with great enthusiasm how he rode his scooter to Starbucks that day, bought a cup of coffee, and read *The New Yorker,* as if it were the most exciting thing anyone had ever done. Another day he told me, "I went to Marshall's today and bought a bright pink t-shirt and new socks! That place is wonderful, Liz!"

George taught me one of the key elements to a happy life: acceptance. Acceptance of what *is*. It is something all of the happy elders I met had. Acceptance of their hip replacements, loss of vision, constipation, lack of money or friends, the political climate, whatever.

Carlotta Delucca had that acceptance in droves. She taught me through her example, to make the most of the hand we are dealt, change what we can, and accept what we cannot. Carlotta grew up in San Francisco with a domineering mother who never allowed her to date, let alone get married. Her mom was from old-world Italy, where the youngest daughter was expected to take care of the mom and then get married. The problem was, Carlotta's mom lived to 98. By the time she died, Carlotta was 68 and had Parkinson's.

There would be no career, travel, husband, or adventure for Carlotta. She had lived an isolated, sad life, literally a slave to her mother until her late 60s. By the time she came to Casa Amanecer, she was 82 and could no longer walk. It was difficult to understand Carlotta when she spoke because her voice was very soft from the Parkinson's. Looking at her, one would think she was a complete invalid. But she was not. Not at all.

Carlotta seemed frail, but she was strong mentally, emotionally, and to the extent that she could manage, physically. I had seen Parkinson's lead to severe dementia in some residents rather quickly, but not Carlotta. She insisted on showering and toileting alone (what she called "doing her business"). She washed and styled her own hair, ironed her own clothes, and cleaned her own apartment, even though housekeeping was included in her rent. She polished her furniture, purses, and electric scooter every night before bed. That was her routine. She had a motorized scooter so she wouldn't need someone to take her to and from the dining room. She said to me, "It's not a wheelchair. It's a traveling chair." Everything comes down to perspective.

Carlotta was almost completely alone in the world. She had no kids, no nieces or nephews, just her older sister and a few friends. She had never had a life of her own, yet I sensed no bitterness, not even a trace of it. Carlotta smiled a lot. She laughed. She told witty, great jokes that made me laugh out loud. She beamed at even the slightest bit of attention. I loved Carlotta. She was enough motivation for me to drag myself to that job every day, despite the fact that I was feeling burnt out by sales.

One day I was walking to my office, coffee and fruit in hand, ready to dig into my emails, and there was Carlotta making her way towards me in her scooter. She was crying and her head was turned down and sideways, trying to hide her tears. It surprised me because I had never, in the six months I had known her, seen Carlotta upset over anything. I coaxed her into my office where she sobbed cathartically, unable to speak. I grabbed a napkin from my top drawer, handed it to her, and waited.

Finally, she said, "I lost my wallet. I'm afraid someone may have stolen it." Together, we mentally retraced her moves to the last time she saw it. I told her we had never had any thefts at Casa Amanecer. All of our staff, residents, and families were highly trustworthy. I promised, though, to thoroughly investigate. Carlotta continued to cry and continued to apologize for crying. She did such a good job of keeping her chin up and making the best of things, but there had to be deep wells of sadness in her. How could there not be? It was as though the lost wallet was the final blow. She just couldn't take anymore.

I went with her and we searched her apartment, every nook and cranny, yet did not find the wallet. A half hour later, I was in my office calling the bank to cancel her ATM and credit cards when Carlotta came back and told me she had found her wallet wedged in the seat of her traveling chair. We had not looked there because she was sitting in it the whole time. She found it when she got out to take a shower.

After that day, Carlotta went back to smiling, raising her hand at Resident Council meetings, telling her funny jokes, polishing her furniture, making the best of her life. She had her meltdown and then got on with the business of living. I try to remember Carlotta when I start to bitch and moan about my life. I try to follow her example and ask myself, *okay, what is right in front of me today? What can I do to make my situation or someone else's a little better? What do I have control over?* Then I work towards focusing my energy on that. When I think of Carlotta, I am a bit ashamed that I have ever complained about a single thing in my life.

Working with elders showed me that we can be young and alive at 100 or we can be old and lifeless at 30. Pablo Casals, the musician said, "The man who works and is never bored is never old. Work and interest in worthwhile things are the best remedy for age. Each day I am reborn. Each day I must begin again." Betty Friedan said, "Aging is not 'lost youth' but a new stage of opportunity and strength."

Frank Edwards, a 92-year-old retired concert pianist, embodied both of these quotes. Prior to becoming a professional pianist, Frank had enjoyed a career in minor-league baseball. (He often showed me photos of himself in his uniform.) He loved Shakespeare and since I love Shakespeare, too, we talked about that a lot. A typical day for Frank started with Qi Gong in the morning, followed by breakfast and an hour of playing piano. Then he would take the senior transit van to the community center where he volunteered "helping the old people." Frank spent two hours teaching Spanish to the people who participated in the Adult Daycare Program. He would eat lunch there, then head back to The Gables where he took a nap, read Shakespeare for an hour then visited his friend, Katherine Conway for a discussion on literature or politics. After that, it was dinner and bed.

Frank had all of his mental faculties but was physically frail. Watching Frank get out of a chair was a sight. It sometimes took him 15 minutes. The typical sequence was that he shifted in his seat then scooted to the front of the chair. Then he would place his hands on the chair arms and brace himself. Next, he would push up with all his might, lift himself a couple inches and fall back onto the chair. This usually happened two or three times before he made it to his feet. Then, still holding onto the arms, he would spend about 5 to 10 minutes steadying himself before taking a step.

If someone tried to help him out of his chair, Frank got annoyed. He insisted on doing it himself. Frank was cantankerous and did not suffer fools. In fact, he was downright mean to most people whose intellect was beneath his own, except for dementia residents. For them, he had deep reservoirs of compassion. Perhaps it was his way of expressing gratitude to the universe for the clear mind he was allowed to keep into his later years.

Rosalind Mirowitz, whose son had lived with her at The Gables, was 87, and had both her physical and mental capacities intact. Rosalind chose The Gables over the phone. She decided to move across the country, sight unseen, after a few telephone conversations with me. The day of her move, she got on an airplane at JFK airport in New York City at 4:30 in the morning, flew to Chicago, changed planes, and arrived in Santa Barbara at 3:00 in the afternoon, where I was waiting to pick her up. She told me she would be wearing a red hat.

I waited in the terminal, watching the plane on the tarmac, expecting to see a woman being escorted in a wheelchair. Instead, I saw a spry woman wearing a large, red straw hat, bouncing down the steps of the plane. *That can't be her*, I thought. She almost walked right past me because I kept looking back at the plane for someone in a wheelchair.

"Rosalind?" I said.

"Yes, you must be Liz! Let's go get my bag from baggage claim." *What the what?*

Gloria Armstrong was 100 years old and also thriving. She was living a full, exciting, and productive life. Gloria painted oils three days a week, entertained regularly, and traveled to Maui for vacation. She went there for a month one winter because it was too cold for her in Ojai. She called us and said she might come home early because the food was weird and the people were too relaxed.

On her 100th birthday, we got a call from the local inn saying we should come pick Gloria up. She should not drive, they said, because she'd had two martinis instead of her usual one. Gloria had taken herself out for martinis as her own personal celebration after the party we held for her earlier in the day. Gloria drove better than many of the 75-year-olds who lived at our place. Her body, mind, and spirit glowed. At 100, Gloria was one of the youngest people I had ever met.

Gloria's daily regimen consisted of one martini, a vitamin C tablet, and three small meals. That was it. My face involuntarily went into a smile whenever I saw her coming towards me. I relished Saturday afternoons when we could sit in her apartment and chat over a glass of iced tea. She told me stories about the summers she spent in France with her painting group. We talked about politics, agreeing on everything since we were both lefties.

At 85, Richard O'Leary was yet another who was still full of energy and wit. Before retiring and eventually moving to Casa Amanecer, Richard had been a project manager at the San Francisco Building Department. One day, Richard invited me out to Westlake Joe's, one of my favorite restaurants, for lunch. When I met Richard in the lobby that day, I noticed he was more dressed up than the khakis and polo shirt he wore on most days. He was wearing a tweed sport coat, white dress shirt, and a blue tie for our Saturday lunch.

Richard opened the door to the restaurant for me, ordered my soda for me, and stood up when I went to the bathroom to wash my hands. I ordered my favorite dish, fettuccini alfredo, and he ordered the roast beef. Richard picked up his knife and fork, hands trembling from Parkinson's Disease, and tried to cut a piece of the juicy, rare beef that sat in front of him. After an unsuccessful attempt, he set down the utensils and said with a smile, "You are a lovely gal. It's a shame you're married."

"Thanks, Richard, that's very sweet of you to say."

"Your husband is a lucky man," he said, trying to cut the meat again. The knife rattled against the plate until he again gave up. I enjoyed my pasta and talked easily with Richard. I had gotten to know him quite well during the months since he moved in.

"Tell me about working at the Building Department, Richard. I imagine you had some interesting experiences there."

"Indeed, I did. We saw some corruption in my day—let me tell you, people getting kickbacks left and right. At one point, about 30 or so years ago, some city officials high up were involved in the bribes and it made the papers. Things got tense around that office and some heads rolled. Those higher-ups weren't going to take the fall, though, you could be sure of that. I saw some of my good friends, people who were innocent, lose their jobs. Somehow, I was spared."

"Do you think that sort of thing still happens today?" I watched Richard struggle again with trying to cut his meat and felt conflicted about whether or not to offer help. It is a fine line we walk with elder care: how much support to give a grown man or woman without taking away their dignity or last shred of independence. I decided not to offer to cut up his food.

Richard shrugged, "I suppose it does. People are people, Liz. There are honest ones and not so honest ones everywhere. I am glad both my boys turned out to be good seeds. I just wish the eldest would find himself a woman. I worry about him ending up alone for the rest of his life, no kids, no one to grow old with."

When the bill came, Richard had eaten one small bite of his roast beef. The waitress asked if he would like a "To Go" container for it and he said no. The meal came to forty-six dollars and he looked at the bill, then counted out cash, then looked back at it and put down more cash, then took some back then put more down, ultimately leaving eighty dollars. I thought about correcting him, telling him he was leaving too much money, but I decided to let it go. Richard had plenty of money and I did not want to draw attention to his confusion, another symptom of his worsening Parkinson's. Better to make the waitress's day than to embarrass him.

We got back to his apartment and Richard hugged me and said,

"Thank you." I felt a warmth rise in my chest from a lovely afternoon of connecting with this sweet man.

"I had a great time, Richard," I said. "And why are you thanking *me*? You paid!"

"Because you made my day," he said.

This was the gift of service. I remembered my friend, Claire, talking about it when we worked together at Sunset Oaks and I remembered not really understanding what she was talking about at the time. Finally, I got it. We give comfort and receive comfort sometimes at the same time. I learned to be of service by helping the people who did not want to ask for help but who found themselves old, vulnerable, and needing assistance, some in big ways, some in small ways. I also learned by watching elders support one another. The seniors who were the happiest and most fulfilled were the ones who, despite their own challenges, got up every day and tried to help those around them.

Edith Wetzler, for instance, played the piano every morning, rain or shine. Each morning when I walked through the door of Casa Amanecer at 8:50 a.m., the first thing I heard was Edith drumming away at those keys. She played beautifully, despite her severe arthritis. Some days it was excruciatingly painful for Edith to play, but she did it anyway. On one particularly cold, damp day, I saw Edith and she told me how badly her fingers hurt. "Why did you play piano, then?"

"It cheers everybody up," she said. "There are people here suffering worse than me. And, if I stop playing, I will cease to be useful and then I'll die."

Being useful and giving back can be healing. I thought back to my years in Ojai and how every December, I prepared holiday baskets with the Santa Barbara Healthcare Association. Those of us in this networking group saw each other all year round, but when we did those baskets, something magical happened. Teams of us would negotiate free donations from local vendors and raise money to buy things like jarred asparagus, special cheese, tins of cookies, wine, tea, lotion, and bath salts from the dollar store.

The baskets were for elderly shut-ins, most of whom were low-income people in their 80s and 90s who were all alone. For many of them, it was the only Christmas gift they received. Our networking group met twice a week for the first two weeks of December to assemble the baskets, and the joy in the room was palpable.

Many studies show that humans often actually get better with age. We mature. The Mills Study tracked a group of 123 women beginning at age 21. It watched them change throughout their lives. The study showed that the women's highest scores in inductive reasoning occurred from their 40s to their early 60s. They also got better at expressing the positive aspects of their personality and restraining the less desirable ones. In their 50s and 60s, they got better at remaining objective. And they got better at handling ambiguity and managing relationships. This is why, throughout history, many of the great theologians and peacemakers have been older people, not young idealists. A *Time Magazine* article about the Mills Study said, "Not everyone achieves the sharp thought and serene mien that can come with age. But for those who do, the later years can be the best years they have ever had."

Jeanne Calment was a French woman who had the longest confirmed human lifespan in history, 122 years. She remained alert and cognitively engaged in life until the end.

Dr. Ethel Percy Andrus, founded both The Gables and AARP after her 46-year career as a teacher and school principal. Dr. Andrus was proof that we can be productive and alive at any age and at any stage of our lives. Colonel Sanders was another one who inspired me, starting Kentucky Fried Chicken at age 62 after numerous disappointments, failures, and defeats in his life. I'm glad he didn't give up because I love that chicken!

One Memorial Day, when my friend George was 83, I went to meet him at the Veteran's Hospital in San Francisco where he was having some tests done. George's latest book had been nominated for an award. In two weeks, he would be traveling to Croatia on a trip to meet distant cousins for the first time. We were getting together for our monthly lunch. Almost two months had passed since our last one, though, because of our busy schedules. George traveled to promote his book about being an off-Broadway playwright during the 1960s.

I was swamped with my travel as vice president of sales and marketing for Elder Care. Getting ready to meet George that day, I felt the cortisol levels rising in my body. I had an early flight to catch the next morning and a long list of things to do before leaving. *I don't have time to meet George.* I didn't have time to go to the bathroom, let alone meet George. I was a big-shot executive now, a far cry from the sad and struggling young woman who had met George 11 years earlier. *George saw beauty in me at a time when I was full of self-hatred most days. He took me under his wing and helped me navigate life, he guided me towards the light,* I reminded myself.

I rushed around the house, gathering my purse and car keys, then hurried out the front door. I forced myself to go, despite being short on time. George was one of the most vibrant people in my life, yet I knew he would not live forever and my time with him was precious. I did not want to find myself sitting at his funeral thinking, *what the hell is wrong with me? I've seen George twice during the past year and we live seven miles from each other.* I refused to let that happen.

I walked around the grounds of San Francisco's Veteran's Hospital, a beautiful setting overlooking the Pacific Ocean. It was quiet that day and felt like a ghost town because of the holiday. I went to the cafeteria where I was supposed to meet George. The doors were locked, closed for the holiday. *Shit. What do I do now?* George didn't have a cell phone. I called his house and left a message. "Hi, George, it's me. I'm here at the VA but the cafeteria is closed. Not sure how to find you. I'll walk around a bit and see if I spot you." I hung up and stared at the ocean.

If I didn't find him, I figured I would head home and deal with the 190 emails in my inbox that were screaming to be answered before I boarded my flight the next morning. I had not packed for my trip. I had not run the marketing reports I would need to present to the CEO. I felt the stress mounting in my stomach.

I walked around the corner, towards the entrance and there was George, walking towards me in a bright turquoise and hot pink plaid jacket. He popped in the foggy distance. I waved. He seemed steady with his cane and I was pleased. *He's getting stronger.* I walked towards him. We hugged and a wave of calm washed over me. The stress was gone and I was there, in the moment. I have heard that people with an elevated consciousness can calm others just by walking into a room. George had this effect on me. He had a remarkable ability to bring me completely into the here and now.

"My tests went great, Liz! My emphysema has actually gotten *better* and the medical equipment company is coming to pick up the oxygen tanks because the pulmonologist said I could take a break from using it."

"Wow, George. When does *that* happen?!"

We drove to the Seal Rock Inn for a late lunch. George ordered a chef's salad and I had fish and chips. We talked about the success of his book and I was delighted for him. We chatted for two hours over a leisurely lunch. I felt joyful. I felt like the kind of woman I had always wanted to be: beautiful, fun, unafraid of my own power, a good person. It was not so much in what George said to me, although he did give me regular compliments and often told me, "Embrace your power, Liz!" It was more a feeling I got when I was around him. I respected him. He saw the best in me and I felt it when I was with him.

I drove George home and during the drive, he told me again how to meditate. "Just sit. Just sit and let your thoughts wash over you. Just observe them. Don't try to stop yourself from thinking. It doesn't work." Four hours had gone by since I left my house that day and I didn't care.

"I'll try, George. You know I'm so intense about these things. About everything."

"I know you are. Quit being so fucking hard on yourself." I dropped him off at the Starbucks near his apartment. He was going in to read *The New Yorker* and have a cup of coffee. We hugged.

"I love you, George."

"I love you, too, sweetie. Have a good trip."

Three years later, as I was seriously pondering the thought of leaving my marriage, I met George for our monthly lunch.

"George, I'm 42 years old. I'm afraid if I don't leave Dave soon, I'll never have another romantic partner. Men in their 40s want women in their 30s."

He laughed out loud. "Honey, listen to me. I have been around women my whole life, actresses on Broadway, show girls, writers, intellectuals, you name it. You are one of the sexiest women I have ever met. You'll be getting laid when you're 70. Yes, you do need to leave Dave and you need to do it soon, but not because you'll end up alone and sex-deprived if you wait."

So, I left Dave and George held my hand through the divorce, heartbreak, court proceedings, and the trauma of losing my life partner and all my money. Every step of the way, George was there. He was my rock and my favorite person to spend time with throughout that year. He was safe. He loved me and he was delightfully fun company. We went to movies, museums, restaurants, and the beach. When George's health started to slip and it dawned on me that I might lose him in the not-so-distant future, I talked with my therapist about it.

"Well," he said, "it has always been somewhat inevitable that you will outlive George. I mean, he was elderly when you met him."

"No," I replied, "George was *never* elderly."

The next week, while George and I were having lunch at a French bistro after seeing a movie, he said to me, "Liz, I am in love with you."

"I'm in love with you, too, George," I replied matter-of-factly.

"But I'm an 88-year-old gay man. It has been a year since you left Dave. You NEED to go on Match.com."

I sighed, "I know, George. I will. I'm just afraid to date again. I promise I'll go online and check it out next week."

"You'll go on there tonight and you will come to my apartment next week and show me the guys you found. Understood?"

"Yes, sir."

I went to his place the following week. We looked through profiles of the men who had emailed me. We laughed, we drank mint tea, I criticized the men, and George told me to be more open-minded.

"You're being negative, dear. I mean look at him, I'd go out with that guy. He's cute. He has a job. He likes to dance."

"Okay, George, let's email him back, then." Together we composed an email to the cute dancing guy with a job, then I got my stuff together to head home. We hugged goodbye and made plans to meet for a museum outing a few days later. As I was leaving, George thanked me for taking him out into the world.

"I have a lot of friends, Liz, as you know. They come to visit me. They spend time with me here in my apartment. But no one takes me out. I need to get OUT into the world and DO things! They say it's too hard. You've worked with old people; you're not afraid of the wheelchair, the walker, the oxygen tank. You and Steve are my only friends who take me out. Thank you, honey."

"You're welcome, George."

I drove home thinking of this dear man, who at age 88 was one of the most alive and youthful people I knew. I felt deep gratitude that he had lived this long and I still got to enjoy him. My heart smiled as I said out loud, "Thank you."

Thank you, God, for all the wise, funny, kind, and interesting seniors I have met over the years. Thank you that people live longer than they used to live. Thank you for thrusting me into a situation where I learned to see elders not as a burden, but as a gift.

Appendix

Research on Dementia and Brain Fitness

Alcohol-Related Dementia

Long-term excessive drinking sometimes leads to what the DSM-5 calls "alcohol-induced neurocognitive disorder,"[1] also known as alcohol-related dementia.[2] Alcohol-related dementia affects the brain in similar ways as Alzheimer's. It is associated with difficulty processing information and making decisions, memory loss, impaired judgment, and eventually, motor impairment.[3]

Wernicke-Korsakoff Syndrome

Two syndromes sometimes result from alcohol misuse. Symptoms of the first, Wernicke's encephalopathy, include abnormal eye movements, unsteady walking, and mental confusion.[4] The second, Korsakoff syndrome, presents when alcohol misuse results in insufficient thiamine levels leading to brain cells that are unable to produce sufficient energy to function properly. Symptoms include difficulty learning, impaired short-term and long-term memory, confabulation (making up stories to fill in the gaps left by memory loss), and hallucinations.[5] Sometimes these two syndromes occur together in what is known as Wernicke-Korsakoff syndrome (WKS).[6]

Alcohol abuse can impair cognition because of resulting nutrition problems, and can also damage the brain by means of the following:

- *The direct toxic effects of alcohol on brain cells.*
- *The biological stress of repeated intoxication and withdrawal.*
- *Alcohol-related cerebrovascular disease.*
- *Head injuries sustained when inebriated.*[7]

Neuroplasticity and Neurogenesis

The concepts of neuroplasticity and neurogenesis are a hopeful aspect of brain health and aging. What are neuroplasticity and neurogenesis? According to researchers, "Neuroplasticity is the brain's ability to transform its shape, adapt, and develop a new neuronal connection provided with a new stimulus"[8] and "neurogenesis is the process by which new neurons are formed in the brain."[9] Neuroplasticity and neurogenesis are prominent during early life, but are also part of the brain throughout the lifespan.[10,11] The fact that there are various lifestyle choices and treatments that may increase neurogenesis and neuroplasticity is good news for those with dementia and Alzheimer's disease.[12,13,14,15]

Dementia Risk, Sleep, Exercise, and Nutrition

Taking care of one's physical body helps reduce the risk of developing dementia and Alzheimer's Disease. Regular physical exercise is strongly associated with reducing the risk of developing dementia and Alzheimer's Disease.[16,17,18,19] Studies have shown that sleeping too long (10 hours or more) or not getting enough sleep (less than 5 hours) are associated with dementia and decreased life expectancy.[20] Studies also show that eating blueberries,[21,22,23] Omega-3s[24,25,26,27] (in fish oil and foods such as salmon), and curcumin[28,29,30] (in turmeric and curry) help prevent, and in some cases treat, dementia or Alzheimer's disease.

Bibliography

Merriam-Webster. 2024. "Sage." Accessed August 19, 2024. https://www.merriam-webster.com/dictionary/sage.

Picasso, Pablo. Quoted by The Socratic Method. https://www.socratic-method.com/quote-meanings/pablo-picasso-it-takes-a-long-time-to-become-young. Accessed May 29, 2024.

Chapter 1

AARP. 2022. "Our History: The Chicken Coop Story That Led to AARP." AARP Website. November 15, 2022. https://www.aarp.org/about-aarp/history/chicken-coop-inspires-mission.

Ojai Valley News. 2023. "Go Inside History of Grey Gables." *Ojai Valley News*, March 23, 2023. https://www.ojaivalleynews.com/culture/go-inside-history-of-grey-gables/article_fe144ff4-c9f4-11ed-a010-e79c6c909a8c.html.

Swift, Jonathan. 1726. *Gulliver's Travels.* Book 3, Chapter 10.

Chapter 2

The Assisted Living Federation website. See https://webharvest.gov/peth04/20041117234400/http://www.alfa.org.

The Bible, King James Version. Matthew 22:39 and Matthew 7:1–3.

The Carol Burnett Show. American variety/sketch comedy television show. Network CBS. 1967–1978.

The Chicks. 1998. "Wide Open Spaces." Song written by Susan Gibson. Lyrics copyright held by Pie Eyed Groobee Music.

Long, Michelle, Karen Diep, Laurie Sobel, and Alina Salganicoff. 2023. "Over-the-Counter Oral Contraceptive Pills." 2023. *KFF*, September 14, 2023. https://www.kff.org/womens-health-policy/issue-brief/over-the-counter-oral-contraceptive-pills.

Matthew Shepard Foundation. "Our Story." Accessed February 11, 2024. https://www.matthewshepard.org/about-us/our-story.

The Milton Berle Show (comedy-variety television show). Network NBC. 1948–1956.

Wikipedia. 2002. "Matthew Shepard." Last modified February 9, 2024. https://en.wikipedia.org/wiki/Matthew_Shepard.

Willour, Margaret. Quoted in 1982, *Reader's Digest*.

Chapter 3

Davis, Bette. Quoted by Chandler, Charlotte. 2006. *The Girl Who Walked Home Alone: Bette Davis, a Personal Biography*. New York: Simon & Schuster, 277–78.

Galan, S. "Countries with the Highest Average Life Expectancy for Those Born in 2024, by Gender." *Statista*. February 13, 2025. https://www.statista.com/statistics/274519/countries-with-the-highest-life-expectancy-worldwide.

McCumber, Ashley. 2008. Letter to Liz Breen from Ashley C. McCumber, Executive Director, Meals on Wheels of San Francisco, about December 2008. 1375 Fairfax Avenue, San Francisco, California.

Winton, Richard, and Martha Groves. 2008. "Case is Closed on Deadly Day at Market." *Los Angeles Times*, May 22, 2008.

Chapter 4

Alonzo, Aly. (n.d.). "Some Simple Do's and Don'ts to Remember When Working with Alzheimer's." Ojai memory care center handout.

Bavarsad, Nazanin Hatami, Shokufeh Bagheri, Masoumeh Kourosh-Arami, and Alireza Komaki. 2023. "Aromatherapy for the Brain: Lavender's Healing Effect on Epilepsy, Depression, Anxiety, Migraine, and Alzheimer's Disease: A Review Article." *Heliyon*, 9(8), July 20, 2023. https://pubmed.ncbi.nlm.nih.gov/37554839.

Berry, Steve, and Greg Krikorian. 2003. "Bail Depends on Alleged Crime." *Los Angeles Times*, February 5, 2003.

Edgerly, Elizabeth, Alvaro Fernandez, and Beverly Sanborn, moderated by Nancy Schier Anzelmo. 2008. "Delaying the Progression of MCI & Dementia." Panel discussion at the California Assisted Living Association Conference, June 9, 2008.

Gomes, Filomena, and Howard Fillit. 2005. "A Practical Guide to Achieving and Maintaining Cognitive Vitality with Aging." *Institute for the Study of Aging (ISOA)*, 8–9.

Guccione, Jean, and Andrew Blankenstein. 2003. "Blake Ordered to Stand Trial but is Granted Bail." *Los Angeles Times*, March 14, 2003.

Holmes, Clive, Vivienne Hopkins, Christine Hensford, Vanessa MacLaughlin, David Wilkinson, and Henry Rosenvinge. "Lavender Oil as a Treatment for

Agitated Behaviour in Severe Dementia: A Placebo Controlled Study." *International Journal of Geriatric Psychology*, 22(5), pp. 305–8, April 2002. https://pubmed.ncbi.nlm.nih.gov/11994882.

Kurlowicz, Lenore, and Meredith Wallace. 1999. "The Mini Mental State Examination (MMSE)." *Try This: Best Practices in Nursing Care to Older Adults from the Hartford Institute for Geriatric Nursing*, no. 3, January, 1999. https://cgatoolkit.ca/Uploads/ContentDocuments/MMSE.pdf.

Merzenich, Michael M. 2005. "Change Minds for the Better." *The Journal on Active Aging* 4, no. 6 (November/December 2005).

Shakespeare, William. 1623. *As You Like It.* Act II, Scene VII. (First published in *Mr. William Shakespeare's Comedies, Histories, & Tragedies*, London: William Jaggard and Edward Blount).

Snowdon, David A. 2003. "Healthy Aging and Dementia: Findings From the Nun Study." *Annals of Internal Medicine* 139 5, Pt 2 (September 2, 2003), 450–54. https://pubmed.ncbi.nlm.nih.gov/12965975.

Sommerlad, Andrew, Mika Kivimäki, Eric B. Larson, Susanne Röhr, Kokoro Shirai, Archana Singh-Manoux, and Gill Livingston. 2023. "Social Participation and Risk of Developing Dementia." *Nature Aging*, 3, (May 2023), 532–45. https://doi.org/10.1038/s43587-023-00387-0.

Unknown Author. 2007. "Body. Old Wives' Tales." *Real Simple*, October 2007, 228.

Troxel, David, and Virginia Bell. 2002. *The Best Friends Approach to Alzheimer's Care.* Baltimore, MD: Health Professions Press. https://bestfriendsapproach.com/about/about-the-best-friends-approach.

Wang, Caroline, and Mary Ann Burris. 1997. "Photovoice: Concept, Methodology, and Use for Participatory Needs Assessment." *Health Education & Behavior*, 24 (3), June 1997, pp 369–87. https://pubmed.ncbi.nlm.nih.gov/9158980.

Wan-ki Lin, Pamela, Wai-chi Chan, Bacon Fung-leung Ng, and Linda Chiu-wa Lam. 2007. "Efficacy of Aromatherapy (Lavandula Angustifolia) as an Intervention for Agitated Behaviours in Chinese Older Persons with Dementia: A Cross-Over Randomized Trial." *International Journal of Geriatric Psychology*, 22(5), pp. 405–10, May 2007. https://pubmed.ncbi.nlm.nih.gov/17342790.

Yoffe, Emily. 2006. "Body Wise: Memory Boot Camp." *Oprah Magazine* (October 2006), 191.

Chapter 5

Alma Via. "2005 Non Exempt Positions by Grade." Last updated 26 September, 2006.

King, Martin Luther, Jr. 1963. "Strength to Love." *Three Dimensions of a Complete*

Life. New York: Harper & Row, 72.

The LTC Solution. "Create A Focus That Calms." 2007 Handout.

The LTC Solution. "Show Respect, Offer Dignity." 2007 Handout.

Chapter 6

AARP. 2022. "Our History: The Chicken Coop Story That Led to AARP." November 15, 2022. https://www.aarp.org/about-aarp/history/chicken-coop-inspires-mission.html.

Andrus, Ethel. 1958. *Modern Maturity Magazine*, October/November 1958. As quoted by AARP in "Modern Maturity Magazine Disrupts Stereotypes About Aging." Access 26 March 2024. https://www.aarp.org/about-aarp/history/modern-maturity-aarp-the-magazine.html.

Basler, Barbara. 2006. "Assisted Living: 10 Great Ideas. Homemade Wine, Calligraphy, Your Own RV—You Can Have It Your Way." *AARP Bulletin*, February 2006.

Jenkins, Robert, Paula C. Carder, and Lindsay Maher. 2005. "The Coming Home Program: Creating a State Road Map for Affordable Assisted Living Policy, Programs, and Demonstrations." *Journal of Housing For the Elderly*, 18(3–4), 2005, pp. 179-201. https://www.tandfonline.com/doi/abs/10.1300/J081v18n03_08.

Kohn-Johnson, Carissa. 2020. "Before Founding AARP: How a Retiree in a Chicken Coop Inspired Dr. Ethel Percy Andrus." March 5, 2020. https://www.relias.com/blog/before-founding-aarp-what-inspired-dr-ethel-percy-andrus.

McCumber, Ashley. 2008. Letter to Liz Breen from Ashley C. McCumber, Executive Director, Meals on Wheels of San Francisco, about December 2008. 1375 Fairfax Avenue, San Francisco, California.

Mission statements from various assisted living facilities, including Emeritus Senior Living, Sunrise Senior Living, Senior Care Communities, and others.

Stackpole, Irving. 2010 California Assisted Living Association Conference. Sacramento, California. Used with permission.

Chapter 7

Kenan, Joanne. 2007. "Aging Parents: Parenting Your Parents." *Real Simple*. October 2007, 265–272.

Mithers, Carol. 2007. "Inner Life: Be Good To Yourself." *Ladies' Home Journal*, July 2007, 22–26.

National Alliance for Caregiving in Collaboration with AARP. 2009. *Caregiving in the U.S. 2009*. December 8, 2009. https://www.aarp.org/pri/topics/ltss/family-caregiving/caregiving_09.html.

Shakespeare, William. 1608. *King Lear*. Act I, Scene IV. Quarto I. London: Nathaniel Butter.

Chapter 8

Bärebring, Linnea, Maria Palmqvist, Anna Winkvist, and Hanna Augustin. 2020. "Gender Differences in Perceived Food Healthiness and Food Avoidance in a Swedish Population-Based Survey: A Cross Sectional Study." *Nutrition Journal*, 19, Article number: 140 (2020). https://nutritionj.biomedcentral.com/articles/10.1186/s12937-020-00659-0.

Deeks, Amanda, Catherine Lombard, Janet Michelmore, and Helena Teede. 2009. "The Effects of Gender and Age on Health Related Behaviors." *BMC Public Health*, 9, 213 (2009). https://bmcpublichealth.biomedcentral.com/articles/10.1186/1471-2458-9-213.

Dickens, Charles. 1859. *A Tale of Two Cities*. London: Chapman & Hall, p. 1.

Kingsolver, Barbara. 2009. *The Lacuna*. New York: HarperCollins.

Kirkwood, Thomas. 2010. "Why Women Live Longer: Stress Alone Does Not Explain the Longevity Gap." *Scientific American*, November 1, 2010. https://www.scientificamerican.com/article/why-women-live-longer.

Li, Yanping, An Pan, Dong D Wang, Xiaoran Liu, Klodian Dhana, Oscar H Franco, Stephen Kaptoge, Emanuele Di Angelantonio, Meir Stampfer, Walter C Willett, and Frank B Hu. 2018. "Impact of Healthy Lifestyle Factors on Life Expectancies in the US Population." *Circulation*, April 30, 2018. https://pubmed.ncbi.nlm.nih.gov/29712712.

Luo, Shan, Shiu Lun Au Yeung, Jie V Zhao, Stephen Burgess, and C Mary Schooling. 2019. "Association of Genetically Predicted Testosterone with Thromboembolism, Heart Failure, and Myocardial Infarction: Mendelian Randomisation Study in UK Biobank." *BMJ*, 2019, 364. https://www.bmj.com/content/364/bmj.l476.

Population Reference Bureau. 2001. *Around the Globe, Women Outlive Men*. September 1, 2001. https://www.prb.org/resources/around-the-globe-women-outlive-men.

Robson, David. 2015. "Why do women live longer than men?" *BBC*. October 1, 2015. https://www.bbc.com/future/article/20151001-why-women-live-longer-than-men.

Schmidt, Megan. 2018. "A Second X Chromosome Could Explain Why Women Live

Longer Than Men." *Discover Magazine.* December 17, 2018. Updated January 9, 2020. https://www.discovermagazine.com/health/a-second-x-chromosome-could-explain-why-women-live-longer-than-men.

Chapter 9

Beckett, Samuel. 1958. *Endgame.* Act 1, Scene 1, p. 69. New York: Grove Press.

Bernstein, Ellen. 2024. "Jack Kevorkian." *Encyclopedia Britannica*, March 5, 2024. https://www.britannica.com/biography/Jack-Kevorkian.

Cartwright, Mark. 2015. "Chimu Civilization." *World History Encyclopedia Chronicle*, April 14, 2015. https://www.worldhistory.org/Chimu_Civilization.

CBS 60 Minutes. 2007. "Kings of Congo, Prescription for Addiction, LT MVP." Season 40, episode 12, December 9, 2007.

Coates, Rick. 2004. "Dr. Kevorkian Breaks His Silence after Five Years in Prison without a Word to the Outside World." *The Northern Express.* March 10, 2004. https://www.northernexpress.com/news/feature/article-323-dr-kevorkian-breaks-his-silence-after-five-years-in-prison-without-a-word-to-the-outside-world.

Davidson, Keay. 2006. "Entrepreneur Backs Research on Anti-Aging." *San Francisco Chronicle*, September 18, 2006.

Gershon, Livia. 2021. "Mass Grave of Women, Children Found in Pre-Hispanic City in Peru." *Smithsonian Magazine*, November 12, 2021. https://www.smithsonianmag.com/smart-news/mass-grave-found-in-prehispanic-south-american-city-180979058.

Keith, Kent M. 1968, 2001. (Quoted by Mother Teresa). *Anyway: The Paradoxical Commandments.* See https://www.kentmkeith.com/paradoxicalcommandments.

Plato. 1966. *Apology of Socrates* 38a. In *Plato in Twelve Volumes*, Volume 1. Translated by Harold North Fowler. Cambridge, MA: Harvard University Press.

Russell, Ruth. 1999. *Pastimes: The Context of Contemporary Leisure, 1st ed.* New York: McGraw Hill.

Schneider, Keith. 2011. "Dr. Jack Kevorkian Dies at 83; A Doctor Who Helped End Lives." *The New York Times*, June 3, 2011, 1. https://www.nytimes.com/2011/06/04/us/04kevorkian.html.

Shakespeare, William. 1603. *Hamlet.* Act III, Scene I. London: Nicholas Ling and John Trundell.

Chapter 10

Atwal, Sanj. 2024. "Oldest Person Ever: 122-Year-Old Jeanne Calment's Extraordinary Life." *Guinness World Records.* February 21, 2024. https://www.guinnessworldrecords.com/news/2024/2/oldest-person-ever-122-year-old-jeanne-calments-extraordinary-life-765016.

Basler, Barbara. 2006. "Assisted Living: 10 Great Ideas. Homemade Wine, Calligraphy, Your Own RV—You Can Have It Your Way." *AARP Bulletin*, February 2006, 7.

Birimisa, George. 2011. "Old-Old Age Bulletin." Gay George Official Blog, Accessed October 26, 2011. See also https://en.wikipedia.org/wiki/George_Birimisa and https://www.ebar.com/story.php?ch=news&sc=&id=242547.

Buettner, Dan. 2008. *The Blue Zones: Lessons for Living Longer from the People Who've Lived the Longest.* Washington, DC: National Geographic.

CNN News18 Business Desk. 2023. "There's No Age for Starting a Business and KFC Founder Colonel Sanders' Story Is Proof." May 3, 2023. https://www.news18.com/business/theres-no-age-for-starting-a-business-and-kfc-founder-colonel-sanders-story-is-proof-7700251.html.

Ehrlich, Genya. 2011. "Happy." Printed in Nader R. Shabahangi, *Gems of Wisdom: A Book of Elder Poetry and Prose.* Bloomington, IN: iUniverse, 2011, p. 36.

Gold, Stephanie. 2008. "My Father, the Late-blooming Lover." *More Magazine.* September, 2008, p. 166.

Gomes, Filomena (Howard Fillit, ed). 2005. "A Practical Guide to Achieving and Maintaining Cognitive Vitality with Aging." *Institute for the Study of Aging (ISOA)*, 3, 11.

Helson, Ravenna. "The Mills Longitudinal Study: Following the Lives of Mills Women for Forty Years and More." Mills Quarterly, Fall 2001, pp. 18 ff.

Institute of Personality and Social Research. The Mills Longitudinal Study. https://millslab.berkeley.edu.

Kluger, Jeffrey. 2006. "The Surprising Power of the Aging Brain." *Time Magazine.* January 16, 2006, 87.

Loren, Sophia, quoted by Gomes, Filomena (Howard Fillit, ed). 2005. "A Practical Guide to Achieving and Maintaining Cognitive Vitality with Aging." *Institute for the Study of Aging (ISOA)*, 15.

Merriam-Webster. 2024. "Generativity." Accessed May 7, 2024. https://www.merriam-webster.com/medical/generativity.

Slatalla, Michelle. 2008. "How to Live Longer Without Really Trying." *The New York Times*, April 24, 2008, Styles section p. 1.

Thomas, Bill. 2015. "Green House Project & Eden Alternative." NIC Talks.

December 4, 2015, YouTube video. https://www.youtube.com/watch?v=bDwssGSj_rA. See also https://www.edenalt.org/who-we-are and https://www.ioaging.org/aging/eden-alternative-dr-bill-thomas-nature-therapy-redefine-aging.

Appendix

[1] American Psychiatric Association. *Diagnostic and statistical manual of mental disorders* (5th edition, text revision). Arlington, VA: American Psychiatric Association, 2022. https://doi.org/10.1176/appi.books.9780890425787.

[2] Buddy T & Steven Gans. 2024. "What Is Alcoholic Dementia?" *Verywell Mind*. January 6, 2024. https://www.verywellmind.com/alcohol-dementia-62980.

[3] Buddy T & Steven Gans, 2024, "What Is Alcoholic Dementia?"

[4] Buddy T & Steven Gans, 2024, "What Is Alcoholic Dementia?"

[5] Alzheimer's Association. n.d. "Korsakoff Syndrome." Accessed January 16, 2024. https://www.alz.org/alzheimers-dementia/what-is-dementia/types-of-dementia/korsakoff-syndrome.

[6] Buddy T & Steven Gans, 2024, "What Is Alcoholic Dementia?"

[7] Alzheimer's Association, n.d., "Korsakoff Syndrome."

[8] Reeju Maharjan, Liliana Diaz Bustamante, Kyrillos Ghattas, Shahbakht Ilyas, Reham Al-Refai, & Safeera Khan. 2020. "Role of Lifestyle in Neuroplasticity and Neurogenesis in an Aging Brain." *Cureus* 12 no. 9 (September 2020): e10639. https://www.cureus.com/articles/39860-role-of-lifestyle-in-neuroplasticity-and-neurogenesis-in-an-aging-brain.

[9] Queensland Brain Institute. n.d. "What is Neurogenesis." The University of Queensland Australia. Accessed January 18, 2024. https://qbi.uq.edu.au/brain-basics/brain-physiology/what-neurogenesis.

[10] Queensland Brain Institute, n.d., "What is Neurogenesis."

[11] Emily Underwood. 2019. "New Neurons for Life? Old People Can Still Make Fresh Brain Cells, Study Finds." *American Association for the Advancement of Science*. March 25, 2019. https://www.science.org/content/article/new-neurons-life-old-people-can-still-make-fresh-brain-cells-study-finds.

[12] Queensland Brain Institute. n.d. "Adult Neurogenesis." The University of Queensland Australia. Accessed January 18, 2024. https://qbi.uq.edu.au/brain-basics/brain-physiology/adult-neurogenesis.

[13] María Colavitta & Francisco Barrantes. 2023. "Therapeutic Strategies Aimed at Improving Neuroplasticity in Alzheimer Disease." *Pharmaceutics* 15 no. 8 (August 2023): 2052.

https://www.ncbi.nlm.nih.gov/pmc/articles/PMC10459958.

[14] Maharjan et al., 2020, "Role of Lifestyle in Neuroplasticity and Neurogenesis in an Aging Brain."

[15] Lingyu She, Hao Tang, Yuqing Zeng, Liwei Li, Li Xiong, et al. 2024. "Ginsenoside RK3 Promotes Neurogenesis in Alzheimer's Disease through Activation of the CREB/BDNF Pathway." *Journal of Ethnopharmacology* 321 (March 2024). https://www.sciencedirect.com/science/article/abs/pii/S0378874123013326.

[16] Alzheimer's Society. 2023. "Physical Activity and the Risk of Dementia." December 2023. https://www.alzheimers.org.uk/about-dementia/managing-the-risk-of-dementia/reduce-your-risk-of-dementia/physical-activity.

[17] Sukai Wang, Hong-Yu Liu, Yi-Chen Cheng, & Chun-Hsien Su. 2021. "Exercise Dosage in Reducing the Risk of Dementia Development: Mode, Duration, and Intensity—A Narrative Review." *International Journal of Environmental Research and Public Health* 18 no. 24 (December 2021). https://www.ncbi.nlm.nih.gov/pmc/articles/PMC8703896.

[18] John Omura, Lisa McGuire, Roshni Patel, Matthew Baumgart, Raza Lamb, et al. 2022. "Modifiable Risk Factors for Alzheimer Disease and Related Dementias Among Adults Aged ≥45 Years — United States, 2019." Centers for Disease Control and Prevention Morbidity and Mortality Weekly Report 71 (2022): 680–685. http://dx.doi.org/10.15585/mmwr.mm7120a2.

[19] Maharjan et al., 2020, "Role of Lifestyle in Neuroplasticity and Neurogenesis in an Aging Brain."

[20] Tomoyuki Ohara, Takanori Honda, Jun Hata, Daigo Yoshida, Naoko Mukai, et al. "Association Between Daily Sleep Duration and Risk of Dementia and Mortality in a Japanese Community." *Journal of the American Geriatrics Society*, 2018. DOI: 10.1111/jgs.15446.

[21] Robert Krikorian, Matthew Skelton, Suzanne Summer, Marcelle Shidler, & Patrick Sullivan. 2022. "Blueberry Supplementation in Midlife for Dementia Risk Reduction." *Nutrients* 14 no. 8 (April 2022): 1619. https://www.ncbi.nlm.nih.gov/pmc/articles/PMC9031005.

[22] Robert McNamara, Wilhelmina Kalt, Marcelle Shidler, Jane McDonald, Suzanne Summer, et al. 2018. "Cognitive Response to Fish Oil, Blueberry, and Combined Supplementation in Older Adults with Subjective Cognitive Impairment." *Neurobiology of Aging* 64 (April 2018): 147–156. https://www.sciencedirect.com/science/article/abs/pii/S0197458017303974.

[23] Yuye Wang, Xiaoqian Niu, & Dantao Peng. 2023. "Eat for Better Cognition in Older Adults at Risk for Alzheimer's Disease." *Nutrition* 109 (May 2023): 111969. https://www.sciencedirect.com/science/article/abs/pii/S0899900722003811.

[24] Robert McNamara et al., 2018, "Cognitive Response to Fish Oil, Blueberry, and

Combined Supplementation in Older Adults with Subjective Cognitive Impairment."

[25] Yuye Wang et al., 2023, "Eat for Better Cognition in Older Adults at Risk for Alzheimer's Disease."

[26] Ibrahim Dighriri, Abdalaziz Alsubaie, Fatimah Hakami, Dalal Hamithi, Maryam Alshekh, et al. 2022. "Effects of Omega-3 Polyunsaturated Fatty Acids on Brain Functions: A Systematic Review." *Cureaus* 14 no. 10 (October 2022): e30091. https://www.ncbi.nlm.nih.gov/pmc/articles/PMC9641984.

[27] Maharjan et al., 2020, "Role of Lifestyle in Neuroplasticity and Neurogenesis in an Aging Brain."

[28] Min Chen, Zhi-Yun Du, Xi Zheng, Dong-Li Li, Ren-Ping Zhou, & Kun Zhang. 2018. "Use of Curcumin in Diagnosis, Prevention, and Treatment of Alzheimer's Disease." *Neural Regeneration Research* 13 no. 4 (April 2018): 742–752. https://www.ncbi.nlm.nih.gov/pmc/articles/PMC5950688.

[29] The Alzheimer's Organization. n.d. "Turmeric Curcumin and Alzheimer's Disease." Accessed January 18, 2024. https://www.alzheimersorganization.org/turmeric-curcumin-and-alzheimers.

[30] Maharjan et al., 2020, "Role of Lifestyle in Neuroplasticity and Neurogenesis in an Aging Brain."

About the Author

At a relatively young age, Liz Renshaw-Breen fell into the world of senior citizens when she became the marketing director for an assisted living community in Southern California. She continued working in the industry for the next eight years at various levels of management. Through her work, she gleaned a behind-the-scenes look at the elder care industry and was privileged to learn from the many older adults she met. They taught her about dementia, family dynamics, the pleasures and heartbreaks of aging, and how to die with dignity, grace, and even joy.

Liz has spent 20 years working in elder care, first in retirement communities and subsequently in home health, hospice, hospitals, and primary care. She has a degree in Latin American Literature from UCLA. She lives with her husband, Marcos, in Northern California.

Photo credit: Chris Conroy Photography

www.ingramcontent.com/pod-product-compliance
Lightning Source LLC
Chambersburg PA
CBHW051645040426
42446CB00009B/989